WORLDS OF DIFFERENCE

WORLDS

CARY J. NEDERMAN

OF DIFFERENCE

EUROPEAN DISCOURSES OF TOLERATION,
C. 1100–C. 1550

The Pennsylvania State University Press
University Park, Pennsylvania

Library of Congress Cataloging-in-Publication Data

Nederman, Cary J.
    Worlds of difference: European discourses of toleration, c. 1100–c. 1550 /
Cary J. Nederman.
        p.   cm.
    Includes bibliographical references (p.) and index.
    ISBN 0-271-02016-4 (cloth: alk. paper)
    ISBN 0-271-02017-2 (pbk.: alk. paper)
    1. Toleration—History—To 1500.   2. Religious tolerance—History—To 1500.
3. Toleration in literature.   4. Religious tolerance in literature.   5. Literature,
Medieval—History and criticism.   6. Civilization, Medieval.   I. Title.

HM1271.N44 2000
179'9—dc21   99-042596

For Donnalee
Amor gignit amorem

CONTENTS

Acknowledgments   ix

Introduction: Toward a More Tolerant Middle Ages   1

1   Beyond Intolerance: Sources and Sites of
    Medieval Religious Dispute   11

2   Demonstration and Mutual Edification in
    Inter-religious Dialogue   25

3   Skepticism, Liberty, and the "Clash of Ideas" in
    John of Salisbury's Writings   39

4   Negotiating the Tolerant Society:
    The Travail of William of Rubruck   53

5   Heresy and Community in Marsiglio of
    Padua's Political Thought   69

6   Nationality and the "Variety of Rites" in Nicholas of Cusa   85

7   Equality, Civilization, and the American Indians
    in the Writings of Las Casas   99

    Conclusion: Tolerating Different Worlds   117

    Notes   123
    Bibliography   143
    Index   153

ACKNOWLEDGMENTS

Some books are written by design. This present one was entirely an accident. The idea for it came from a passing remark by Chris Laursen that I had inadvertently written almost an entire book on ideas of toleration in the Latin Middle Ages. Although I scoffed at the time, I later admitted to myself that he was right and decided to finish off what I had unintentionally begun. I owe Chris a large debt of thanks, not only for inspiring this project but also for nearly a decade of fruitful scholarly collaboration and for his unflagging support of my research.

Most of the chapters in this volume were presented to professional audiences, including conferences, seminars, and public lectures sponsored by: the Advanced Studies Center of the International Institute at the University of Michigan, Ann Arbor; Baylor University; the University of California, Riverside; the Arizona Center for Medieval and Renaissance Studies; Villanova University; the American Political Science Association; and the Medieval Institute of Western Michigan University. Many individuals have aided me by commenting on the drafts and soundings that found their way into this book. Among those deserving of praise (but no blame) are Dwight and Wendy Allman, Albrecht Classen, Ed Curley, Steve Darwell, Chris Laursen, Tom Mayer, Jim Muldoon, Gordon Schochet, and Simone Zurbuchen. The readers for Penn State University Press, Gary Remer and Paul Sigmund, and my editor there, Sandy Thatcher, are to be credited for many helpful and productive suggestions. I must also acknowledge the Arizona Center for Medieval and Renaissance Studies Summer Program at Saint Catharine's College, Cambridge, for providing me with a stimulating environment in which to think and write during the summers of 1997 and 1998. Finally, my dear friend Edd Whetmore afforded me luxurious and scenic surroundings in the mountains of Nevada to complete final revision of the text in the summer of 1999.

Donnalee Dox first entered my life as a result of our mutual interest in medieval attitudes toward difference. It is entirely appropriate and fitting, therefore, that this volume is dedicated in deepest love to her.

South Lake Tahoe
June 1999

INTRODUCTION

Toward a More Tolerant Middle Ages

The subject of toleration enjoys considerable vogue at present among philosophers, political theorists, and intellectual historians, if the number of books and articles recently published on the topic is a reliable gauge.[1] The extensive current interest in tolerance (a term that I use interchangeably with toleration in this work)[2] may be explained in a number of ways. The global resurgence during the 1980s and 1990s of religious, racial, ethnic, and social intolerance has stimulated a reassessment of existing political institutions and practices. Moreover, new schools of thought, including communitarianism, postmodernism, and feminism, have challenged ingrained liberal doctrines, such as freedom of expression and the neutrality of the state. Likewise, numerous social movements devoted to promoting human diversity and identity (in regard to such matters as sexuality, gender, race, and culture) have drawn attention to issues of respect for group differences. Taken together, these developments raise profound and serious questions about the viability of the concept of toleration.[3]

Many voices have contributed to the renewed and reinvigorated reflection on the meaning of tolerance. Nearly every participant, however, seems to be in agreement about two basic points—one historical, the other theoretical. First, toleration is overwhelmingly viewed as a doctrine (applying to institutions as well as persons) that initially emerged in early modern Europe as a pragmatic response to the fragmentation of Christianity at the time of the Reformation.[4] Accordingly, the West before the Reformation, and all other world cultures untouched by modern Western values, universally accepted that social unity and public order demand adherence to a single, fixed body of beliefs or doctrines, often (but not necessarily) religious. A multiplicity of ways of life was deemed to be dangerous as well as evil; diversity was, so to speak, the devil's work, and where it existed it was to be stamped out. The Reformation was the watershed in eliminating the identification of social harmony with rigid conformity of thought and action. A century or more of bloody conflict throughout Europe, fueled by fierce and unremitting religious dispute, made clear that insistence on any strict orthodoxy as a precondition of social and political inclusion was untenable. The only practical solution was some form of official tolerance for persons and groups of differing (albeit still Christian) religious viewpoints. Increasingly, this path was followed over the course of the seventeenth and eighteenth centuries, as much from expediency as from a principled commitment to diversity. Toleration was forced on European states and their citizens by ineluctable confessional divisions, a clear example of practice preceding theory.

The second point to which virtually all recent contributors to the discussion about tolerance subscribe is the integral association (conceptual as well as historical) between toleration and the political theory of liberalism.[5] Few scholars dispute the claim that the first truly theoretical defense of tolerance was proposed by John Locke in his *Epistola de Tolerantia*.[6] What distinguished Locke is said to be his treatment of toleration as grounded on a conception of the human individual that was absolute and non-negotiable. Intolerant conduct on the part of governments and private parties constituted an illegitimate use of power, which could properly be resisted. The consequences of toleration were not directly of concern to Locke: Although he believed that a tolerant society was in fact more likely to be a stable one, the validity of tolerant practices could not be judged on utilitarian grounds according to their results. Locke focused specifically on matters of religion (and more narrowly, on Christian religion), and he perhaps did not envisage a wider application of his principle. But others soon speculated that what was true of differences in Christian faith could also be true of other forms of human thought and conduct. Hence, the eighteenth and nineteenth centuries saw more ways of life brought under the umbrella of toleration: preferences of thought, association, and speech; worship of non-Christian deities and refusal of religion altogether; and eventually rights of privacy and of experimentation in personal lifestyle. Clarion calls of the expanded conception of toleration came in the writings of Wilhelm von Humboldt, Benjamin Constant, and John Stuart Mill. In all their theories, liberal convictions about the individual person and the neutral quality of the state support and justify the insistence on tolerance as an ineradicable attribute of a well-ordered social and political system. Indeed, many thinkers have come to view toleration as a principle whose philosophical foundations rest solely and uniquely on liberalism.

The clear implication of these two assumptions about toleration is that the Christian Middle Ages has nothing whatsoever to contribute to our understanding—philosophical or historical—of tolerance as a worthy principle or practice. Indeed, a veritable chorus of scholarly voices endorses this viewpoint. Preston King bluntly states, "Christians . . . persecuted dissident sects. No Christian writer during the Middle Ages can readily be described as an opponent of intolerance."[7] Henry Kamen is even more succinct: "The Middle Ages had not tolerated dissent."[8] Ole Peter Grell and his coeditors affirm the same claim in the opening sentence of their volume: "Religious intolerance was the norm throughout the Christian Middle Ages."[9] Consequently, as Brian Tierney asserts, "In this area [of tolerance] the stance of the medieval church was harshly antithetical to the growth of modern freedom."[10]

The reason most often cited for the supposed medieval antipathy to toleration is the unitary nature of Latin Christianity itself as a faith as well as an institutional mechanism. Mario Turchetti remarks: "Christianity in medieval times simply reinforced the bond of religious concord, extending it to all aspects of communal life, in its construction of the monolithic *Respublica Christiana*."[11] This observation is echoed by Klaus Schreiner, for whom the "consensus-shaping *viniculum societatis*" of medieval Christendom formed "a closed system of belief" lacking "free spaces of action in which individuals and groups could realize their rights of freedom of belief and conscience."[12] Bernard Hamilton likewise points out that "medieval Western society was based on religious assumptions, and the Church was taken entirely for granted by everybody. Like or dislike of the institutional Church, fervor or indifference in religious practice, were irrelevant in such a society, where the church was regarded as a fundamental part of life, not as an optional extra."[13] Thus, in the usual interpretation of the matter, the Middle Ages posited in a single moment a universal faith, a universal governance, and a universal culture—in sum, an overarching unity of human experience in which diversity had no place. As an "authoritarian religion," medieval Christianity was utterly unprepared to cope with religious division.[14] "Medieval people," Tierney declares, "were so convinced of the truths of their faith that they could never see dissent from the faith as merely an intellectual error, a mistake of judgment."[15] In sum, medieval Europe hardly seems very promising terrain on which to advance the study of the history of the idea of toleration.

Yet concentration on a mania for unity and a fear of difference may be misleading. Indeed, the claims made on behalf of an authoritative *Respublica*

Christiana capture only one aspect of a more comprehensive "struggle between tolerance and repression in the Middle Ages."[16] As Waugh and Diehl observe, "Latin Christendom had always encompassed great variety within its nominal unity of religious faith. The vision of a uniform Christendom under the leadership of a single Church barely concealed the heterogeneity of the peoples it embraced or the diversity of the beliefs that they held."[17] The intellectual terrain of the Middle Ages, Alasdair MacIntyre points out, was constituted not by the unity of a single form of life but by the sheer multiplicity and diversity of such forms.[18] Consequently, any conception of a unified Christian life had to contend with what Constantin Fasolt describes as "a plethora of actors jostling side by side to assert their particular ideas of the highest good."[19] Raoul Vaneigem offers a contemporary analogy: "The Middle Ages were, in short, Christian in the same way that the countries of Eastern Europe were communist."[20] Beneath the veneer of religious singularity, European Christendom during the Middle Ages struggled endlessly with manifestations of difference.

The historical diversity of forms of life in medieval Europe was matched by a vocabulary suited to defending and exploring difference. As István Bejczy has ably documented, the term *tolerantia* was widely circulated in works of canon law and scholasticism and came to be applied "to justify the existence of all social deviance, especially in the urban community."[21] Similarly, languages of individual conscience, human rights, and liberty—extending a basis for personal refusal to defer to superior authority—formed ingrained features of medieval theology and philosophy as well as law and politics.[22] These discursive weapons, properly deployed, afforded a sizable armament to those who might wish to thwart the persecutorial impulse and to advocate a measure of forbearance in matters of intellectual (or even practical) difference.

The purpose of the present book, then, is to challenge and modify the conventional wisdom about the role of tolerance in the Latin Middle Ages. In particular, I argue that long before the Reformation—indeed as early as about 1100—religious toleration (sometimes in conjunction with other forms of tolerance, such as forbearance of philosophical, cultural, and political difference) received reasoned defense from various quarters in Latin Christendom, orthodox as well as dissenting. The figures and texts examined in this volume are by no means the only ones to take up the cause of tolerance: My primary intent is to offer illustrations rather than a comprehensive account. Many other medieval sources—some of which have recently received attention from scholars[23]—contributed as well to the formation of a body of literature sympathetic to tolerant thought and conduct. Yet an important theme draws together the array of writings addressed in the present volume, namely, their recognition that by God's own ordination, the human world is composed of difference. In other words, the claim shared by all the works surveyed here is that some form of toleration is rendered necessary by the conditions—physical, psychological, or both—imposed by divinely-created (if flawed) human nature itself. Whether because of the frailties of the human mind and understanding (as conceived, for example, by Peter Abelard and John of Salisbury), or the material needs of the members of the human community (Marsiglio of Padua), or the ordained patterns of sociocultural development (Nicholas of Cusa, William of Rubruck, and Bartolomé de Las Casas), these authors embraced, if only indirectly, some policy of toleration as a result of their conception of the natural predicament of humankind. Tolerance is required because intolerant practices are not and cannot be efficacious in light of some significant and irremovable dimension of human existence. Toleration is, therefore, not a good or an end in itself, but a course of action or inaction sanctioned, ultimately, by God himself inasmuch as He created and endowed humanity with certain capacities and frailties.

Does this medieval approach I describe amount to a strictly pragmatic or "concordant" concept of forbearance, such as is commonly associated with the Reformation?[24] I do not think so. Although all the authors under discussion were convinced Christians who believed in the ultimate truth of their faith, they also each recognized that the forcible imposition of a narrow and monolithic orthodoxy could not be achieved precisely because of one or another aspect of humanity's God-given nature. They advocated in the main what Michael Sandel labels "judgemental toleration," according to which tolerance is worthy of pursuit to achieve or maintain some other valuable or necessary human good.[25] While every figure examined in the present study may have longed for universal acceptance of a single body of Christian doctrine and rite, none was especially confident about the possibility of reaching this end, certainly not in a foreseeable future. What specifically animated these writers, however, was concern that the systematic practice of intolerance, because it is based on mistaken premises about human beings, affords a misguided path to attain the goals of religious unanimity and consensus. It is in this sense that the critique of intolerance took precedence among many medieval advocates of toleration: They sought to demonstrate why tolerance was necessary by revealing the flawed assumptions on which nontolerant attitudes were founded.

The emergence of such criticism of intolerance in the High Middle Ages may be charted, at least in part, against important developments in Latin Christendom itself. R. I. Moore speaks of the twelfth and thirteenth centuries in terms of "the formation of a persecuting society," characterized by the extension of ecclesiastical control, sometimes by force, over the hearts and minds of the European populace, with the intention of stamping out forms of religious diversity and dissent that had grown popular during the early Middle Ages.[26] Quite possibly, the doubts raised by medieval thinkers about a program of intolerance constitute a reaction (directly or indirectly) to the persecuting society that was being formed. Just as in early modern Europe, where the violence and instability caused by religious divergence stimulated some theorists to articulate cases for toleration, so in the Middle Ages abhorrence of concerted policies of intolerance generated a similar response among certain authors. The discovery of voices supporting toleration in the medieval world may, ironically, confirm elements of Moore's thesis that Christianity after about 1100 became more aggressive and confident in suppressing dissent.

Moreover, granted that the Latin Church, in cooperation with various secular authorities, did seek to enforce orthodoxy more vigorously, there were numerous practical impediments to the success of this project. As the first chapter shows, the depiction of Europe during the Latin Middle Ages as a monolithic "persecuting society" is something of a caricature. Medieval culture was far too diverse and complex in its religious and intellectual views to be reduced to a single set of rigid doctrines. Christian tradition itself was ambivalent about the appropriate treatment to be accorded heretics and unbelievers. Moreover, the facts of daily life in the Middle Ages, including the continuing presence in some locales of non-Christians, resisted the imposition of orthodox uniformity. Lingering pockets of diversity (in matters of sociocultural identity as well as religious conviction) thus provided a framework in which critics of intolerance could oppose policies of uniformity and repression, rendering viable the positing of forms of tolerant discourse, personal liberty, and free debate.

Among the earliest medieval expressions of reservations about intolerance may be counted the genre of the inter-religious dialogue, which entered a phase of popularity around 1100. Chapter 2 surveys a number of examples of this literary form, arguing that it embraces a principle of rational discussion that ultimately encourages tolerance. Even though inter-religious dialogues, particularly those stemming from the circle around Archbishop Anselm of Canterbury, did not at first fully realize this requirement of reasoned debate, later contributors to the genre, such as Peter Abelard (c. 1130) and Ramon Llull (c. 1275), realized that rational discussion was an open-ended process that demanded (perhaps indefinite) deferral of a final resolution. The nature of human intellectual and linguistic capacities points to deep difficulties in achieving complete mutual understanding in matters of religion. Thus, participation in discourse was indeed necessary and valuable even when interlocutors did not become convinced of the rectitude of one or another faith.

Another important dimension of the history of toleration has been its association with the doctrine of skepticism. As the third chapter reveals, an acceptance of a skeptical method in philosophy, such as John of Salisbury's dedication to the Ciceronian New Academy in his writings of the 1150s, could produce a notable degree of tolerance for the freedom to think and dispute for oneself. Adopting Cicero's principle that the human mind is poorly equipped to know very many truths with certainty, John advocates a probabilistic position with regard to a wide range of theological, moral, and metaphysical issues. Indeed, he asserts that human beings enjoy a right to draw their own conclusions in connection with those numerous questions about which uncertainty remains. This principle, in turn, undergirds John's advocacy of a large measure of public free expression, including even the criticism of rulers and other superiors.

Of course, thinkers such as Abelard and John of Salisbury were working within a framework of essentially "intellectual" disputes, implying the extension of toleration only to a small group of literate, well-educated churchmen who already accepted the primary values of the Latin Christian faith and culture. By contrast, Chapter 4 investigates the written account of the real-life encounter of a mid-thirteenth-century Franciscan missionary, William of Rubruck, with a religiously and culturally diverse and tolerant society, the Mongol empire. William reports the impediments to achieving a genuine interreligious dialogue among adherents to various faiths and rites (Christian as well as non-Christian). These obstacles are not to be ascribed merely to the ignorance or willfulness of unbelievers and the heterodox but reflect ingrained cultural patterns as well as reasoned arguments. In turn, William's narrative also demonstrates that it was possible for a Latin Christian to negotiate the terms of a tolerant society, where the Roman Church lacked any significant following, without surrendering his own convictions. By learning to live harmoniously with adherents to beliefs he abhors, William reveals the practicability of achieving tolerance.

For the medieval Christian, ironically, it was perhaps easier to tolerate non-Christians than heretics. The heretic, while claiming to be a true Christian, posed a direct threat to the unity of orthodox faith that was regarded as the hallmark of the universal church. Hence, heresy would seem to be so serious a challenge to Christianity that it could never be tolerated. Yet as we discover in the fifth chapter, Marsiglio of Padua, writing in the first half of the fourteenth century, argues that heretics should be tolerated for the sake of the temporal welfare of the community. Constructing a firm division between the needs of the body and those of the soul, Marsiglio associates the good of the political order primarily with the former. Although he accepts excommunication as the necessary sanction for heresy, he contends that it is a spiritual punishment only, not a secular one. Therefore, the heretic retains his status in the civil body, and faithful Christians can and should be permitted to have intercourse with him in this temporal capacity for the economic benefit of everyone in society.

All the authors discussed thus far perhaps regarded toleration as necessary and unavoidable, but still not entirely desirable. However, the fifteenth-century cardinal Nicholas of Cusa, whose ideas are investigated in Chapter 6, departs in some measure from this viewpoint by proposing a case that a "variety of rites" may in fact be beneficial to the worship of God. Horrified by the violence that accompanied the fall of Constantinople in 1453, Nicholas promotes a vision of inter-religious harmony among various Christian sects as well as non-Christian groups. Although he admits that such harmony requires agreement on a few basic truths, he allows that the diverse conditions of human history and culture inevitably produce a multiplicity of forms of worship (including both Christian and non-Christian ceremonies and sacraments). Not only is it impossible to eradicate this diversity, according to Nicholas, but the pride taken by various confessions in their distinct rites would spur them to compete with one another in serving God, thus enhancing the faith of all.

By the close of the Middle Ages, then, thinkers had criticized intolerance and sought alternatives to it, in a number of contexts. But the European encounter with the native peoples of the Americas raised questions of toleration from another perspective. Whereas for some authors the Indians appeared so barbarous that they could be evaluated only in Aristotelian terms as "slaves by nature," the Spanish Dominican Bartolomé de Las Casas, whose writings are discussed in the seventh chapter, devoted much of his career to making a case for affording extensive tolerance toward their culture and religion. Despite the fact that his work dates to the first half of the sixteenth century, Las Casas remains firmly grounded in the source materials and languages of the Middle Ages. In particular, he appeals to the arguments of Cicero to support his contention that all human beings are fundamentally equal in their mental faculties—in their reason, their understanding of divinity, and their sociability. Consequently, he insists that European attempts to destroy the Indians' civilization and to impose Christianity on them are contrary to nature, because they must follow for themselves the process of cultural development that will prepare them to accept the truth of the Christian faith. It is indeed an affront to God, who has endowed human beings with their equal natures, to intervene by force in the societies and cultures that the Indians have created.

It should be evident that my purpose is not to hunt in medieval texts for the ancestry of post-Reformation approaches to tolerance. My investigation thus instead adopts the spirit expressed by Michael Walzer in *On Toleration*: "I mean to defend . . . a historical and contextual account of toleration and coexistence, one that examines the different forms that these have actually taken and the norms of everyday life appropriate to each . . . a close and circumstantial account of the different regimes of toleration, in both their actual and their ideal versions."[27] Not surprisingly, the body of medieval writing about toleration promotes doctrines standing well outside the now-standard modern, liberal vision. Medieval thinkers come to their conclusions about toleration on grounds quite different from various modern authors, who make a positive case *for* toleration based on liberty (e.g., Locke), utility (Mill), human rights, and so on. This approach distinguishes the medieval from the modern route to tolerance: Whereas the latter believed tolerance to be among the worthy goals of human life, the former held toleration to follow from the unfortunate limits imposed on human beings by their common nature. According to the view I attribute to the Latin Middle Ages, we are compelled to accept some form of tolerance once we have recognized the realities and shortcomings of humanity's mental powers or physical capacities. This more modulated and circumscribed conception of tolerance perhaps reflects the circumstances in which medieval authors were working, that is, under conditions of intolerance in which, nonetheless, possibilities of toleration remained.

For theorists and philosophers concerned with the problems associated with intolerance in the contemporary world, this historical lesson ought to offer encouragement. Too often, recent debates surrounding toleration have been polarized between laconic restatement of traditional liberal views about the inviolability of human freedom of thought and belief, on the one hand, and strident assertion of the theoretical as well as practical limitations of the liberal stance, on the other. What seems required instead is the vigor to fashion new theories of toleration that learn from both sides, avoiding the pitfalls of conventional liberalism while still promoting the goals of mutual respect and understanding (if not acceptance) among disparate groups and individuals. One may enlarge the horizons of current toleration theorists by means of a careful examination and appreciation of how earlier thinkers dealt with similar issues about the diversity of human conviction and action. In turning our gaze toward the Middle Ages, we encounter a rich and complex reality, in which thinkers as early as the twelfth century challenged the validity of repressive practices, proposed remarkably tolerant doctrines, and were some-times prepared to respect deep differences among personal and group beliefs and actions, especially in religious matters.

I must emphasize that I do not regard the study of medieval discourses of toleration to be simply an academic exercise. The authors whose writings are analyzed in this volume were actively engaged in the politics associated with the criticism of intolerance. Many were dissenters (and even heretics) them-selves—for example, Abelard, Llull, and Marsiglio—while others (such as Anselm, John of Salisbury, Nicholas of Cusa, and Las Casas) were members of the established order whose intellects and experiences led them to recognize the difficulties inherent in pursuing intolerant policies toward differing groups or ideas. All demonstrated great courage in standing up against oppression, and some paid a large price in personal reputation and physical safety for stat-ing their positions. Beyond the conceptual horizons that may be opened up by study of the earliest advocates of tolerance, political theorists and philoso-phers today might well draw some inspiration from the sacrifices of their fore-bears. As news reports illustrate with horrifying frequency, the issues of four or five or six centuries ago—intolerance, human hatred, and the violence these breed—are still very much a part of the global landscape. Although it may be less dangerous for authors at the moment to voice reasoned opposition to intolerance and support for toleration (at least in some parts of the world), it is no less urgent a task than in earlier times.

1

Beyond Intolerance

Sources and Sites of Medieval Religious Dispute

A Persecuting Society?

Toleration has seldom been taken as a hallmark of Christian thought or practice in medieval Europe. The common impression is perhaps best summarized by the title of R. I. Moore's influential study of religious conformity during the High Middle Ages: *The Formation of a Persecuting Society*.[1] Moore's main thesis—that a decided trend toward the enforcement of orthodox faith against a range of medieval dissenters can be detected during the High Middle Ages—has considerable evidence to support it. From the late eleventh century onward, the Roman Church, generally in collaboration with secular powers, certainly pursued a systematic policy of imposing a unified set of Christian beliefs on the inhabitants of Europe—and beyond. Heresies were stamped out, infidels were attacked, dissonant voices were quieted.[2] This tendency perhaps culminated in the Fourth Lateran Council of 1215, at which the institutional Church took direct aim at many expressions of religious difference, ranging from heresy to Judaism to intellectual dispute. The goal was the realization in practice of the *Respublica Christiana*, the universal community of the faithful that had been posited in theory by generations of clerics.

Yet the picture sketched by Moore, while accurate in its general outline, depicts only part of the terrain. Even as the church spurred on persecutorial activities, its own traditions that militated against repression and violence could not be entirely forgotten. Moreover, it was often difficult to discern the demarcation between enthusiasm for reform and heretical zeal. Nor could ecclesiastical authority stem the effect of the flood of non-Christian writings that were pouring into Western Europe from the twelfth-century onward. The continued presence of and coexistence with unbelieving groups, especially the Jews, in the Latin West suggest that Christians were willing and able in everyday life to tolerate non-Christian communities. In sum, careful investigation of the historical record shows that forms of religious diversity, at an intellectual as well as a practical level, subsisted throughout medieval Europe, even when the institutional Church made a concerted attempt to eliminate them. In turn, recognition of these pockets of tolerant attitudes and behavior provides a crucial context for understanding the emergence of medieval criticisms of intolerance and concomitant defenses of toleration.

Faith and Persecution in Imperial Rome

The Christianity of Roman antiquity is said to be a religion both persecuted and persecuting, but this statement requires some qualification. Although the persecution of Christians occurred before the Christianization of the Roman Empire, it was seldom conducted on a systematic basis coordinated by imperial authorities (the Great Persecution of 303–12 was exceptional in this regard).[3] Rather, persecution of Christians happened in a sporadic and localized manner and was sometimes even discouraged by imperial officials who sympathized with persons accused of holding Christian beliefs. To the modern mind, perhaps the most horrifying aspect of Roman persecutions was the nature of the charge: Merely to be "Christian," rather than to commit some definite offense, was sufficient to be prosecuted for a capital crime. It must be recognized, however, that this harshness stemmed from the very odd character of Christian belief when judged by pantheistic and indifferent Roman standards: It was universalistic and exclusivist. That is, Christians claimed the validity of their faith for all people at all times and in all places and were unwilling to accommodate other deities or public rites associated with the Roman cults. Indeed, Roman society regarded Christianity as atheistic in precisely the sense that its adherents refused to "pay cult to the gods."

The Roman reaction to Christianity may usefully be contrasted with the reaction to Judaism. The Jews had a long history of living and thriving in non-

Jewish civilizations in both the Eastern and Western worlds, while nonetheless maintaining their own cultural and religious identity.[4] Although it would be difficult to argue that Judaism was warmly welcomed, Louis Feldman's analysis of a census of ancient Greek and Latin texts (including Christian works) reveals a nearly even split between negative and positive opinions about the Jews.[5] It is apt thus, according to Peter Garnsey, to "use the term 'toleration' in good conscience with respect to the Jews" when discussing their treatment under pagan Rome.[6] In general, when Rome conquered a people, it stipulated that the new provincials make sacrifice to the approved Roman deities in addition to their own gods—a relatively unproblematic request to pantheist or pluralistic religions. In the case of the Jews, however, Rome even tolerated nonworship of its cult, provided that the unbelievers were prepared to pray to their own God for the sake of the emperor. Although the Roman establishment was by no means fond of the peculiar beliefs and rites of Judaism, the antiquity of that religion earned its adherents the respect and forbearance of authorities.

The religious landscape changed dramatically in the fourth century, as Christianity moved rapidly from a proscribed faith to an officially protected and subsidized sect. Yet the public privileging of Christian religion cannot be equated with the state-sanctioned imposition of strict orthodoxy on the lands under the control of the Roman Empire. Beyond the myriad practical problems involved with eliminating paganism and heretical Christian movements, Christianity's universalistic and exclusivist elements were tempered by biblical teachings about charity, patience, nonviolence, and the like. Jesus had advocated preaching and example as the appropriate techniques for disseminating his message. The employment of Church-endorsed state compulsion to enforce Christian conformity fit uncomfortably with scriptural lessons that advocated personal free choice and commended turning the other cheek in response to one's enemies.

As early as the end of the fourth century, Saint Augustine grappled with the issue of whether he should call on the resources of the Roman state to assist him in suppressing the Donatist heresy. Although Augustine ultimately embraced persecution and intolerance as the only practicable solution to the persistence and strength of Donatism, he did so only as a last resort, after nearly a decade of promoting less extreme measures. As he later explained in one of his letters:

> It seemed to certain of the brethren, of whom I was one, that although the madness of the Donatists was raging in every direction, yet we

should not ask of the emperors to ordain that heresy should absolutely cease to be, by sanctioning a punishment on all who wished to live in it; but that they should rather content themselves with ordaining that those who either preached the Catholic truth with their voice, or established it by their study, should no longer be exposed to the furious violence of the heretics.[7]

These are hardly the words of a man to whom intolerance came easily. In his initial view, at least, the role of the state should be strictly limited to the protection of peaceful persons from religiously motivated attacks, in other words, a function essentially consistent with publicly approved toleration. In open debate with Donatists, Augustine even attacked those among his own Church who sought to persecute heretics, citing scripture in support of a policy of patient correction, forbearance, and prayer. Persecution, he says, is "the work of evil men" who do not comprehend the nature of the faith to which they pretend.[8]

A similar approach was adopted for the problem of the appropriate relation between Christianity and the writings of non-Christians, especially the pagan classics.[9] In patristic times, considerable discussion occurred about whether the words and ideas of unbelievers could possibly contribute anything to deepening the Christian faith. Were not such uninspired texts corrupt and useless for salvation? Saint Jerome cautioned against the unbridled use of pagan writings on the grounds that they were tainted with the stain of worldliness. Jerome was echoing a concern that Tertullian had articulated (albeit more dramatically) two centuries earlier: "What is there in common between the philosopher and the Christian, between the pupil of Hellas and the pupil of Heaven?"

This lack of forbearance toward pagan thought professed by Tertullian and Jerome did not ultimately prevail, however. It was rather Saint Augustine's position, stated in his widely influential treatise *De doctrina christiana*, that guided Christian scholars. Augustine, who possessed an excellent classical education, drew an analogy between pagan learning and the Egyptian gold taken by the Israelites in their flight described in Exodus. Just as the Hebrews were justified in removing the gold from an "unjust possessor" and converting it to righteous uses, so Christian intellectuals may rightfully seize on those elements of non-Christian teaching that are of assistance to them in the work of spreading the gospel.[10] Thus, Augustine counseled the study of a range of pagan philosophical, literary, historical, and rhetorical texts to improve the pedagogical and evangelical skills of Christian preachers and authors.

On the whole, the impression of early Christianity as a religion whose traditions were persecutorial demands modification. Even at the apex of their influence under the late Roman Empire, Christian leaders demonstrated ambivalence toward the use of their authority to achieve doctrinal purity. Heresy was always a concern, and proper reaction to religious deviation (whether popular or intellectual) stood as one of the central issues of the patristic age. Yet the lessons of scripture, along with respect for the many important accomplishments of the pagan past, exercised powerful effects on the minds of the Church Fathers, leading them to resist the impulse to suppress all forms of religious dissent.

Reform and Heresy

The official status of Latin Christianity, and the growing intersection of the interests of ecclesiastical magistrates and secular rulers, meant that during the Latin Middle Ages political power remained available to enforce orthodox faith.[11] We have noted already the increasing efforts during the course of the Middle Ages to impose and extend control on Europeans both as political subjects and as faithful Christians, but such efforts were not uniformly successful. Indeed, the evidence suggests that persecution did not halt dissent and in some instances may have only hardened the resolve of dissidents. This is true at all levels of medieval society: Theologians and philosophers did not forgo the reading of Aristotle because the Church proscribed many of his teachings and texts; peasant Cathar heretics did not surrender their beliefs even when a crusade was preached against them; kings and princes did not renounce their claims to political autonomy in secular (and even some spiritual) matters simply because the pope anathematized them. The centralized authority of the *Respublica Christiana* whose rhetoric has been well documented was often too frail in practice to realize the claims made by and for it. It is easy to be so dazzled by tales of the Crusades and stories of inquisitional procedures (formal or informal) that one neglects the mundane realities of Christian Europe during the Middle Ages.

Chief among these realities was the sheer diversity of religious life that simmered near the surface of sanctioned Roman Christendom. Most important perhaps were the regional and even local differences of belief arising from the imposition of a literate, text-based religion on an illiterate, custom-bound population. To make Christian doctrine comprehensible, it was often imbued or admixed with elements of traditional pagan superstition. Raoul Vaneigem has plausibly questioned whether it is even possible to speak of the vast mass of the medieval European populace as recognizably Christian at all in the sub-stance of their faith.[12] Except in rare instances where such popular belief broke out into full-fledged heresy—as in the case of the Cathars—we know far too little about the content of the versions of Christianity practiced in the parish to form hard and fast judgments.[13] But one of the greatest frustrations of the ecclesiastical hierarchy remained the difficulty of ensuring that orthodoxy was disseminated to and adopted by the body of the Christian faithful.[14]

The fractured condition of religious life in medieval Europe thus rendered possible the wide airing of dissonant voices in Christianity. It is a crude cari-cature to depict the Roman Church as a ceaseless fount of monolithic faith and guidance until Martin Luther and his fellow reformers tumbled the structure. This view overlooks, for instance, the unwavering medieval desire for reform, expressed in any number of movements, from the Gregorian renovation of the church to the Cluniac call for reform in "head and members" to the Franciscan glorification of evangelical poverty as a clerical ideal to the conciliarist agenda pursued by ecclesiological reformers in the Age of the Councils.[15] The con-dition of the Church at almost any moment in European history formed a source of dissatisfaction for a large number of faithful Christians, among them leading theologians and scholars, who saw it as their duty to edify the repro-bates—clerics as well as laity—to the end of restoring ecclesial purity. This reforming zeal was assuredly respectful of and deferential to authority, but it stubbornly opposed "real or apparent corruption and decline."[16] Indeed, if Giles Constable is correct, the medieval mania for reform changed perspective some-time during the twelfth century from a conservative, backward-looking phe-nomenon to a progressive, perfectionist orientation.[17] "Renovation" and even "innovation" became bywords of reform movements.

The religious reformers of the High Middle Ages generally made every effort to remain within the pale. Scholarship has revealed, however, that the mainstream reform movement associated with the rise of scholastic thought shared many important preconditions and characteristics with the more fanat-ical of the popular heresies.[18] Indeed, medieval heresy might sometimes be appropriately characterized as reforming sentiment that found itself in polit-ical disfavor with institutional Church authorities. Official response to out-right heresy was by no means a simple and settled matter. In her recent study of the Cathar heresy in thirteenth-century Orvieto, Carol Lansing has demon-strated that heretics flourished even in the face of inquisitional procedures.[19] Informal social intercourse as well as some of the formal legal strictures of Orvieto's commune, Lansing observes, favored toleration in practice and (at least occasionally) in policy. Indeed, in Orvieto and elsewhere in medieval

Italy, inquisitional repression fostered popular resistance to clerical authority among a population already inclined toward skepticism about central tenets of the orthodox creed, not to mention about the motives of the inquisitors.

Excommunication and anathematization were the approved responses to the obdurate heretic.[20] Yet the fact that the body of canon law on excommunication grew significantly during the twelfth and thirteenth centuries may not be a sign that the Church was clamping down on heresy and dissent so much as an indication that excommunication itself had become a tool in coping with civil matters such as indebtedness and violence.[21] Even in cases of heresy, however, excommunication was based on standards that were ambiguous and difficult to enforce. Alexander Murray has pointed out that the very principle of excommunication stood in "an inevitable tension" with Christian teachings "that enemies had to be loved" and that the sacraments had a "medicinal" effect on the sick soul of the heretic.[22] Moreover, the social realities of medieval Europe "corroded" the impact of proclamations of excommunication: Growing mobility and commercial intercourse rendered the ostracizing implications of excommunication increasingly obsolete, whereas the continued fragmentation and pluralization of ecclesiastical (and secular) jurisdictions made it difficult to ascertain where authority for declaration of excommunication lay.[23]

Of course, in the most extreme instances of heresy, excommunication was unlikely to carry much weight with religious dissidents in any case, because such heretics were relatively unconcerned about the condition of life in the present world. Rather, they believed that the Church itself had become utterly corrupt and that their mission was to restore the faithful to some higher or more primal purity away from which the degraded priesthood had led them. Heretical sects generally claimed to enjoy privileged access to the revealed word of God, setting their followers in direct opposition to the established Church. Hence, they did not even acknowledge the legitimate authority of the Church to deny to them sacraments and salvation.[24] This may help to explain the "increasing lay apathy toward excommunication" and its diminishing force in the secular sphere, developments that Elisabeth Vodola has detected, for example, in recurrent popular demands for the "guarantee of the civil rights of excommunicates" evident in the High Middle Ages.[25] It may not be too far-fetched to conclude that the expansion of the law of excommunication during the twelfth and thirteenth centuries actually reflects a decline in the effectiveness of excommunication as a method of ecclesiastical control of dissent.

In sum, it is simply incorrect to conflate the Church's war on heresy with the stifling of all religious dissent. The urge to reform enjoyed a venerable lineage in ecclesiastical circles, and criticism of the practices of churchmen was widely regarded as worthy of forbearance. In general, the line between calling for reform of ecclesiastical practices and questioning central articles of faith was sufficiently blurred to permit a wider band of debate than is often supposed.

Academic Dispute

The Roman Church had only slightly more success in regulating open differences of opinion among Christian teachers and scholars, theologians prominent among them. The medieval intelligentsia was in fact permitted reasonably wide latitude in debating fundamental issues about the faith, whatever our uninformed impressions may be. This becomes especially apparent after about 1100, when the pace of academic dispute picks up rapidly. By the turn of the twelfth century, one can find profound disagreements among Christian theologians about important metaphysical questions that touched on both the divine nature and the nature of God's creations.[26] Only the most obdurate thinkers and the most extreme positions were threatened with official condemnation, and then the decision to proscribe certain doctrines seems to have been as much the result of petty academic and ecclesiastical rivalries and jealousies as of any intrinsic danger posed by the ideas themselves.[27] If never quite formally institutionalized, freedom of intellectual inquiry into matters of central concern to orthodoxy seems to have been remarkably well preserved in medieval Christendom.

Intellectual independence was in some measure legitimated by the predominance of the Augustinian attitude toward classical learning throughout the Latin Middle Ages. Even those medieval churchmen such as Saint Bonaventure who were deeply suspicious of extensive reliance on the ideas of the pagan classics never proposed complete prohibition of their circulation. No one questioned that a Plato or an Aristotle, a Cicero or a Seneca, a Virgil or even an Ovid, could teach the Christian scholar a great deal. Indeed, it was deemed senseless to shun pagans simply because they had the misfortune to be born before the Christian era and thus to have missed the opportunity to receive the word of Jesus (although it was sometimes suspected that Plato's thought must have enjoyed at least a little direct divine inspiration).[28] Ecclesiastical authorities generally moved to proscribe pagan doctrines only in cases where they directly conflicted with such established and fundamental tenets of Christian faith as the finite nature of creation or the eternity of the soul. Even then, there was no concerted attempt to suppress the classical texts harboring such ideas.[29]

Two institutional factors perhaps helped to reinforce the intellectual autonomy of Christian scholars. First, the rise of universities throughout Europe after c. 1200 provided a measure of protection against the intrusion of the Church into the dissemination of ideas. Before the formation of university communities, teachers were usually directly subject to the authority and regulation of ecclesiastical superiors, whose judgments of intellectual innovation could be harsh. As relatively orthodox theologians such as Gilbert de la Porrée—not to mention genuine freethinkers such as Peter Abelard—discovered,[30] even the slightest perceived misstep could render their teachings susceptible to inquisitional procedures and public condemnation. The university, as a free and self-governing community of scholars, was better prepared to resist ecclesiastical incursions into the classroom, because it exercised its own discipline over its masters and students. As Jacques Le Goff has argued, universities from c.1200 until the early fifteenth century remained relatively insulated from external pressures exerted by "public authorities."[31] Somewhat ironically, it was only at the very end of the Middle Ages that exercise of control over institutions of advanced learning became more intensive. Attempts to intrude into the daily operations of the university tended to be rebuffed or ignored. Witness the general ineffectiveness of various condemnations of Aristotelian learning.

The organization of university instruction on the basis of a scholastic curriculum necessarily encouraged open debate about nearly every topic in theology as well as the liberal arts.[32] No less a figure than Saint Thomas Aquinas vigorously defended the view that the attainment of true knowledge, even on basic theological issues, depended crucially on a process of free and rational discussion and argumentation: "Anyone who wants really to understand and know some truth will find it very helpful to know the doubts and objections raised about it. By resolving doubts one discovers truth, and so, if one is to know the truth about something, it is very important for one to see the reasons for holding a contrary opinion."[33] Aquinas maintains that public disputation in the university community, conducted on the basis of reason alone rather than through citation of authority, constitutes the most effective method of learning from conflicting points of view.[34] "There is no better way of disclosing truth and refuting error," Thomas observes, "than by opposing the opposition."[35] The scholastic method pioneered and refined in European universities thus afforded wide scope for fundamental disagreement and continuing contestation about the most profound questions of the age.

The other institutional development conducive to intellectual freedom in the Middle Ages was the growth in the authority and size of secular governments. Throughout Europe, kings and other lay rulers and communities increasingly required literate servants to perform the everyday tasks of administration, adjudication, and diplomacy. These offices were commonly filled by university-educated men—often, but not exclusively, lawyers—who, regardless of their clerical status, owed their careers to their temporal masters and who served them unfailingly. In many cases, such persons were behind plots to enhance the political or financial power of lay rulers at the expense of the Church: For example, the Paris-trained counselors to the French king Philip the Fair largely precipitated and guided his conflict with Pope Boniface VIII.[36] The protection afforded by temporal lords also permitted authors to engage in hearty public debate about the foundations and legitimacy of ecclesiastical power and to propound with aplomb doctrines that were clearly heretical as well as damaging to the Church. At the most extreme, a ruler such as the German king Ludwig of Bavaria might gather around him a large retinue of infamous schoolmen to employ as an arsenal in a war of words with the papacy.[37]

The Latin Middle Ages, then, produced a vital intellectual culture that proved capable of accommodating disagreement and dispute over fundamental questions. Such questions concerned not merely arcane scholastic topics, but extended to matters of deep and immediate religious and political significance. Educated individuals in medieval Europe may not always have been happy about the cacophony of opinions expressed, but they seem to have accorded sufficient respect to their opponents that they ordinarily responded with reasoned treatises, rather than seeking direct suppression of ideas with which they took exception.

Medieval Christianity and Non-Christians

Another token of forbearance during the Latin Middle Ages stems from the open dissemination of Islamic learning. Islam posed a challenge to medieval Christianity different from that of pagan antiquity: Islam was a vital religious force with which the Christian West had repeatedly clashed over the salvation of souls. The Crusades and religious violence in the Middle East, however, formed only one side of the story. The Western presence in the Holy Lands also produced fruitful contact and growing familiarity with Islamic culture.[38] Moreover, the Muslim presence came to be felt at least at the southern fringes of the Latin world. That Christians and Muslims were capable of coexisting in relative proximity is demonstrated by the circumstances of Spain, where *convivencia* was the watchword for adherents to the various sects residing there.[39] (Of course, much of the explanation for such peaceful coexistence in Spain doubtless lies with Islam itself, which had already established a fuller tradition of tolerance than was known in the medieval West.)[40] Yet it remains true that no medieval Christian would have dreamed of living in complete equality with Muslims in the heart of Europe.

At the same time, however, the Church did permit scholars to study the writings of their Islamic counterparts, especially commentaries on the pagan classics.[41] Unlike Christianity, Islam had maintained a vigorous intellectual life, stimulated by familiarity with the ancient Greek philosophers, throughout the Middle Ages: Islamic scholars read Greek, translated pagan texts into Arabic, and produced voluminous commentaries and original studies. It was largely through contact with Islam, in turn, that the Latin West renewed its acquaintance with the learning of the ancient Greek world. In this process, not only were original texts translated into Latin (sometimes from an Arabic intermediary rather than directly from Greek), but also a large body of related Islamic literature. In certain cases, Islamic writings were mistakenly thought to be the genuine work of Greek antiquity (as with the pseudo-Aristotelian *Secreta secretorum*); more often Latin readers were fully aware of the Islamic provenance of a text, as in the instance of the writings of Avicenna (Ibn Sina) and Averroes (Ibn Rushd), both of whom were revered in the West. Indeed, Averroes quickly earned the title "The Commentator" for his authoritative textual analysis of the corpus of Aristotle, "The Philosopher." It is perhaps not too great an exaggeration to say that Islam played a major role in shaping the way in which Latin Christendom assimilated and embraced the wisdom of the ancients from the twelfth century onward. The intellectual importance of Islam in the Latin West is hardly compatible with an attitude of intransigence and indiscriminate intolerance toward all infidels.

Of course, one might say that the toleration accorded to Islam was "merely theoretical," because the ideas promoted by Islamic texts were just as disembodied in the Christian West (at least outside of southern Europe) as the teachings of the long-dead ancient pagans. That is, an important distinction perhaps ought to be made between permitting a few Christian scholars to read non-Christian writings and an officially Christian society's ability to live on a daily basis with people who practice a non-Christian faith. Even if this is so, however, Christianity throughout the Middle Ages did coexist in just such fashion with another prominent religion, Judaism.

Judaism was as much an anomaly in medieval Europe as it had been during the period of Roman ascendance. Jewish communities existed in many European cities, and although their members lacked rights identical to Christians, the common image of medieval Jews as under constant threat of pogrom or expulsion is now regarded as overdrawn.[42] Despite the fact that they were never integrated into the mainstream of Latin society, Jews could not be entirely expunged from it either.[43] Consequently, canon lawyers commonly defended a range of fundamental rights for Jews living under Christian jurisdiction in the West.[44] Jews formed a stable presence in the West, their numbers fluctuating at about the same rate as the general European population.[45] Medieval Jewry may have been reviled and despised, but it played a vital role in the social, economic, and intellectual life of the Middle Ages.

Much of the explanation for this situation must be referred to the historical resilience displayed by Jewish communities, to their ability to adapt to circumstance, but some of the reason for the perpetuation of Judaism in Western Europe rests with Christianity itself. The Jews, of course, enjoyed a special place in the history of the Christian religion, inasmuch as Christianity styled itself the fulfillment of traditional Judaic prophesies. From the patristic era onward, it was argued that Christian forbearance toward Jewish communities was justified by their function as witnesses to the law of the Old Testament as well as by the scriptural promise of Jewish conversion at the end of the world.[46] Although hardly sufficient to halt popular expressions of anti-Semitism, it did afford the Jewish faith a formal (albeit limited) toleration, the significance of which should not be disparaged.

The comparison of Judaism with heresy is instructive. Heretics remained, technically speaking, members of the Church through their baptism, their very marginality in this regard rendering them "dangerous" to the faithful. Somewhat ironically, the outsider status of Jews shielded them from the treatment afforded to heretics. According to canonists and theologians, "The faithful were not required to shun pagans and Jews in the same way as excommunicates, not only because the former 'did not care much' when they were ostracized . . . but also because the church had no responsibility or authority to discipline non-Christians."[47] Although Innocent IV may have claimed for the papacy the right to impose on those outside the church the law appropriate to them (for instance, the law of Moses on Jews),[48] there seems to have been little serious attempt to apply this principle. If the incidence of intolerance toward the Jews was on the rise during the later Middle Ages, as has been documented,[49] then this may well have been due to the erosion of ecclesiastical influence over secular government, rather than the result of pressure brought to bear on temporal authorities by the Church.

Conclusion

Granted that medieval Christendom was not an entirely open society, when judged by post-Enlightenment standards, neither was it the closed and monolithic "persecuting society" that it has been portrayed. Rather, the Latin Middle Ages harbored opportunities to pursue and defend different understandings of religious faith without their necessarily suffering complete suppression or exclusion. Many expressions of dissent from religious authority, as we have seen, occurred in a closed and essentially academic sphere, but some, at least, had public and even popular dimensions. Once we come to realize that the unitary *Respublica Christiana* was at best an aspiration of medieval life—an ideal that was perhaps so revered because it seemed so unattainable—we may begin to perceive the diverse strands of thought and practice that lay beneath the veneer of unity.

None of this is to gloss over the difficulties and dangers associated with resistance to the rigid uniformity esteemed by the Roman Church during the Middle Ages. Yet an appreciation of the context may help to explain how and why some medieval writers were able to criticize dull devotion to the image of a single universal faith, governance, and culture and thus to consider strategies for coping with the worlds of difference that dotted the religious landscape. Observing the persistence of deep divisions, intellectual as well as cultural, in the beliefs held by Christians as well as non-Christians, these authors came to articulate principles to explain and justify the existence of diverse forms of human life, rather than simply seeking to eliminate all such difference. In criticizing the theory and practice of intolerance, some medieval thinkers began (if only implicitly) to conceive of toleration as an object of theoretical reflection and as a permanent and necessary feature of the social and intellectual terrain, not just a temporary or expedient measure. Once writers confronted the inherent diversity of human life and hence admitted the practical impossibility of narrowly enforced religious conformity, they naturally started to consider ways in which people with divergent beliefs and practices could live together. Here may be found the germ of various theories of tolerance generated in Europe from the twelfth to the sixteenth centuries.

2

Demonstration and Mutual Edification in Inter-religious Dialogue

Debating Intolerance

Beneath the veneer of confidence exuded by the rhetoric of the monolithic *Respublica Christiana,* Latin Christianity after the turn of the millennium became increasingly anxious and insecure about its doctrines and institutions. Contact with non-Christian cultures, transmission of pagan classical learning, demands for the moral regeneration of the Church and its officers—all these developments may be viewed as contributing to a general trepidation about the foundations of Christian religion. The Church reacted to such circumstances by closing ranks, clinging to its self-proclaimed unity, and enhancing its efforts to suppress and persecute its enemies (real or perceived).

But not every medieval thinker was entirely comfortable with repression as a response to religious nonconformity. For some, instead, the tenets of Christianity, not to mention the lessons of philosophy and history, suggested that differences in belief ought to be addressed from the standpoint of patience and charity, manifested through dialogue and discussion. Thus, the very period in which the rise of persecution has been detected also witnessed an upsurge in writings that took the form of inter-religious dialogue, that is, discussion between persons of different faiths, sects, or both, directed toward the discovery of truth or, at least, common ground. Inter-religious debates had debuted in the patristic era, pioneered by writers such as Minucius Felix, Justin Martyr, and Tertullian, and were revived during the High Middle Ages by Christian authors; Jews and Muslims likewise employed the format.[1] Among the salient contributions to the medieval dialogue genre may be counted the *Disputatio Judei et Christiani* and *Disputatio cum gentili* (c. 1092–93) of Gilbert Crispin, Peter Abelard's *Dialogus inter philosophum, Judaeum, et Christianum* (c. 1130), and the *Liber de gentili et tribus sapientibus* (c. 1275) by Ramon Llull. In these works, characters representing two or more confessions discuss the relative merits of their beliefs and rites, either among themselves or before some appointed arbiter.

Is it fair to classify these dialogues as expressions of religious toleration? It is certainly an overstatement to assert a necessary relation between dialogue and tolerance. As Gary Remer observes in his analysis of Reformation-era inter-religious discourses, "Not all dialogues are tolerant." Nonetheless, one may identify a "long-standing connection" between dialogue and toleration, based on precepts of prudence and rhetoric as well as on logic.[2] Jay Newman remarks that "in a pluralistic society, the main way in which people of different faiths come to co-operate and to be tolerant of one another is through religious dialogue."[3] The alternative, Newman notes, is the mutual suspicion and hostility engendered by constant monological proselytizing (or worse, overt violence) among diverse religious groups.[4] Although Europe in the Middle Ages was certainly not a fully "pluralistic society" in the sense Newman means, we have seen that it was sufficiently diverse that open exchange of views afforded the opportunity to diffuse anxiety and to promote a settled spirit of cooperation and tolerance.

Of course, one might wonder whether works in the medieval inter-religious genre deserve to be labeled "dialogues" at all. After all, they were not records of actual discussions, but fictive constructions by Latin Christian authors writing for an audience already sharing essentially identical religious convictions.[5] It might be thought that the dialogue format was purely heuristic; and some of the earliest of the medieval exponents of inter-religious dispute, such as Odo of Tournai,[6] did use non-Christian characters simply for expository purposes. Yet a number of Latin writers seem to have realized that a necessary characteristic of genuine dialogue is human reason, the ability to comprehend rational proofs and also to question the adequacy of such proofs. To the extent that they held all human beings, regardless of their faith, to possess powers of reason, instilled in them by God and nature, medieval thinkers could accept a rational standard of intellectual debate that did not overtly favor the author-ity of Christianity over other religious persuasions.[7] Reason afforded a clear alternative to intolerant oppression and violence. Indeed, a measure of toler-ation must be assumed for any inter-religious dialogue (even an imagined one) to move forward: Engaging in rational comparison of divergent beliefs pre-supposes some (minimal) respect for differences of conviction. Such a con-nection was acknowledged by a wide range of medieval authors from the late eleventh century onward.

At the same time, not all medieval inter-religious dialogues were identical in character and approach. Where many such writings (including the earli-est of them) were largely didactic in nature—what may be termed a "dialogue of demonstration"—some of them displayed a higher degree of sensitivity to the complexities of debate, and thus less readiness to seek closure—which shall be called the "dialogue of mutual edification." The former type of dialogue demonstrates to readers (and to participants) the absolute and final truth of a single dogma. The latter sort defers the determination of such ultimate judg-ment in the name of mutual respect and openness to learning through dis-course. Hence, the "dialogue of demonstration" is overtly concordant, in Mario Turchetti's sense of granting temporary forbearance in the name of establish-ing permanent unity.[8] By contrast, the "dialogue of mutual edification" is more properly and completely tolerant, ceding to disputants an open-ended oppor-tunity to pursue their disagreements with an extended and deepened under-standing of their interlocutors' (and their own) convictions. The "dialogue of mutual edification" is thus stimulated by a "practical educational motive" iden-tified by Newman: "By talking with men of other faiths, by being prepared to learn from them, we can enrich our own faith."[9]

Principles of Rational Dialogue

The medieval use of the dialogue genre as a means for developing theological and philosophical precepts owed a great deal to Anselm of Canterbury, who produced a large body of such works in the course of his long career. Anselm's dialogues were generally of the "master and pupil" variety and thus narrowly didactic in character, although one treatise that may be from his hand involves a debate between a Christian and a Gentile.[10] Yet the operative principle throughout Anselm's writings is that at least some matters of Christian doc-trine may be discussed and demonstrated rationally, that is, without direct dependence on either authoritative texts or inspired faith. As the Gentile in the Anselmian *Disputatio inter Christianum et gentilem* proclaims, in asking of the Christian why God humbled himself through the Incarnation, "I do not want this to be proved by the authority of your Scriptures, in which I do not believe, but, if this has been done rationally, I desire the reason for this event."[11] The Christian's response is framed by this request, and the Gentile eventually submits as a "faithful disciple" based on the compelling rationality of the explanations given to him.[12]

The aim of demonstrating religious truth by reason alone is typical of the inter-religious dialogues of the twelfth and thirteenth centuries. Gilbert Crispin, a close associate and student of Anselm, emphasized the rational quality of discussion with non-Christians in both his popular dialogues. The philosophically trained Gentile in the *Disputatio cum gentili* insists that reason must be the sole criterion for debate, because "truth and reason can be refuted by no one."[13] The Christian, in his turn, agrees to the limitation to "leave out of account the authority of our scriptures."[14] For Gilbert, the consequence of a rationally based dialogue is the disputants' forbearance in relation to their differing beliefs. The educated Jewish character of the *Disputatio Judei et Christiani* remarks to his interlocutor (supposedly Gilbert himself), "Since Christians claim that you are learned in letters and ready with the faculty of speaking, I should like you to deal with me in a tolerant spirit."[15] Rational dialogue, it seems, entails a measure of decorum, a level of mutual respect among the participants, or, as Gilbert says, "conversation in a friendly spirit."[16] To proceed otherwise is to invite invective and the breakdown of the entire rational enterprise through appeal to exclusive authority and revelation. Gilbert thereby admits a direct link between inter-religious dialogue and tolerance.

A similar connection is drawn more extensively in Abelard's *Dialogus inter philosophum, Judaeum, et Christianum*. The *Dialogus* (or *Collationes*, as it is titled in one early manuscript)[17] occurs in three parts. In the opening, prefatory section, Abelard recounts a dream in which he is visited by three wise men—a philosopher, a Jew, and a Christian—who agree on only one point: the existence of a single deity.[18] They ask him to arbitrate their remaining differences of faith and way of life, a request to which he somewhat reluctantly consents. The second portion contains a conversation between the Jew and the philosopher about Jewish teachings, and the final part recounts a discussion of the philosopher with the Christian. The *Dialogus* ends without Abelard rendering his judgment, and it has consequently been counted among his several unfinished works (a contention that is examined later).

As with Gilbert's inter-religious dialogues, which may have provided the model for Abelard, the *Dialogus* stipulates that the discussion will be guided wholly by the standards of reason. The dispute between the three characters is motivated by the concerns of the philosopher, who regards it as his "proper task . . . to search into the truth by rational means and in all things not to follow the opinion of human beings but the lead of reason."[19] Having first acquired learning in moral philosophy, he says, he undertook examination of "the different religious schools of thought around me into which the world is now divided," only to be disappointed: "I discovered the Jews to be stupid and the Christians insane."[20] Neither confession, he repeatedly contends, adds anything to moral learning that cannot be discovered by rational reflection on natural law; and indeed both sorts of worship teach many doctrines that cannot be demonstrated by reason, but depend on authority or pure faith. The philosopher in fact evinces doubt about whether either Jews or Christians have any rational precepts standing behind their convictions, rather than merely the force of uncritical tradition and the threat of persecution.[21] Consequently, "the one who does not go beyond the common understanding of the people is said to be most steadfast in the faith. Surely the result of this is that no one is allowed to inquire into what is to be believed or to doubt what everyone affirms, without fear of punishment. . . . Hence, they take the greatest glory in their apparent belief in what can be neither expressed in words nor conceived by the mind."[22] The challenge posed by the *Dialogus*, then, is for the representatives of the two faiths to reveal the reasons for their teachings under the scrupulous questioning of the philosopher.

Abelard recounts that his arbitration is sought to put an end to the debate, even though it is acknowledged that he himself is a Christian. But because any judge, the philosopher says, is bound to be from one of the three sects, better it be someone who excels "in intellectual acumen" and is renowned for "broad learning," as well as a person who has prevailed "under persecution" of his own writings.[23] Abelard accepts the commission to arbitrate in part because he recognizes the free and symmetrical foundation of the discussion: "You have set this up by agreement and mutual consent, and I see that each of you has confidence in his own powers."[24] In other words, the conditions of unobstructed rational debate have been met: Each party may express himself openly and without fear, invoking only the standards of reason. Abelard also contends that dialogue is conducive to education: "I believe that I will learn something from this. In fact, as one of your own [Saint Augustine] reminds us, 'There is no teaching so false that there is not some true teaching mixed in.' And I believe that there is no disputation so frivolous that it does not contain some instructive lesson."[25] If it is too much to detect here the spirit of John Stuart Mill's defense of liberty of speech, Abelard is still advocating the principle that open discussion is always conducive to the ongoing quest for truth. His dialogue is a tolerant one, inasmuch as all parties to the dispute are to be permitted the free expression of their views within the parameters set by a reasoned exchange of ideas. Even the Jew, whose teachings come under the harshest criticism, is presented sympathetically as one whose people has sustained itself despite the "great contempt and hatred" inflicted by both sects, Gentile and Christian alike.[26]

In the next century, Ramon Llull's *Liber de gentili et tribus sapientibus* continued to subscribe to the attitude of tolerance pioneered by the dialogues of Gilbert and Abelard. A Spaniard who lived under the reality of *convivencio* among Christians, Jews, and Muslims, Llull's interest in inter-religious dialogue was more practical and realistic than was that of his Northern predecessors. (The work may have been composed as a teaching tool for Llull's Christian missionary school.) He announces early in the Prologue his intention to write not a work of "speculative science," but rather "a book for laymen," expressed "in plain words."[27] As a result of his circumstances, moreover, Llull enjoyed greater familiarity with the actual teachings espoused by members of non-Christian sects. Consequently, the *Liber* more nearly reflects the complexities, socially and culturally as well as doctrinally, of multireligious experience.

Llull's sensitivity is captured, most obviously, in the great lengths to which he goes to establish the dramatic setting of the dialogue. The main discussion of the *Liber* arises from the convergence of two narratives. First, he recounts the tale of "a Gentile, very learned in philosophy, who began to worry about old age, death, and the joys of this world," and who became so agitated about his situation that he resolved to leave his homeland and travel abroad to find answers to his unsolved questions.[28] By coincidence, three wise men—a Jew, a Christian, and a Saracen—were setting off from their city along the same route as the Gentile. These three were clearly acquainted, for, Llull tells us, "When they were outside the city and saw each other, they approached and greeted one another in friendly fashion, and they accompanied one another, each inquiring about the other's health and what he intended to do."[29] Llull thereby establishes at once the tone of mutual respect and decorum for which the *Liber* has become known: Although members of competing faiths, the wise men conduct themselves in a dignified and convivial manner.

Initially, the three wise men encounter a lady, named Intelligence, who explains to them the principles of Llull's famous "Art," that is, his "new method and new reasons" of scientific demonstration.[30] The details of this Art need not detain us here; it forms the basis of the so-called Llullism that was to be expounded (and condemned) by later generations of medieval philosophers and theologians.[31] The lady Intelligence explains the operation of the Art in what Llull evidently intends to be exoteric terms, by reference to a metaphor of five trees, each of which represents one category of analysis.[32] After Intelligence departs, the wise men express awe and admiration for her system of rational demonstration, which they realize affords the opportunity to achieve some concordance on those points of religious dispute that have long separated them. One of the wise men remarks, "Since we cannot agree by means of authorities, let us try to come to some agreement by means of demonstrative and necessary reasons."[33] As they prepare to discuss their differences, however, they are immediately interrupted by the wandering and despondent Gentile, whom they greet in a friendly manner, and who consequently unburdens his woes before them.[34] Having discovered that the philosopher is completely innocent of revealed religion, the wise men concur that they must teach him what they know of God and His saving powers to rescue him from his misery. They resolve to do so by employing "the method shown us by the Lady of Intelligence [sic]," that is, by rational Art.[35]

In the first book, the three wise men defend the basic principles of monotheistic religion and the afterlife shared in common by Judaism, Christianity, and Islam, in contrast to Abelard's *Dialogus*, where the existence of one deity is taken for granted by all the interlocutors. As they enlighten the Gentile, the wise men's speeches are presented interchangeably, with no reference to the identity of the speaker. Indeed, they discourse with such unanimity that the Gentile has no idea that they subscribe to differing confessions: "'What!' cried the Gentile, 'Are the three of you not of a single religion and belief?' 'No,' replied the wise men, 'we differ as to belief and religion, for one of us is a Jew, the other a Christian, and the other a Saracen.' 'And which of you,' asked the Gentile, 'has the better religion, and which of these religions is true?'"[36] The three wise men immediately begin bickering about the superiority of their respective convictions, leading the Gentile back into his pit of despair. Finally, the Gentile induces them to "debate before him and . . . each give his arguments as best he could, so that he could see which of them was on the path to salvation."[37] The ensuing discussion, which takes up the remaining three books of the *Liber*, is consciously and carefully structured according to rules that all freely accept in advance: The dialogue will proceed according to the method of the Art; none of the speakers will "contradict the other while he was presenting his arguments"; and the Gentile himself will serve as questioner of the representatives of each faith.[38] The second book contains a defense of Judaism; the third, Christian apologetic; and the fourth, a polemic on behalf of Islam—the order of presentation determined solely by reference to the antiquity of the religion under scrutiny.

The decorum of rational dialogue is enforced throughout the *Liber*. When, at the beginning of Book 4, the Christian becomes upset with the Muslim's denial of the Trinity and attempts to interrupt, "the Gentile said it was not his turn to speak, and that he himself would answer the Saracen."[39] Moreover, Llull demonstrates noteworthy sympathy for the doctrines of the non-Christian sects. Like Abelard, he is eloquent about the sufferings inflicted on the Jews by their Christian and Islamic masters;[40] and he provides a balanced account of the Muslim's sensualistic conception of Paradise.[41] In sum, the tolerant tone of rational dialogue evident in Lull's twelfth-century predecessors is maintained and advanced in the *Liber*. Llull evidently believed that rigorous adherence to his Art alone would be sufficient to produce a satisfactory result.

From Demonstration to Mutual Edification

It may plausibly be objected that there is nothing about the rational inter-religious dialogues of the Middle Ages that is truly tolerant at all, in the sense of extending permanent and inviolable protection to those who dissent from ultimate religious (Christian) truth. Rather, the inter-religious writings that we have surveyed might seem to be better described as "concordant" in Turchetti's aforementioned sense. Thus, Gilbert Crispin's dialogues end in much the same manner as the Anselmian *Disputatio*, with the demonstration of the absolute validity of Christian belief over Judaism and natural religion: The Jew and the Gentile are silenced. Near the end of the *Disputatio cum gentili*, in particular, the Gentile is replaced by a character identified as a "disciple"; the dialogue reverts to a more traditional "master and pupil" format.[42] Likewise, Abelard's express purpose in the *Dialogus* is to reach some final judgment about which of the three convictions represented is true.[43] As the philosopher remarks, "We are conferring together in the search for truth."[44] Even Llull prefaces the *Liber* by stating as its goal that "those in error might be shown the path to glory without end and the means of avoiding infinite suffering."[45] The desire for unity is confirmed by the wise men themselves: "What a great good fortune it be if . . . we could all—every person on earth—be under one religion and belief, so that there would be no more rancor or ill will among people, who hate each other because of diversity and contrariness of beliefs and sects."[46] None of these inter-religious debates, then, seems to conceive of tolerance as much more than a practical measure, a grant to be withdrawn when truth shines forth as the result of rational dialogue.

Certainly, this charge has merit in the case of the earliest texts we have examined: Little in Gilbert's writings suggests that toleration is anything more than an expedient to facilitate the process of rational demonstration and, it is hoped, conversion. The Christian faith is shown to be unquestionably superior to its competitors. In the instances of Abelard and Llull, however, there is reason to suppose that a different and subtler model of dialogue—a discourse concerned with edification rather than merely demonstration—is being employed. With Abelard and especially Llull, we encounter recognition that the truth or falsity of a confession is not easily established, so that dialogue is better conceived of as an open-ended process, the purpose of which is the instruction of the participants (and implicitly the audience).

In Abelard's *Dialogus*, the evidence for this edificatory approach to dialogue is partial and tentative. He gives us a glimpse of his intentions in a personal aside that occurs after the first discussion between the philosopher and the Jew, but before the discourse of the Christian with the philosopher. Having been asked to render his decision about the merits of the Jew's position in comparison to the philosopher's, the judge (Abelard himself) replies: "I, however, more desirous of learning than of judging, answer that I first wish to hear the arguments of all so that the wiser I become by listening, the more discerning will I be in judging. . . . All unanimously agreed to this, inflamed with the same desire to learn."[47] The clear message is that wise judgment depends on full knowledge of the issues to be arbitrated, and thus that the preemptive closure of discussion impedes education. Abelard regards the very purpose of the debate as instructional, both for himself and for the interlocutors. Judgment is therefore deferred and is, of course, never rendered at the end of the *Dialogus*.

Scholars have generally assumed that the latter feature of Abelard's treatise is simply the result of his failure to complete the work.[48] Certainly, the *Dialogus* does break off rather abruptly, and there is no evidence in any of the extant manuscripts that further passages are missing. Constant Mews has, however, lately argued that a number of grounds exist for the alternative view that Abelard's text is indeed complete as he conceived it: "The lack of a firm conclusion to this treatise is not an accident due to external circumstances beyond Abelard's control, but a characteristic of his thought."[49] On Mews's account, Abelard provided no final judgment because, given his philosophy of language and of mind, matters of doctrine were not susceptible to ready settlement. Rather, in a sense, Abelard defers his own judgment so that readers may make an independent determination. In this connection, Mews assimilates the rhetorical technique of the *Dialogus* to that of *Sic et Non*, a work that contains contradictory and unreconciled statements by major Church Fathers about the divinity of Christ. Abelard explains in the Preface to *Sic et Non* that only by "persistent and frequent questioning" is it possible to understand these conflicting statements and hence to achieve wisdom.[50] Abelard himself, however, provides only the riddles, not the solutions. Therefore, Mews argues, "The *Sic et Non* is like the *Dialogus* in being an invitation to thought. . . . Judgement on the questions under debate is left to the reader, rather than imposed by Abelard himself."[51]

If Mews is correct about the completed state of the *Dialogus*, then Abelard has taken a considerable step toward transforming the inter-religious dialogue from a polemical to an edificatory tool. This fact has profound significance, in turn, for tolerance: Without denying that ultimate truth may be attained, Abelard in effect renders concordance problematic inasmuch as he postpones judgment because of the uncertainties and obscurities of doctrine (as well as the infirmities of human mental faculties). We must take seriously Abelard's claim that the value of dialogue is "learning." We discover the range of human beliefs, and their basis in reason, and thereby sharpen our ability to discriminate falsehoods and insupportable superstitions. We do not, however, establish truth, except perhaps provisionally, on condition that our understanding may be further deepened and transformed by additional debate and inquiry. The deferral of final judgment consequently implies the necessity of continuing toleration of questioning and dissent.

The model of dialogue as mutual edification is far more completely and elaborately developed in Llull's *Liber*. As in the case of Abelard's *Dialogus*, discernment of the validity of competing confessions is the stated purpose of the work. Yet the role of judge is played not by a potentially interested party (the Christian Abelard), but by the neutral Gentile, who has only the purest of motives in choosing the true faith. More significantly, the Epilogue to the *Liber*, in which final judgment is to be proclaimed, is filled with intriguing ambiguity. Having listened closely to the respective discourses of the Jew, the Christian, and the Muslim and having understood each of their teachings so precisely that they praise him, the Gentile has clearly come to his final decision. He offers to his new God a lengthy prayer, which still contains no clue as to his determination because it is couched in the terms of Lull's rational method of the Art.[52] He is about to proclaim his choice, when he is interrupted by the distant sighting of two compatriots whom he recognizes and in front of whom he wishes to declare his new faith. The three wise men, however, decline to remain and, in a surprise ending unprecedented in inter-religious dialogue, take their leave before judgment is rendered.

The Gentile asked them in astonishment why they did not wait to hear which religion he would choose in preference to the others. The three wise men answered, saying that, in order for each to be free to choose his own religion, they preferred not knowing which religion he would choose. "And all the more so since this is a question we could discuss amongst ourselves to see, by force of reason and by means of our intellects, which religion it must be that you will choose. And if, in front of us, you state which religion it is that you prefer, then we would not have such a good subject of discussion nor such satisfaction in discovering the truth."[53]

The decision remains unstated, and readers never discover the confession to which the Gentile converts. Just as remarkable is the rationale given by the three wise men for wishing to remain in ignorance. First, they assert something that sounds very close to a principle of liberty of conscience: All people must be free to choose their religion for themselves. The principle is left ungrounded, but it may contain echoes of the traditional Christian view that genuine consent, not external compulsion or force, must dictate one's convictions. Moreover, the wise men appeal to the ongoing nature of their own discussions as reason to depart without hearing the Gentile's decision. They express a wish to pursue the debate among themselves, unencumbered by prior knowledge of his choice, which would only tip the scales in one or another direction. In sum, they recognize that the choice of the true religion is a complex process, even after all that has been said to the Gentile on behalf of their respective faiths.

Nor does the *Liber* close with the departure of the three wise men from the company of the Gentile. Rather, Llull recounts their talk on the way back to the city. They again bemoan the harm that comes from inter-religious strife and agree on the desirability of achieving concordance.[54] The wise men ascribe the diversity of confessions to earthly causes, such as the deference human beings pay to "the faith in which they found themselves, and in which they were raised by their parents and ancestors," as well as to their love "of temporal possessions."[55] As the three enter the city gates, they apologize to one another for whatever insult or slight each might have given to the religion of his companions. Then, most intriguingly of all, they agree to perpetual continuation of their dialogue. "When they were about to part, one wise man said: 'Do you think we have nothing to gain from what happened to us in the forest? Would you like to meet once a day and . . . discuss according to the manner the Lady of Intelligence showed us, and have our discussions until all three of us have only one faith, one religion, and until we can find some way to honor and serve one another, so that we can be in agreement?'"[56] The dialogue closes with a consensus on this proposal, assigning "a time and place for their discussions, as well as how they should honor and serve one another, and how they should dispute. . . . Each of the three wise men went home and remained faithful to his promise."[57] The latter words are the final ones of Llull's narrative, to which is appended only a short coda in which the author expresses hope that he has adequately illuminated a rational method "for entering into union with and getting to know strangers and friends."[58]

Although Llull's *Liber* never surrenders the conviction that religious truth exists and unity of faith remains possible (indeed, desirable), it can hardly be construed as a work of concordance. His message, instead, is that agreement cannot be forced and must be postponed (to a seemingly indefinite future) while rational discussion and comparison of various creeds continue. The three wise men are not presented simply as missionaries full of conversional zeal. They recognize that, even with the possession of a commonly accepted rational method, the discovery of the truth is a process shrouded in difficulty and uncertainty. No one should give up the quest for truth on account of these obstacles, but Llull offers no guarantees that even the wisest of persons will be able to attain it absolutely to the point that he may convince others without dissent. Toleration must be the norm, because a tolerant attitude forms the inescapable condition for the ongoing, open-ended, and free dialogue that alone holds the potential for universal religious harmony. Mutual edification may remain a means to the end of concord, but the potential for reaching that end is so deferred by Llull that dialogue comes to be virtually a goal in itself, a worthy alternative to the hostility and misery that inter-religious conflict generates.

Conclusion

In what was perhaps the most tolerant inter-religious dialogue of the Reformation era, Jean Bodin's *Colloquium*, the various characters, having praised and debated their own disparate convictions, resolve never again to discuss the matter among one another.[59] Whether this signifies Bodin's belief that religious issues are inherently resistant to rational scrutiny (as some scholars suggest[60]), or that each of the adherents has come to an improved understanding of his own and his fellows' faith (as others contend[61]), the *Colloquium* still sets limits on the dialogical enterprise. By contrast, the medieval inter-religious dialogues of mutual edification composed by Christians seem more sanguine about the value of continued discussion and more inclined to accept the open-ended nature of the debate. Granted that the many inter-religious dialogues were largely hypothetical and didactic, their authors nonetheless subscribed to an ideal of rational discussion that stands at a distance from the commonplace conception of monolithic medieval Christianity. They promoted a spirit of tolerance that enabled some authors (quite possibly Abelard and certainly Llull) to raise rational debate among competing religions to a high level of openness.

Hence, as a philosophical and literary genre, medieval inter-religious writing seems to meet the conditions of genuinely tolerant dialogue, understood from the perspective of education rather than conversion. As Newman explains, "Religious dialogue, or any other form of dialogue, requiring as it does a talking *between* rather than a talking *at*, requires that those who enter into it be full-fledged, sincere *listeners*, as well as full-fledged, sincere *speakers*, that they be prepared to learn as well as to teach. In effect, it requires that one respect the integrity and rationality of one's partner in discussion."[62] Although Newman plausibly shows that not all medieval conceptions of interfaith communication met this standard (Aquinas, for example, holds fast to a "conversionist" idea[63]), the works of Abelard and Llull seem congenial to this educational goal. Nor ought it to be objected that the open-ended quality of their dialogues conveys a covert message: namely, to teach the impossibility of achieving any rational agreement whatsoever. Both Abelard and Llull explicitly upheld the possibility of reaching agreement about the truths of faith through reason alone. Rather, the doubts they expressed were about the ease of such consensus, because of the complexities of the subject matter as well as the frailties of human mental faculties. It is this humility in the presence of diverse and well thought-out faiths that forms the cornerstone of truly tolerant dialogue during the Latin Middle Ages.

3

Skepticism, Liberty, and the "Clash of Ideas" in John of Salisbury's Writings

Skepticism's Challenge

The recognition that human beings are capable of engaging in rational dialogue, and hence of reaching agreement (eventually) about matters of religion, affords one powerful model on the basis of which intolerance may be dismissed and toleration justified. A very different contention about the human intellect—that mental powers are so weak that certain knowledge is impossible, or at least extremely difficult, to attain—provides an alternative framework for criticizing intolerant practices and attitudes. Such skepticism calls in question the very foundation for the suppression of the ideas to which one is opposed: If one cannot be absolutely certain about the truth of one's own doctrines, then one loses a vital source of legitimization for the condemnation of other teachings.

Philosophical adherence to the skeptical thesis has already been closely associated with the development of ideas of religious toleration in early modern Europe.[1] As Preston King explains, there appears to exist a

> symbiotic relationship . . . between *tolerance* and *scepticism*. The tolerance involves an antipathy towards certain ideas combined with the conviction that one should not exclude from consideration that they

may be correct; the scepticism involves the approval of (meaning "agreement with") certain ideas combined with the conviction that one should not exclude from examination arguments which might prove those views mistaken. . . . *Tolerance*, although it begins with a negative assessment conjoined with a suspended negative act, always involves *scepticism*, conceived as a positive assessment conjoined with a suspended positive act.[2]

Although an automatic connection between skeptical and tolerant stances has been convincingly challenged on historical grounds by some recent scholarship,[3] skepticism still often supported principles of toleration toward religious differences in the early modern world. A wide range of thinkers, from Sebastian Castellio and Jean Bodin in the sixteenth century to Voltaire in the eighteenth, reasoned that the recognition of human fallibility in matters of religion must entail a program of tolerance and respect for dissenting points of view.

Philosophical skepticism itself was by no means an invention of early modern thought. Versions of the skeptical thesis had been popular in pagan antiquity and had been disseminated (via critics such as Saint Augustine as well as by proponents such as Cicero) without a break in medieval and Renaissance Latin Christendom.[4] It has, however, been generally (if somewhat uncritically) assumed that the Christian reception of ancient skepticism was of a largely negative character: a straw man against whom to reaffirm the absolute indubitability of God's revelation and of the moral and metaphysical truths flowing therefrom. This position was adopted by Saint Augustine in his polemic *Contra Academicos*, which sought to refute the methodological skepticism that had been championed by Cicero and other adherents to the Academic School. The unquestioned acceptance of Augustine's attack on the skeptical position by medieval thinkers has been taken as a virtual article of faith. As Richard Tuck remarks, "At the back of many people's minds is a rough history of the modern world in which the dissolution of strongly held beliefs (typically, the relatively unified Christianity of the Middle Ages) was a precondition for extending toleration to men who would once have been attacked as heretics."[5] Hence, the presumption runs that, although medieval Europe was familiar with skepticism, a skeptical outlook could have not been embraced to such an extent as to generate the principles from which toleration (understood as something like a defensible right to freedom of inquiry, conscience, and dissent) might be admitted.

Medieval thinkers were, however, not entirely oblivious to the connection between skeptical and tolerant attitudes. It is possible to detect a direct linkage between skepticism and tolerant attitudes, for instance, in the work of the twelfth-century "humanist" churchman John of Salisbury,[6] who is recognized to be one of the most prominent medieval champions of the moderate skepticism of the New Academy that had been promoted by Cicero.[7] John's political theory incorporates a compelling defense of liberty of thought and speech (and hence of forbearance and toleration) in a wide range of moral matters. In turn, his position is directly tied to his advocacy of Ciceronian skepticism as the appropriate stance to be adopted by the wise person when confronted with complex and difficult philosophical issues. John's interpretation of the Academic School leads to a defense of *de jure* freedom to dispute and dissent in those matters about which rational minds may disagree. His perspective in many ways resembles that of another, later Northern humanist: Desiderius Erasmus of Rotterdam. Like Erasmus, John defends *on principle* a remarkably extensive right on the part of wise individuals to uphold differing points of view about issues of fundamental importance. This resemblance should not be surprising because both thinkers drew heavily on Ciceronian conceptions of mind and speech.[8]

John on Liberty

Without question, John of Salisbury maintained a central role for human liberty in his moral and political thought.[9] The force of his claims made on behalf of such liberty is evident in his *Policraticus* (composed between 1157 and 1159). John defends there a conception of open personal expression that is vast even judged by far later standards. He counsels a doctrine of "patience" for the opinions and deeds of others, which becomes difficult to distinguish from toleration. "The best and wisest man is moderate with the reins of liberty and patiently takes note of whatever is said to him. And he does not oppose himself to the works of liberty, so long as damage to virtue does not occur. For when virtue shines everywhere from its own source, the reputation of patience becomes more evident with glorious renown."[10] The patient man respects the liberty of others to state their own honest opinions, and he attempts to improve himself by patiently regarding his fellows. "The practice of liberty," John observes, "displeases only those who live in the manner of slaves."[11] Free men are reciprocally tolerant of the freedom of others, even when they are the objects of criticism. John praises the Romans for "being more patient than others with censure," because they adhered to the principle that "whoever loathes and evades [criticism] when fairly expressed seems to be ignorant of restraint. For even if it conveys obvious or secret insult, patience with censure is among wise men far more glorious than its punishment."[12] The *Policraticus* supports this claim in characteristic form with numerous *exempla* of wise people who spoke their minds in a straightforward manner and of wise rulers who permitted such free expression to occur.

At one level, John's praise of liberty of thought and speech reflects his conception of decorum and "civility": The refined person permits civilized speech in his presence, and such speech may involve personal criticism and admonitions. But more is at stake than simple good manners. John posits an intimate relation between liberty and morality. "[Virtue] does not arise in its perfection without liberty, and the loss of liberty demonstrates irrefutably that virtue is not present. And therefore anyone is free according to the virtue of one's dispositions, and, to the extent that one is free, the virtues are effective."[13] Freedom makes virtue possible, for no one who is unfree (i.e., unable to make decisions) can ever be counted as capable of moral action. A virtuous (and also presumably a vicious) act is one that an individual has intentionally chosen to do and thus for which one can be held responsible. No such intentional choice is possible in the absence of liberty; the slave merely does as he is told, so that his master must bear the blame for his conduct.

John therefore denies that it is possible to achieve virtue through coercive means. Enforced virtuous actions are not really virtuous at all and do more harm than good to subjects. It is for this reason that he condemns the immoderation (and immorality) of zealous rulers who compel their subjects to perform good deeds and who excessively punish evildoers.[14] Does this imply the view that "every man has the right to go to hell in his own way"? By no means.[15] Although John maintains that there must be a realm of personal discretion in decision making with which no one may interfere, he also insists that patient endurance of the liberty of others must be matched by a liberty of critical speech. John asserts that "it is permitted to censure that which is to be equitably corrected."[16] If we may not properly force people to do good, then we must equally be respected and tolerated when we point out the error of their ways. In other words, if you are free to do wrong, then I must also be free to correct or reprove you. John emphasizes this point: "Liberty . . . is not afraid to censure that which is opposed to sound moral character. . . . Man is to be free, and it is always permitted to a free man to speak to persons about restraining their vices."[17] The *Policraticus* indeed practices what it preaches. John describes an encounter between himself and Pope Adrian IV, in which he recounted to the pontiff all the evils that were commonly ascribed to the

Roman Church and curia.[18] Moreover, John does not shy from lamenting at great length the many sins and vices committed by priests, monks, and other members of the ecclesiastical hierarchy.[19] In fact, John claims that his liberty to censure is not merely a privilege: "It is not necessary to obtain confirmed permission for such remarks which serve the public utility."[20] Freedom to speak one's mind about the ills of society, whether spiritual or temporal, parallels the legitimate liberty to act without restraint.[21]

Of course, the toleration of liberty proposed by John is by no means unlimited. He asserts that the "vices" of individuals, which we ought to endure if we are unable to correct them through free speech, must be distinguished from "flagrant crimes," that is, "acts which one is not permitted to endure or which cannot faithfully be endured."[22] Similarly, he acknowledges that statements made "rashly," that is, without respect for the persons to whom they are addressed and with the intent of harming another's reputation, are deserving of censure and condemnation.[23] The intent must be pure for liberty of action and expression to be tolerated; manifestly irreligious or dishonorable conduct and words have no claim on our patience. Still, individuals are afforded a remarkably large realm of personal freedom not simply in private but as part of their public roles and perhaps even responsibilities.

The political ramifications of John's doctrine of liberty become especially evident when we turn to his well-known conception of the body politic. The *Policraticus* articulated a complex and influential version of the organic metaphor for the political community whose full statement occupies two books and over two hundred pages of text.[24] John compares the ruler to the head, the counselors to the heart, the various administrators and officials to the several organs and limbs, and the peasants and artisans to the feet.[25] Central to this analogy is the construction of civil order on the principle of the social division of labor while rejecting the strictly hierarchical values of the Platonic polis (the outlines of which John would have been familiar with via the opening section of the *Timaeus*).[26] John designed his body politic as a system of harmonious cooperation based on reciprocal interdependence and social and political inclusion.

The recognition and toleration of personal liberty are crucial to the successful operation of the political organism. John insists that all the relations between the members of the community ought to be governed according to a principle consistent with reciprocity. Adapting the advice of Terrence in regard to the treatment of the evils of one's spouse, he proposes that "the vices of princes and subjects ought to be either endured or removed."[27] John points out that "removal" here does not imply coercion or punishment. Rather, according to his interpretation, "'Removing' is meant in the sense of correction. . . . What cannot be removed is to be endured."[28] John thus argues that we ought to attempt to restore erring members of the body politic to the path of virtue, but that, so long as their vices do not disturb the material or spiritual well-being of the whole, they are to be tolerated when they cannot be convinced of their errors. This principle entails both aspects of liberty discussed previously: not only the freedom to speak to people about their vices, but also the liberty to act, at least within the limits of public order.

Several implications follow from the general principles of liberty and toleration espoused in the *Policraticus*. First, the ruler must carefully respect the liberty of his subjects. Indeed, John's famous distinction between the true prince (or king) and the tyrant turns on his doctrine of liberty. By definition, "the prince fights for the laws and the liberty of the people; the tyrant supposes that nothing is done unless the laws are cancelled and the people are brought into servitude."[29] The good ruler necessarily governs so as to promote the liberty of subjects: Liberty "has spurred on all outstanding princes; and none has ever trampled on liberty except for the manifest enemies of virtue."[30] It is perhaps for this reason that John places the prince under the strict dictates of law,[31] because "laws were introduced in support of liberty."[32] That is, law assures men that they will not be subject to the arbitrary will of a ruler and thus that they will be free to act within the fixed and equitable restraints imposed by legal standards.

One consequence of this legally (as well as morally) assured liberty is that a measure of public criticism of superiors, even rulers and priests, must be permitted. John takes great pains to distinguish between "high treason" (*crimen majestas*) and proper free expression. "High treason" has the express purpose of separating the head from its members and thus of violating the reciprocity vital to the life of the body politic. Such an attack on the head is a violation of the whole.[33] John enumerates all the deeds that count as cases of high treason, citing copious legal texts in support of his definition,[34] but it is noteworthy that liberty of conscience, construed as public criticism of the ruler, is excluded as an example of traitorous activity. For this reason, John insists that he is exempt from the charges that he himself is committing high treason by criticizing the bad morals and frivolities of princes and courtiers: "I myself will not be accused unfairly by anyone of having presumed against the authority of the prince."[35] Of course, just as princes (and indeed all people) must endure those vices that cannot be corrected in their fellow human beings, so subjects must tolerate the vices of their superiors. "Even if the ruler is too loose in the virtues of his office, still he has to be honored; and . . . subjects, whom we have said to be the feet and members, should exhibit subservience to him in every way, so long as his vices are not pernicious. For, even if he is afflicted with vices, he is to be endured as one with whom rests the hopes of the provincials for their security."[36] Note, however, that such "subservience" is not slavery. The liberty to speak openly to superiors about their vices in hope of achieving correction cannot be suppressed by a ruler without the enslavement of his subjects, at which point he ceases to be merely vicious and commits a flagrant crime against the body politic. The liberty of the individual members is the life blood of the political organism and is violated only by the tyrant. The proper response of the good ruler is illustrated by the *Policraticus*'s account of the reply of Pope Adrian IV to John's own honest and stinging criticisms of the papal curia: "The pontiff laughed and congratulated such great candor, commanding that whenever anything unfavorable about him made a sound in my ears, he was to be informed of this without delay."[37] Free speech, even of a highly critical nature, is always welcomed at the court of the good ruler.

The Medieval Academy

It might be objected, however, that John's functional or communal defense of personal liberty constitutes an insufficient basis for a full-blooded theory of toleration, inasmuch as it does not include some rights-based conception of individual liberty of conscience or belief.[38] To adopt terminology suggested by Hans Guggisberg, John's position reflects a "politico-pragmatic" or perhaps an "economic" vision of toleration, rather than a "theologico-philosophical" one.[39] Lacking firm principles by means of which an individual may claim a right to exercise liberty apart from direct considerations of some moral or public good, it might be argued, John's account of tolerance remains susceptible to the charge that it permits a political authority to revoke the exercise of liberty when deemed incompatible with standards of virtue or the perceived needs of the community.

Whatever the merits of this objection, it does not pertain to the idea of toleration proposed in the *Policraticus*. John in fact promotes such a philosophical grounding, yielding a *right* of dissent quite apart from communal considerations. The locus of this foundation is to be discovered in John's abiding dedication to the teachings of the Academic School of philosophy, espoused in several works by Cicero available during the Latin Middle Ages. Cicero's defense of a version of Academic philosophy known as the "New

Academy" (sometimes filtered through his Christian critics Augustine and Lactantius) was the primary brand of skepticism with which medieval thinkers were familiar. In a number of his mature writings (including *De natura deorum, De officiis*, and the two versions of the *Academica*), Cicero professed a moderate skepticism about matters in which probability rather than dogmatic certitude seemed the best course.[40] Cicero thus distanced himself from the more radically skeptical method of the so-called Old Academy, which denied that anything whatsoever could be known with certainty.

The fundamentals of Ciceronian skepticism are too well known to require lengthy rehearsal.[41] Cicero succinctly states his guiding principle in the Prologue to *De natura deorum*: "The philosophers of the Academy have been wise in withholding their consent from any proposition that has not been proved. There is nothing worse than a hasty judgment, and nothing could be more unworthy of the dignity and integrity of a philosopher than to adopt a false opinion or to maintain as certain some theory which has not been fully explored and understood."[42] As Cicero explains in the *Academica*, this is not to deny the *possibility* of the human mind attaining truth (*pace* the Old Academy), but only to insist that the criteria for knowing truth and falsity are not inborn or intuitive and that the senses can be deceptive.[43] Cicero's skepticism hence has the character of antidogmatism, not of absolute doubt.

John of Salisbury clearly understood this difference between a moderate and a complete skeptical stance. In his early didactic poem *Entheticus de dogmate philosophorum* (the second section of which, containing a discussion of the Academy, may have been written while studying in Paris during the 1130s and 1140s, but was probably not finished any later than 1155),[44] he chides the radically skeptical Academic view that "the human race is deprived of light."[45] Instead, he prefers the alternative position of the more enlightened Academic that one should

> hesitate in all things except those which are proved by living reason. . . . These things, he declares, are known; he passes doubtfully on other things, of which more certainty is to be had from experience. For the usual course of events makes probable what you always see under a similar pattern. Yet, since it sometimes happens otherwise, these things are not sufficiently certain, and yet not without evidence. What he, therefore, affirms to be true, he thinks to be necessary; for the rest, he says "I believe" or "I think it to be."[46]

Thus, John clearly recognizes the epistemological underpinnings of the rival versions of skeptical philosophy. This fact has been missed, for instance, by

Charles Schmitt, who, concentrating only on the later *Policraticus*, concludes that John "really gives us little detail regarding those aspects—e.g., sense deception or the fallibility of normally accepted logical doctrine—which were central to ancient writings on skepticism. . . . On the whole, . . . his treatment has little philosophical sophistication."[47] On the contrary, if John in his later writings did not dwell on these epistemological issues, it is only because he had previously acknowledged and examined them in the *Entheticus*.

John's expression of admiration for temperate Academic skepticism reinforces another key theme of his work: *modestia* or *moderatio*. He was a convinced adherent to an Aristotelian-tinged doctrine that virtue necessarily consists in the mean and that moderation in all things is therefore the most valid standard for judging human thought and action.[48] As John points out in the *Entheticus*, the Academic stance is consonant with "a modest mind . . . that no one may accuse it of being guilty of falsehood; it thus tempers all words with qualifiers, so that it should always be rightly credible."[49] John stresses that the possessors of such a modest mind "restrain their words according to condition, time, cause, and manner [and] they avoid speaking with too much simplicity."[50] Academic moderation results in rhetorical as well as intellectual humility, if not caution, consistent with the virtuous mean.

John's later work on the current state of scholastic education, the *Metalogicon* (probably written between 1157 and 1159), reiterates the Academic position articulated in the *Entheticus*. He repeatedly proclaims his explicit commitment to the philosophical program of the New Academy. In the Prologue, he announces, "Being an Academic in matters that are doubtful to the wise person, I cannot swear to the truth of what I say. Whether such propositions may be true or false, I am satisfied with probable certainty."[51] John again distances his own version of skepticism from more radical views that deny the possibility of knowing truth (or at any rate, very many truths).[52] He admits that even if truth is susceptible to human comprehension the process of achieving knowledge is troublesome. Echoing a remark by Cicero in the *Academica*, John observes, "It is difficult to apprehend the truth, which (as our Academics say) is as obscure as if it lay at the bottom of a well."[53] Although he demonstrates some sympathy for Saint Augustine's criticisms in *Contra Academicos* of Ciceronian skepticism,[54] John returns often in the *Metalogicon* to Cicero's methodological injunction against embracing insufficiently substantiated truth-claims too hastily in the quest for knowledge. Indeed, a main theme of the *Metalogicon* might aptly be characterized as the refutation of the arid argumentation that occurred among the Parisian teachers of his time as a result of their unwillingness to renounce their rigid formulas and fixed dogmas.

Skepticism in the *Policraticus*

John of Salisbury's most extensive discussion and use of the Ciceronian New Academy occurs not in the *Entheticus* or the *Metalogicon,* however, but in the *Policraticus.* There, as we shall see, he appeals to Academic philosophy in ways that are crucial for establishing the principles of his theory of toleration. The *Policraticus* once again contains repeated self-identification of its author with the teachings of the Academy, its Prologue echoing the words of the *Metalogicon:* "In philosophy, I am a devotee of Academic dispute, which measures by reason that which presents itself as more probable. I am not ashamed of the declarations of the Academics, so that I do not recede from their footprints in those matters about which the wise person has doubts."[55] Indeed, this viewpoint is raised to the level of an evaluative standard in Book 7 of the *Policraticus,* which contains a lengthy recounting of the major schools of Greco-Roman philosophy, the stated aim of which is to discover the valuable lessons in each approach as well as to demonstrate the limitations inherent in all of them.[56]

The treatment of the Academic School is given pride of place, opening Book 7's critical history of pagan philosophy. Even as he admits his own devotion to the Academy, John stresses the divide that exists in the School between an extreme skepticism that proclaims the utter fallibility of the human mind and his own moderate Ciceronian stance. In this connection, he offers a kind of *reductio* argument against the radically skeptical position: "Yet I do not say that all those who are included under the name of Academic have upheld the rule of modesty, since even its basic creed is in dispute and parts of it are open as much to derision as to error. . . . If the Academic is in doubt about each thing, he is certain about nothing. . . . But he possesses uncertainty about whether he is in doubt, so long as he does not know for certain that he does not know this doubt itself."[57] Extreme doubt, which refuses any criteria for knowledge, leads to a vicious circle in which the doubter must doubt even his own uncertainty and must thereby at least admit of the possibility of attaining valid knowledge about certain matters. Radical skepticism cannot even attain to the mantle of philosophy, John says, for the philosopher's love of wisdom requires the admission that one may know what is true (even if this is difficult to achieve).[58]

By contrast, John's moderate skepticism, consciously modeled on the lessons of Cicero, accepts that there are three reliable foundations for knowledge: faith, reason, and the senses.[59] Thus, it does not behoove the philosopher to question his faith in the existence of God or the certainty of central postulates of mathematics or a number of other first principles that "one is not permitted to doubt, except for those who are occupied by the labors of not knowing anything."[60] It might seem, then, that John's skepticism is not so very skeptical after all, in the sense that he seems willing to countenance as certain a wide range of knowledge-claims stemming from a number of different sources. But this turns out not to be the case. John in fact generates an extremely lengthy list of "doubtful matters about which the wise person is not convinced by the authority of either faith or his senses or manifest reason, and in which contrary claims rest on the support of some evidence."[61] The topics subject to doubt that John enumerates include major issues of metaphysics and cosmology (such as the nature of the soul and of body, time and place, and the status of universals), ethics (the unity of the virtues, the nature of virtue and vice, legal and moral duties and punishments), natural science (magnitude, friction, the humors, geography), and even theology (free will and providence, punishment of sin, angels, what can be asked of God by human beings).[62] The entire list goes on in Webb's critical edition of the *Policraticus* for twenty-four lines and is clearly meant to be illustrative rather than inclusive. In sum, John opens up to doubt and dispute an extraordinarily broad array of topics that for him are by no means settled and are thus appropriate for philosophical discourse.

In confronting all such debatable subjects, John counsels adherence to the Academic method because "the Academics have doubts regarding these matters with so much modesty that I perceive them to have guarded diligently against the danger of rashness."[63] Unique among all schools of philosophy, the Academy resists the temptation to replace open discussion of uncertain matters with prematurely closed dogma. In John's view, the moderate skepticism of the New Academy alone defends the liberty of inquiry that he evidently regards to be necessary to the quest for truth.

From Skepticism to Toleration

Although the *Policraticus* does not return to the epistemological bases of intellectual fallibility that John had addressed in the *Entheticus* and *Metalogicon*, it clearly takes for granted that the human mind is furnished with only weak powers for comprehending truth. Hence, John rejects the Augustinian claim that even Cicero's moderate skepticism "piles up darkness from some hidden source, and warns that the whole of philosophy is obscure, and does not allow one to hope that any light will be found in it."[64] Indeed, in a surprising twist,

John attempts to enlist Augustine himself in support of those who evince Academic doubt: "Even our Augustine does not assail them, since he himself somewhat frequently employs Academic moderation in his works and propounds many matters as ambiguous which would not seem to be in question to another arguing with greater confidence and just as safely."[65] On John's reading, Augustine practiced the Academic method even while he excoriated it in principle. The validity of this interpretation aside, John seeks any evidence whatsoever to bolster his own view that "mortals can know very little," as he puts it in the *Entheticus*.[66]

This epistemological premise stands at the philosophical core of John's approach to human liberty and toleration. As we have seen, John believes that both personal virtue and good political order assume extensive freedom of choice and expression, and that such freedom must be respected and indeed protected by other individuals as well as by the healthy public body. But why is such freedom necessary at all? The answer must lie with the fallibility of human intellect: Because we cannot be certain in many matters connected with human goodness and earthly well-being what the correct action may be, we must extend tolerance to persons who have different conceptions of goodness and who seek to realize them in different ways. If there were some sure standard for the moral or public good, which could be known and imposed infallibly, respect for liberty would be unnecessary. But because such matters are difficult to ascertain and subject to debate, on account of the nature of the human mind itself, John requires the exercise of forbearance. This view not only applies in the case of toleration in political affairs, but encompasses freedom of inquiry in the full range of philosophical and theological matters detailed above.

John himself is aware of the connection between his Academy-influenced skepticism and the necessity for a wide band of free judgment and expression. In prefacing his critical history of philosophy contained in Chapter 7, wherein he seeks to trace the "footprints of philosophers," John explains the operative principle of the Academic School: "If these inquiries seem to approach formal philosophy, the spirit of investigation corresponds to Academic practices rather than to the plan of a stubborn combatant, so that each is to reserve to oneself freedom of judgment in the examination of truth (*in examinationem veri suum cuique iudicium liberum reservetur*), and the authority of writers is to be considered useless whenever it is subdued by a better argument."[67] The approach of the Academy requires that in all matters not settled beyond reasonable doubt, the force of the evidence alone should prevail. Authorities themselves should not be granted superior wisdom if a more cogent viewpoint opposes them. Likewise, the determination of what position seems most plausible or defensible *lies with the individual*. In view of his skeptical predilections, John raises the priority of individual judgment to a universal principle, not susceptible to revocation in the manner of a privilege conceded by some external authority.

That John recognized this implication of his adherence to the Academy is signaled by his statement on more than one occasion in the *Policraticus* that freedom of judgment is a *ius*, a right that pertains to human beings. The history of rights language during the Middle Ages is a complex one, much debated in present scholarship.[68] At minimum, the medieval understanding of *ius* entailed acknowledgment of a fixed and defensible sphere of activity whose exercise is independent of external infringement or control. This seems to be precisely what John has in mind when insisting on the *right* of free inquiry and determination: "The Academy of the ancients bestows upon the human race the leave that each person by his right (*suo iure*) may defend whatever presents itself to him as most probable."[69] As he remarks in another passage, "It is a very ancient rule of the Academics that each person may of his own right (*suo iure*) defend that which presents itself to him as most probable."[70] The source of this right is surely neither political nor (except indirectly) divine; it is not granted from above and therefore subject to limitation or removal. Rather, one's right to assert one's freedom to form one's own judgments apparently derives from the fallible nature of the human mind and the uncertain character of many knowledge-claims. It is, in short, a result of the human predicament.

In John's reference to the "right" of persons, then, we encounter the philosophical roots of the toleration that he advocates elsewhere in the *Policraticus*. If we each enjoy a right to draw conclusions and construct arguments about those matters open to rational disagreement, then it follows that others (regardless of their status or power) likewise have a duty to respect our thoughts even if they do not endorse them. This is underscored in the *Policraticus* by John's remark that, regarding unsettled issues, "one is free to question and doubt, up to the point where, from a comparison of views, truth shines through as though from the clash of ideas (*quasi quadam rationum collisione*)."[71] Such a statement suggests that John understood very well the implications of his skeptical philosophy: The quest for truth in matters of practical as well as philosophical import demands the maintenance of openness and dissent. It is the responsibility of the wise person, not to mention the wise ruler or prelate, to uphold and defend the grounds of public debate. The realization of truth is hampered, not aided, by the suppression of divergent positions and the persecution of their adherents.

Conclusion

At times, John of Salisbury approaches the position embraced by another English probabilist, John Stuart Mill, seven hundred years later. In *On Liberty*, Mill commented, "There is the greatest difference between presuming an opinion to be true because, with every opportunity for contesting it, it has not been refuted, and assuming its truth for the purpose of not permitting refutation. Complete liberty of contradicting and disproving our opinion is the very condition which justifies us in assuming its truth."[72] Of course, John of Salisbury was no John Stuart Mill. Many issues that Mill regarded as contestable would have fallen under John's rubric of those things known to be true according to faith, reason, or the senses.[73] Yet the example of John of Salisbury demonstrates that a philosophically mature defense of toleration of free thought and debate, based on a probabilistic conception of knowledge, did not have to await the dawn of the Renaissance, let alone the Enlightenment. The materials of Ciceronian Academic skepticism, deployed by an author of John's moderate intellectual temperament, afforded a theoretically cogent starting point for the condemnation of intolerant repression, as well as the maximization and enshrined protection of intellectual liberty.

The case of John of Salisbury should dispel lingering suspicions that Christian orthodoxy was so hegemonic as to render a principled concept of toleration unthinkable. John's work forcefully illustrates the realization on the part of many medieval intellectuals that the persecution of philosophical differences was a retrograde policy if one's goal was discovery of the truth. Like his near contemporaries, John sought to make room for reasoned discussion of those matters about which rational minds can and do disagree. His contribution to this enterprise was to develop a more overt philosophical basis for the defense of such toleration. The skeptical spirit of free inquiry that John explicitly embraced was in many ways the spirit of his times, presaging scholastic as well as humanist forms of dispute and discussion.[74]

4

NEGOTIATING THE TOLERANT SOCIETY

The Travail of William of Rubruck

Encountering Tolerant Practice

The inter-religious dialogues of the High Middle Ages, even those that champion toleration as a direct offshoot of open discourse, may seem susceptible to the accusation that they are "merely theoretical." In other words, a number of preconditions for successful tolerant discussion are simply taken for granted as unproblematic, in particular, assumptions about the willingness and capacity of the parties to enter into rational dialogue as well as the practical viability of achieving mutual understanding among participants. In the works of Abelard and Llull, it was accepted as axiomatic that men of strong faith would nevertheless agree to enter into reasoned debate with one another and would subscribe to identical standards of rational argumentation. Moreover, it apparently did not occur to Latin medieval thinkers that the intellectual and linguistic matrix of Christianity was in any way short of universal: The Jew, the Muslim, and the Gentile are all made to speak (literally as well as figuratively) in the language of the Roman Church. Perhaps such limitations were unavoidable, and they surely do not detract from the aspirations of Abelard and Llull to realize more tolerant and less fractious forms of religious contact. Yet the medieval theorists of inter-religious dialogue do seem susceptible to a potentially damaging charge of extreme naïveté, the direct consequence of which is to undermine the viability of the ideal of greater tolerance based on continuing open discussion.

Regardless of the validity of these objections to the cases of intellectuals such as Abelard and Llull, however, there is significant evidence that the pursuit of inter-religious dialogue was not an entirely theoretical exercise. Beyond the well-known examples of *convivencia* in Spain and of commercial contact between Christians and Muslims in the Middle East,[1] the Middle Ages witnessed numerous missions by Christian emissaries into the terra incognita of Central Asia, especially to courts of various rulers of the Mongols (usually and erroneously called the Tartars by medieval Europeans).[2] When armed bands of Mongols first appeared at and began to menace the eastern borders of Christian Europe around 1222, virtually nothing was known in the West about their culture, beliefs, or social organization.[3] A series of expeditions during the mid-thirteenth century, generally conducted by Franciscans, sought to rectify this ignorance.[4]

As near as may be determined, the success of these missions (when their contingent returned at all) was gauged primarily in terms of military reconnaissance. The report of John of Plano Carpini, who was dispatched by Pope Innocent IV in 1245, is heavily slanted toward intelligence about the Mongol army's conquests, tactics, and plans for the future. John warns of a power bent on establishing global hegemony and advises the creation of a pan-European strike force "to fight against the Tartars before they begin to spread over the land, for once they begin to be scattered throughout a country it is impossible for anyone to give effective help to another."[5] John's *History of the Mongols,* which was perhaps the most widely circulated account in Latin Christendom, thus served to reinforce the fearful tales and rumors that had already spread through Europe about the extent of the Mongol threat.[6]

By contrast, the travel narrative of another Franciscan, William of Rubruck, who was sent eastward by French King Louis IX in 1153 on a journey that eventually lasted two years, paints a less horrific, and altogether more intimate, portrait of the Mongols. The report of this trip, known by the title *The Journey of William of Rubruck,* runs to roughly twice the length of John's text; it sketches not only the qualities of Mongol society and everyday life, but also recounts in detail the movements and activities of the author and his companions (another friar and two servants) as they trek from the court of one Mongol ruler to another, starting in Western Asia with Sartak and Batu and traveling finally to the stronghold of the reigning Great Chan, Mangu. Unlike John, William enjoyed considerable overseas experience with Louis IX's entourage in the Middle East, and he has been justly praised for his lucid and precise descriptions of the persons and events he witnessed. Indeed, the letter in which he narrates to Louis the course of his expedition has most often been cited by scholars either for its factual information about the Mongols and their empire or as a source for Western attitudes about the East.[7]

Acknowledging these dimensions of William's letter should not, however, deter us from the recognition of what is perhaps its most unique feature: its documentation of its author's intensely personal struggle between his own zeal to spread the word of Latin Christian doctrine and his efforts to accommodate himself to the multireligious (and multicultural) world into which he has been sent. As William constantly reminds those whom he meets on his journey, his authority is confined to spiritual matters: Louis has dispatched him as a missionary, seeking the salvation of souls, not as an ambassador or emissary.[8] The distinction is an important one, for it means both that he is accorded less respect by his hosts and also that he is perceived by them as less of a threat. Mindful of his charge, William looks often for opportunities to preach and discourse publicly on Roman Christianity, yet he is persistently thwarted—not by persecution or suppression, but by linguistic and cultural difference as well as by the need to compromise in a world that is not so much aggressively hostile as indifferent to his message. In a sense, William's narrative reveals many of the practical impediments to realizing inter-religious dialogue while suggesting a strategy for negotiating a path through a society untroubled by the presence of religious diversity. His letter, however unwittingly, illustrates how a devout medieval Christian might learn, in the face of circumstance, to conduct himself with a measure of tolerance, without surrendering his certainty about the ultimate rectitude of his own convictions.

Conditions of Religious Toleration

From nearly the beginning of his letter, William of Rubruck registers a sense of awe at the society and culture of the Mongols. His mission had seemed simple enough. Louis sent him to establish the veracity of a rumor widespread in the Middle East: namely, that the future Chan Sartak, the son of the present Chan Batu, had converted to Christianity. Matters become complicated by Sartak's forceful insistence that William continue his journey along to the court of Batu; and Batu in turn passes him on to Mangu, the Great Chan, at whose court he remains for upward of five months. Thus, psychologically as well as geographically, William is drawn into the heart of the Mongol empire and, although he is not generally prone to overstatement, he twice describes his encounter as an experience completely without parallel: "When I came among them [the Mongols] I felt as if I were entering some other world."[9]

What accounts for William's amazement? Certainly, some of it must be attributed to the strangeness of Mongol customs, habits, and rituals in matters of domicile, adornment, economy, and nourishment, all of which he records.[10] But the feature of the Mongols' way of life to which William's narrative returns most frequently is the cosmopolitan quality of the territory under their command. By the mid-thirteenth century, Mongol armies had conquered vast regions of Asia, the Middle East, and Eastern Europe. What William notices, however, is not so much military strength as the bewildering array of ethnic, racial, and cultural groups who live in relative peace and harmony under Mongol rule. William even meets European Christians (captured during forays into Hungary) from Germany, England, and France.[11]

Perhaps most strikingly, the Mongols control their vast empire without any attempt to impose religious uniformity on subject peoples. Rather, William observes that members of virtually every religious group known to the Mediterranean and Eurasian worlds—he mentions Christians (Nestorians, Armenians, Russians, Alans, and Georgians as well as Romans) and non-Christians (Muslims ["Saracens"], Uigurs, and "pagans" of many varieties) alike—may be found in territories under Mongol domination.[12] In some instances, these groups are separated geographically, permitted to practice their pre-existing confessions and rites as long as they submit to the political terms imposed by the Mongols.[13] In most of the cases noted by William, however, adherents to many faiths live side by side with what appears to be a minimum of inter-religious conflict.[14] In the Mongol settlement of Caracorum, for example, "there are twelve idol temples belonging to the different peoples, two mosques in which the religion of Mahomet is proclaimed, and one Christian church at the far end of the town."[15] All faiths engage in their rites openly and without any evident regulation.

This is not to suggest that the rulers of the Mongol empire were indifferent to matters of religion; they seem closest to subscribing to some form of religious pluralism. On the one hand, the Mongols belong to the Uigur sect "in so far as they believe in only one God," although they nonetheless engage in idolatrous practices.[16] Mongol adherence to monotheistic doctrine is affirmed in a profession of faith made by Mangu, the Great Chan, to William: "'We Mongols,' he said, 'believe that there is but one God by whom we have life and through whom we die, and towards whom we direct our hearts.'"[17] Yet monotheism is not regarded as inconsistent with the truth of differing confessions: Mangu proclaims that "'just as God has given the hand several fingers, so he has given mankind several paths. To you God has given the Scriptures.'"[18] Indeed, Mangu openly embraces just such pluralism: "It was his custom to hold court on such days as his soothsayers prescribe feasts or the Nestorians on occasions pronounce holy. On days like this the first to arrive are the Christian clergy with their equipment, and they pray for him and bless his cup. As they withdraw, the Saracen priests appear and do likewise; and after them come the idolator priests, who do the same."[19] The Mongols apparently saw no reason to favor one rite over any other, and their leaders were prepared not merely to endure but to endorse a wide range of convictions. Indeed, monotheism did not constitute the outer limit of Mongol tolerance, because many of the pagan priests who served at the court of the Great Chan seem to have held animistic or pantheistic beliefs.[20] In sum, the Mongols, or at any rate members of their ruling clique, were willing and even eager to follow a policy of broad religious toleration, not only countenancing worship according to personal creed but also incorporating diverse rites into public ceremony. The organization of religion under the Mongols thus reflected a working model of the "multinational empire" regime of toleration described by some recent political philosophers.[21]

The Mongols' tolerant attitudes and practices were in many ways a source of frustration to William (as they no doubt were to other evangelically minded priests of various sects). It is not that the Mongols evinced disinterest in Christianity. William's letter mentions numerous occasions on which Mongols examined the books and raiments that he carried with him and demonstrated curiosity about Christian beliefs.[22] But the Mongols whom William encounters show little inclination toward conversion. As he remarks after his final audience with the Great Chan, "If I had possessed the power to work miracles, as Moses did, he [Mangu] might perhaps have humbled himself."[23] Indeed, judging by the letter to King Louis that Mangu sends with William on his return to the West, the religious convictions of the Mongols are almost indistinguishable from their military pretensions. In the mouths of the Chans themselves is to be found "the order of the everlasting God"—a decree that places "the entire world, from the sun's rising to its setting . . . at one in joy and in peace" under Mongol dominion.[24] To the Mongols, then, strict adherence to any confession would probably appear extraneous to, if not incompatible with, their aspirations for global hegemony.

Barriers to Discourse

If William had imagined at the beginning of his expedition that there might be some hope of converting the elites of the Mongol empire to Roman Christianity, then he was soon disappointed. But it was not simply the ingrained Mongol policy of toleration that created an obstacle to William's missionary zeal. His letter reveals that a range of cultural differences (of language and custom as well as religion) impeded the achievement of mutual understanding necessary for genuine dialogue, let alone conversion. William seems to have a dual motivation for promoting open discussion: First, he recognizes it to be a necessary precondition for spreading his message; but second, he seeks to deepen his appreciation of the nature of the beliefs and practices that distinguish and separate the many sects he encounters. On both counts, however, he is repeatedly frustrated.

Language is perhaps the primary barrier faced by William to entry into dialogue. The problem was twofold. Time and again, the sheer incompetence of William's interpreter is cited by him to explain a breakdown of discussion. William describes the interpreter as "neither intelligent nor articulate"[25] and as one whose own motivations are continually suspect.[26] William claims that during his journey many chances were lost to spread Christianity at the Mongol encampments: "Had I been possessed of a good interpreter, this would have given me an opportunity of sowing much good seed."[27] Likewise, when William attempts to instruct his guides in Christianity, "my interpreter proved inadequate. . . . To speak in doctrinal terms through an interpreter like this was a great risk—in fact, an impossibility, for he was ignorant of them."[28] So troublesome is the poor interpreting that William makes it one of his main recommendations that any future missions to the Mongols "would have need of a good interpreter—several interpreters, in fact."[29]

William's own remarks indicate that his judgment of his interpreter may have been unduly harsh, however, and that much of the difficulty actually resided with problems inherent to translating Roman Christian concepts into the discourse of the Mongols. The interpreter is blamed, for instance, for halting a theological dialogue into which William enters with some Uigur priests: "When I wanted to argue further with them, my interpreter, who was tired and incapable of finding the right words, made me stop talking."[30] Elsewhere, William complains, "When I wanted to do some preaching, . . . my interpreter would say, 'Do not make me preach, since I do not know how to express these things.' He was right. Later, when I acquired some little knowledge of the language, I noticed that when I said one thing he would say something totally different. After that, I realized the danger of speaking through him, and chose rather to say nothing."[31] Where William sees his intentions foiled by a bad translator, however, it may be that his own doctrines simply have no discursive equivalents in the language of the Mongols. Although later in his expedition William undertakes to learn the language for himself (both from one of the wives of Mangu and from an Armenian monk who is also resident at the court of the Great Chan) and also discovers an interpreter who is more capable than the one assigned to him, the Franciscan is no more successful in spreading his message. All of this suggests that linguistic factors per se—the absence of a pre-existing vocabulary—should be held as responsible for William's failures at engendering dialogue as the quality of the interpreter. The interpreter is quite right to assert that he "has no words" to express the tenets of Roman Christian faith. Where William apparently takes for granted the transparency of language, he is thwarted time and again by the complexities of identifying (or probably creating) a coherent terminology into which his conceptual structure may be translated.

The obstacles to dialogue posed by language were only reinforced by differences of custom. Numerous people whom William meets are under the impression that adherence to Christianity is incompatible with their own ways of life, most especially in connection with the consumption of mare's milk, called *comos*, a staple of the Asian diet. One of his Mongol escorts questions him about this early on in the journey: "The Russian, Greek, and Alan Christians who live among them, and who wish strictly to observe their religion, do not drink it, and in fact once they have drunk it they no longer even regard themselves as Christians, their clergy reconciling them as if they had abjured the Christian faith."[32] William and his companion can think of no orthodox justification for this prohibition (they themselves have already partaken of the drink),[33] but they are regularly hounded by the supposed proscription of *comos* and other victuals. A Muslim who expresses interest in converting to Christianity ultimately declines baptism on the grounds that "then he would not be able to drink *comos*: the Christians in this country claimed that nobody who was truly a Christian should drink it, and he could not survive in that wilderness without the drink. I was wholly unable to disabuse him of this idea."[34] Likewise, a group of Alans (described as nonschismatic adherents to the Greek rite) express concern to William about "whether they could be saved, since they were obliged to drink *comos* and to eat carrion and what had been slaughtered by Saracens and other infidels."[35] Such misapprehensions about the dictates of Christian belief are, as William discovers, difficult to eradicate, and they contribute materially to the indifference of peoples under Mongol rule toward Christianity. Much to William's consternation, even discussion and reasoned explanation seem inadequate to sway individuals from their preconceptions.

Confronting Religious Division

Obviously, a major source of these misunderstandings is the other Christian confessions themselves. Although William reassures the Alans that they have not jeopardized their salvation by consuming *comos* or other nourishment, a more fundamental problem is implicitly raised: To what extent must the Romans sacrifice the purity of their own rite to work together with fellow Christians toward the common good of the faith? How far may Latin Christians go in compromising their practices before they endanger orthodox faith? These are questions with which William constantly grapples during his journey. On the one hand, it is clear that he holds the practices and customs of Nestorians, Armenians, and other sects in contempt. The Nestorians, in particular, are excoriated by William for their complete corruption: "Even though they instruct them [the Mongols] in the Gospels and the Faith, nevertheless by their immorality and greed they rather alienate them from the Christian religion. For the lives of the Mongols, and even the *tuins* (that is, the idolators), are more blameless than their own."[36] In a similar fashion, William expresses distrust of the Armenians, who so loathe the Muslims that they distort any teaching to serve their interests in conducting war against Islam.[37] Indeed, throughout his letter we are confronted with detailed descriptions of the errors of non-Latin Christian groups.

Yet, on the other hand, the reality is that these churches formed by far the largest body of Christians in Mongol society. To engage in conflict with them would be both imprudent (because they already enjoy legitimacy among the Mongols) and improper (because it risks alienating people who are baptized Christians). Consequently, William does his best to cooperate with all the Christian sects and even to avoid antagonizing non-Christians. His letter indeed invites us to contrast his own behavior with that of the unnamed Armenian monk with whom he shares living quarters during most of his stay at the court of the Great Chan. The monk described by William seems to relish inter-religious dispute. Even Mangu admonishes the Armenian, asking him "why—since he was a man whose duty it was to pray to God—he talked so much to men."[38] As illustration of this contentiousness, William narrates that the monk entered into a debate with an eminent Nestorian priest over the Creation and introduced a decidedly Manichean element into his own account. When William, called on to arbitrate the dispute, gently corrected the heresy, the monk responded with invective and insult.[39] In a separate incident, the monk is challenged to a religious argument by a group of Saracens and responds violently (threatening to strike his opponents with a whip) rather than "using rational arguments in his own defense." In this case, word of the monk's intolerant conduct is relayed to the Great Chan's court; a dismayed Mangu relieves the Armenian of some of his special privileges.[40] Although William clearly regards the monk as his closest religious ally, the portrayal of the Armenian is hardly flattering. As William remarks, "I would show him the deference due to a superior, since he was familiar with the language. But nevertheless he used to do many things to which I objected."[41] In particular, the behavior of the monk evidently leads William to realize that adopting an impatient and disputatious stance toward adherents to other sects and rites, at least in the context of an officially tolerant society, was unlikely to improve the standing of Christianity and thus was counterproductive.

In his narrative, consequently, William represents himself as the model of tolerance in his dealings with other religious groups as well as with his Mongol hosts. His operative principle, as he explains to Mangu's chancellor, is accommodation within the limits permitted to a faithful Christian: "We shall do as your master wishes, provided that we are given no order contrary to the worship and honor of God."[42] Of course, a precise dividing line between those acts consonant with divine command and those beyond the pale is often difficult to discern, as William himself tacitly acknowledges. The Franciscan tries his best to cooperate with other Christians. When he first arrives at Caracorum, he is summoned, along with the Armenian monk and the Nestorian priests, to the palace of the Great Chan. Uncertain about whether he should accede to the request, William remarks, "I reflected a good deal as to what I should do myself, whether or not to go. But since I was afraid that dissociating myself from the other Christians would cause a scandal, and since it was the Chan's will, and since I feared lest an advantage might be thwarted which I hoped to gain, I chose to go even though I should be observing them engaging in practices that were riddled with superstition and idolatry."[43] William clearly regards his decision as a compromise, justified by what he regards as a set of greater goods. If he is to succeed in furthering the Christian cause in the context of a tolerant society, he recognizes that he must adopt an ecumenical strategy.

A more significant dilemma arises for William in connection with the celebration of Easter. The problem is twofold. First, he is deeply concerned about the orthodoxy of the Nestorian priests, in whose care the Christian church is placed. "I was observing the way the Nestorians consecrated and was very much in agony as to my course: whether to receive the Sacrament at their hands, or to celebrate in their vestments and with their chalice and on their altar, or to abstain from the Sacrament altogether."[44] William clearly fears that acceptance of the Host from the Nestorians, let alone saying Mass with the use of their accoutrements, would constitute a sin. A second difficulty is posed by the large number of Christians of various confessions resident at Caracorum, "none of whom had set eyes on the sacrament since their capture, as the Nestorians would not admit them into their church unless they were rebaptized. . . . These Christians and the [Armenian] monk kept asking us insistently, in God's name, to celebrate."[45] Ultimately, William permits his doubts about the rectitude of saying Mass and conferring Communion to be pushed aside under the force of circumstance. He compels the various Christians first to confess and finds himself forgiving their commission of theft of food and clothes and of killing in battle. (Both acts are excused on grounds of necessity, because as prisoners of the Mongols the Christians were nearly slaves.)[46] The Nestorians agree to lend him their own paraphernalia and a section of the church: "And so on Maundy Thursday I celebrated Mass . . . and likewise on Easter Sunday. And it was with God's blessing, I hope, that we gave the people communion."[47] The last phrase indicates that although William continued to have misgivings about the propriety of his decision, he recognizes that the spiritual good of all the Christians (few of whom subscribed to the Roman rite) warrants following a path potentially dangerous to his own soul and status as a priest in the Latin Church. William reacts with forbearance in his treatment of people whom a less tolerant individual might have treated as unworthy of the risk.

Dialogue and Its Limits

If William comes to display an ecumenical spirit toward his fellow Christians, he also learns important lessons about how tolerant dealings with non-Christians may be possible. This is especially evident in a remarkable chapter of his letter, where he recounts the occurrence of an actual inter-religious dialogue held at the command of the Great Chan—a discussion that illuminates the practical difficulties inherent in such an exchange. Perhaps disturbed by the religious strife he observes, Mangu announces his desire to understand better the conflicting claims made by various confessions. "He sent to me his secretaries, who said: 'Our master is sending us to you with this message: "Here you are, Christians, Saracens, and *tuins*, and each one of you claims that his religion is superior and his writings or his books contain more truth." So he would like you all to assemble together and hold a conference and each one is to put his claims in writing, to enable the Chan to learn the truth.'"[48] Although William views this as an ideal opportunity to further his evangelical agenda, he stipulates that the debate must take place in a framework of tolerance, "without bickering or recrimination," a requirement on which the Great Chan himself insists: "'This is Mangu's decree . . . that no one shall be so bold as to make provocative or insulting remarks to his opponent, and that no one is to make any commotion that would obstruct these proceedings, on pain of death.'"[49] Thus, the convocation is mandated to follow a principle of rational dialogue: Each sect must defend its beliefs according to reasoned argument and logic rather than invective and vituperation.

This requirement is soon revealed to be problematic, however. As William realizes when he coordinates his efforts with the Nestorian Christians, many people of deep conviction lack a rational foundation for their faith. When William asks the priests how, in the midst of the debate, they would demonstrate the existence of God to the *tuins*, he discovers that "the Nestorians were incapable of proving anything, but could only relate what the Scripture tells. I said: 'They do not believe in the Scriptures; if you tell them one story, they will quote you another.'"[50] It is necessary, William points out, to establish a common ground on which to engage in inter-religious discussion, apart from those convictions that are not susceptible to rational support. (This is a point that had been established already in earlier medieval contributions to the inter-religious dialogue genre.) Otherwise, the discourse inevitably breaks down as each of the participants simply reiterates the truth of his own accepted articles of faith.

Yet even unanimity on what constitutes valid reasoning may be difficult to attain, depending on one's theological starting point. When the day of the conference arrives, there is immediately a dispute over the order of the topics according to which the discussion should proceed. The *tuins* insist on initially addressing the creation of the world and the immortality of the soul, "because they consider them more important" points, whereas William asserts that "'we should begin by speaking about God, for you hold a different view of Him from us, and Mangu wishes to learn whose belief is superior.'"[51] The judges— three of the Great Chan's scribes, one from each of the main religious views represented—side with William, who proceeds to assert the unity and perfection of God. The *tuins*, in contradiction, defend a version of polytheism, employing an analogy from the multiplicity of "mighty lords" on earth to a plurality of deities in heaven. William objects, of course, to what he regards as a false comparison, on the grounds that it presumes "arguing from men to God," rather than from the divine nature, which is higher, to earthly conditions, which are inferior.[52] The *tuin* speaker simply refuses to acknowledge that his statement is illogical; indeed, it is not, given his premises. Likewise, dialogue repeatedly grinds to a halt over the issues of the omnipotence and goodness of their respective deities, the *tuins* falling into astonished silence in reaction to the "erroneous and impossible" creed of the Christians.[53]

Ultimately, of course, the practical limitations of rational dialogue prove insuperable. The Muslims simply refuse to engage in discussion at all, preferring instead to capitulate entirely (if somewhat disingenuously). "'We concede that your religion is true,'" they say to their Nestorian interlocutors, "'and that everything in the Gospel is true; and therefore we have no wish to debate any issue with you.'"[54] Still, no one becomes convinced of the rectitude of another's convictions: "Everybody listened without challenging a single word. But for all that, no one said, 'I believe, and I wish to become a Christian.'"[55] Does William mean his reader to draw the conclusion that the debate was a failure? The text offers no remark that explicitly indicates this. Rather, the dialogue (and the chapter) closes with raucous singing and drinking on the part of the participants, an indication of a measure of mutual respect and forbearance even in light of deep religious division. In a sense, the postdisputation celebration restores the status quo of Mongol society: peaceful interaction among members of the various confessions. That people may argue about such matters, disagree, and yet finally share in expressions of conviviality suggests an intriguing model of tolerant dialogue quite different from that pursued by theorists for whom consensus was the eventual, if postponed, outcome.

Lessons of a Tolerant Society

Did the Great Chan in fact ever study any report of the debate whose assembly he commanded? The answer must remain a matter of speculation. The day after the disputation, as William prepares for his return to the West, however, Mangu summons the Franciscan and lectures him on the contentiousness and hypocrisy of the Christians he observes.

"To you God has given the Scriptures and you Christians do not observe them. You do not find in the Scriptures that a man ought to abuse another, now do you?" he said. "No," I said, "but I indicated to you from the outset that I had no desire to be at odds with anyone.". . . "I am not speaking of you," he replied. "So, then, God has given you the Scriptures and you do not observe them; whereas to us he has given soothsayers, and we do what they tell us and live in peace."[56]

Whether the Great Chan has in mind the disputatious behavior of the Armenian monk and the Nestorian priests is uncertain, but he clearly believes that Christianity in practice, if not in principle, fostered turmoil. Hence, in his view, religious pluralism continues to be the best policy for the Mongol empire.

Mangu does not forestall the possibility of William's returning to Mongol lands to minister to Roman Christians already residing there.[57] Yet whatever hopes the Franciscan may have harbored at the outset of his journey about spreading Roman Christianity among the inhabitants of territory under Mongol control appear to have been diminished, if not dashed. Encountering a group of Dominicans on their way to the courts of Sartak and Mangu with a papal commission, William offers a discouraging assessment of the situation: "I told them, however, what I had seen and how I was being sent back. . . . Since their sole mission was to preach, little heed would be paid to them, especially as they had no interpreter."[58] It is not, he insists, that the trip (although arduous) is unsafe for Christians on account of their faith. Rather, his pessimism seems to stem from the level of religious indifference that pervades Mongol society.

Yet William's apparent despair over the magnitude of the enterprise posed by Christian conversion in the East reflects, perhaps somewhat ironically, his recognition that tolerant policies are needed in coping with the Mongol empire. In contrast with John of Plano Carpini, William eschews a military resolution to the "threat" of the Mongols. In the absence of religious fanaticism, he realizes, the armies of the Chans pose no direct danger to the Christian faith. Nor does William demonstrate any sympathy for the alleged Armenian plan to join with the Mongols in the destruction of the "Saracens." Rather, although he has confronted the many obstacles to achieving successful inter-religious discourse, the Franciscan ultimately seems to adopt an irenic and patient approach to the Mongols. Because they show no direct hostility toward Christianity or its missionaries, William can find no grounds for opposing them. If preaching the Gospel alone is insufficient to ensure conversion, in William's view, then the appropriate response is not warfare but a redoubled effort to represent the real nature of the faith and its Western protectors to the Mongols through the appointment of an ambassador whose words will carry authority. In a tolerant society, he realizes, the possibility of peaceful dissemination of Christian doctrine remains available. As William proclaims in his final interview with Mangu, "'It is our desire that the world should be ruled over by those who would govern it most justly, in accordance with the will of God. It is our task to teach men how to live in accordance with God's will, and for that purpose we came to these parts and we should gladly have remained.'"[59] Echoing the doctrine of Pope Innocent IV on the legitimacy of infidel regimes,[60] William in this statement embraces a principle of reciprocity: So long as he retains the ability to proclaim his convictions, he is prepared to respect a social and political order that is not officially dedicated to promulgating Christian beliefs.

Conclusion

Is William's ultimate position, then, merely pragmatic or concordant? Is he holding out for a day when his Roman Christian doctrines will be taken for a final truth in the lands subject to the Mongols? Perhaps this was his intention, but what William's letter teaches (and what he himself apparently learned) is that the road to such universal agreement is an arduous one, blocked by the diverse human cultures and languages that impede the very circulation of Christian doctrines. Assuredly, recognition of these obstacles to successful cross-cultural proselytizing has a practical component, namely, the development of strategies for rendering Christian truths accessible to non-Western civilizations. But a larger theoretical issue is also embedded in the dilemmas posed by William's letter: What are the responsibilities of Christian Europe, and especially the Church, toward the infidels of the East?

This question was widely debated in the middle of the thirteenth century, and William was likely to have known the basic range of opinions, at least in rough outline. The attitudes he expresses in the letter seem to reflect an implicit endorsement of Innocent IV's side in the conflict, namely, that the Latin Church and its members must respect the rights of infidel rulers provided that they do not persecute Christians or command direct violations of natural law. Certainly, William shows no sympathy for the position upheld by the canon lawyer Hostiensis: that the use of force against infidels, such as the Mongols, is justified, because they are in "unjust possession" of their lordship.[61] The only alternative, then, is to accept the tolerant balance achieved by the Mongol empire by its broad admission of all sects and creeds. If, as a Christian, one cannot convert the non-Christians of the East en masse, then one ought to embrace the opportunity to minister to the faithful and to enjoy on equal terms the ear of the ruler. This means, simply put, a readiness to negotiate the social conditions of toleration afforded by a multinational empire for an indefinite time.

5

HERESY AND COMMUNITY IN MARSIGLIO OF PADUA'S POLITICAL THOUGHT

Confronting Heresy

Among the varied forms of religious difference confronted by orthodox medieval Christianity, surely none was so troubling as heresy. Unlike adherents to non-Christian confessions, heretics remained part of the body of the faithful, although they had marginalized themselves because of their heterodox convictions. The often-employed metaphor for heresy was disease: If heretics were permitted to remain in the communal body of true believers, they could (and surely would) infect others with their contagion.[1] Hence, the heretic must be excised from the church, not only through excommunication but also through the imposition of temporal penalties by the secular authorities, whether loss of property or corporal or even capital punishment.[2] Only the complete elimination of the heretic from all contact with Christians was sufficient to ensure the health of the community of the faithful. Over the course of the Middle Ages, the strictures against heresy became more stringent and repressive, a certain sign of the growth of the persecutorial impulse.[3]

Although we must take seriously the suppression of religious dissent in medieval Europe, it is also important to realize that not everyone readily embraced the rationale offered by the Church for the excommunication and physical punishment of heretics. Part of the reason for this opposition was the increasingly pragmatic uses to which excommunication and anathematization were put: During the High and Late Middle Ages, the papacy repeatedly employed its powers of excommunication to attack political enemies and to support its own claims to temporal dominion. The kings of many European nations, not to mention numerous scholars as well as several orders in the institutional Church, found themselves subject to papal condemnation for heresy as a result of conduct or beliefs that challenged nothing more than Rome's inflated self-image. Such manipulation of a legitimate spiritual tool in support of the papacy's campaign for political ascendance in Europe disturbed a considerable number of churchmen, touching off a widespread polemical battle in the late thirteenth and fourteenth centuries against papal claims to *plenitudo potestatis* over laity as well as clergy.[4]

One of the central figures in this war of treatises was Marsiglio (also know as Marsilius) of Padua, a scholastic physician and natural philosopher who doubled as an adviser to several powerful Italian families who were seeking to contain the extension of papal influence.[5] While teaching at Paris, Marsiglio completed the work that was to make him infamous in his own day and for centuries thereafter, the *Defensor pacis*. Finished in June 1324, the *Defensor pacis* is a systematic account of the purely natural basis of secular political power and an extended attack on the papacy's pretensions to possess any form of temporal power or indeed even supreme spiritual authority in the Church. Marsiglio soon found himself officially condemned for publishing such views and was forced to flee to the court of the German king and emperor-elect Ludwig of Bavaria, who was in the midst of his own struggle with the papacy. In his later years, Marsiglio continued to perform polemical favors for his protector, culminating in the composition of the *Defensor minor* around 1340. This treatise was a summary and refinement of the principles that had earlier been articulated in the *Defensor pacis*.[6]

For our purposes, what distinguishes Marsiglio from the many other writers who contributed to the attack on papal power was his readiness to advance the claim that religious differences among members of the Christian Church should neither impede civic intercourse and inclusion nor be subject to public regulation. By no means was this assertion simply a pragmatic or strategic maneuver on Marsiglio's part. Rather, it arose from a clearly defined conception of human nature and its relation to political order. Marsiglio maintained that the fundamental aim of temporal public life was the perpetuation and enhancement of the physical well-being of humanity, rather than the salvation of souls, which he regarded as an essentially personal and inward concern. Thus, in an age when religion, above almost all other standards, determined the dividing line between communal inclusion and exclusion, he took special care to ensure that the "public" character of political life, based on the functional requirements of the community, was strictly separated from the "private" dimension of religion.

The outlines of Marsiglio's theoretical model derive primarily from a widespread medieval conception of the political body, which has been termed "communal functionalism."[7] Stated briefly, if we conceive of the community as an arrangement of functionally distinct parts, each of which is necessary for the well-being of the whole and of the individual members, then the common good can be identified and applied only by the joint participation of all the members in the political process. Any attempt to exclude functional members from public life on the basis of nonfunctional criteria (that is, forms of conduct or modes of belief that are extraneous to the intercommunication of functions) thus directly damages the realization of the common good itself. Interdependence entails inclusion. Likewise, inasmuch as the common good is not all-embracing, but is more narrowly concerned with the performance of function, it remains possible to permit a large private realm. Because there are no valid grounds for regulating differences that do not affect the activities necessary for the public welfare, respect for personal or group difference (including religious diversity) is a logical concomitant of communal functionalism. In the *Defensor pacis*, and even more explicitly in the *Defensor minor*, Marsiglio develops this general model into a theoretical framework capable of defending heretics against the claim that they must be punished and persecuted in the present life for their beliefs.

Marsiglian Communal Functionalism

Although commonly regarded as a quintessentially Aristotelian tract, the *Defensor pacis* departs at important junctures from the principles of Aristotle's political theory.[8] Thus, Marsiglio cites Aristotle's doctrine that the civil body exists both for the sake of living and of living well; that is, it not only meets physical human needs but promotes the exercise of "the virtues of both the practical and the theoretical soul."[9] Marsiglio, however, evinces little concern for questions of what it is to "live well" or how the political community can best advance that goal. Indeed, the end of "living well" soon disappears from his argument altogether. He remarks that "living and its modes . . . form the purpose for the sake of which the civil body (*civitas*) was established and which necessitates everything which exists in the civil body and is done by human association in it."[10] Marsiglio then quotes Cicero (not Aristotle!) in support of a human instinct of biological self-preservation, the realization of which becomes the primary focus of the Marsiglian community. Here, as elsewhere in the *Defensor pacis*, Aristotle's doctrines are subtly revised (if not manifestly distorted). Although Aristotle had asserted that the polis first comes into existence for the sake of living, he insisted that it continues to exist for the sake of the good life, whose pursuit should be its major goal.[11]

The emphasis on the biological rather than moral and intellectual aspects of human life furnishes, in turn, the standard by which Marsiglio classifies political systems. According to the *Defensor pacis*, the best and highest temporal aim to which good regimes can aspire is the provision of a sufficient or materially adequate existence. Diseased governments, on the other hand, impede or retard the sufficient life of their subjects.[12] Consequently, the structure of the Marsiglian community is determined by the wide-ranging socioeconomic functions that human beings are able to perform.

Marsiglio asserts that the emergence of the community is stimulated by the growth of social complexity: "Those first [village] communities did not have so great a differentiation and ordering of parts, or so large a quantity of necessary arts and rules of living, as were gradually to be found afterwards in perfect communities."[13] The chief token of this complexity was the developing social division of labor, which led human beings to concentrate their efforts on specialized tasks. This division derives from human physiology itself: Human beings are "born bare and unprotected from the excess force of the air and other elements, and capable of suffering and destruction." Their vulnerability leads them to invent "arts of diverse kinds and types to avoid these injuries. But since these arts can only be exercised by a large number of men, and can only be made through their association with one another, men had to assemble together in order to attain what was beneficial through these arts and to avoid what was harmful."[14] As the division of labor expanded, the *Defensor pacis* contends, people became more dependent on one another, and yet, as a direct result, they were also more prone to enter into conflict. For as the economic self-sufficiency of households was eroded by economic interdependence, so the opportunities increased for dispute over control of the benefits of association. This event more than any other sparked the creation of the civil community governed by specialized rulers according to law.

The *Defensor pacis* gauges the level of the "development" or "perfection" of a community according to the extent of the differentiation of its parts, where such parts are understood to be the specialized functional divisions in society.

It is only possible to speak of the "perfect community, called the *civitas*, with the differentiation of its parts" once human beings have discovered the variegated activities through which the full range of their needs may be met.[15] "Since diverse things are necessary to men who desire a sufficient life, things which cannot be supplied by men of one order or office, there had to be diverse human orders or offices in this association, exercising or supplying such diverse things which men need for a sufficient life."[16] Marsiglio thus places a premium on reciprocity. The intercommunication of functions should be the goal of the multiplicity of parts. The final cause of each member is the well-being of the whole community rather than simply its narrow self-interest.[17] In turn, every function is itself indispensable for the sufficient communal life that all human beings naturally desire.[18] The parts are consequently regarded as parts *of the civic body*. These parts do not perform their functions in isolation, but rather in the context of and in relation to the other elements of the civil community.[19]

Yet Marsiglio acknowledges that this notion of function is potentially problematic. On the one hand, the specialized parts of the state all have narrowly constituted purposes: The end of each segment of society must be the completion of its own specific task. Hence, "the final cause of the shipbuilding part of the civic body is a ship; of the military part, the practice of arms and fighting."[20] In this sense, the goal of the members is a private, partial good that is exclusive to it and that might even in principle stand in conflict with the aims of the other sections. Yet, on the other hand, no part of the community can survive without the cooperation of the other parts. The intercommunication of functions is necessary for the sustenance of the multiplicity of parts. Understood from this perspective, "these diverse human orders or offices are none other than the many and distinct parts of the civic body."[21] Viewed communally, the final cause of each member must be the well-being of the whole community rather than simply its narrow self-interest. Here indeed is the positive character of the public provision of communal peace. There is a material necessity for all "the parts of the *civitas*, in whose perfect and unimpeded interaction and intercommunication is said to consist the tranquillity of the *civitas*."[22] The parts do not perform their functions in isolation, but rather in the context of and in relation to the other elements of the civil community.

The functional basis of community translates directly into a principle of civic inclusion and citizenship for Marsiglio. The purpose of politics, including government and law, is to maintain the conditions of tranquillity necessary for the interchange of functions and the attainment of a sufficient life.[23] Political institutions attain this goal, however, only when they serve the common good, that is, when they favor no particular segment of the community. How can this impartial orientation toward the public interest be assured? Marsiglio's solution is to insist that all the functional parts of the civil body whose interests are at stake—even humble practitioners of the mechanical, financial, and agricultural arts—must give their consent to all legislation and must elect their rulers.[24] Unlike Aristotle, who distinguishes between the physical necessity of an activity and the excellence necessary for citizenship,[25] Marsiglio's more biological conception of the purpose of communal association leads him to extend a full set of citizen rights to all those whose material contributions are indispensable for a sufficient life. The community of citizens, composed of the "whole body of the people" and termed "the human legislator" by Marsiglio, has within its competence all the crucial political decisions necessary for the public health and well-being.[26] Consequently, to deny full civic identity to any functional part of the community is to risk the dominance of partial interests, an occurrence that leads to dispute, conflict, and ultimately communal disintegration.[27] An extensive, inclusive, and participatory form of citizenship represents for Marsiglio the best protection against contention.

Religion and Politics

The biological and functional orientation of the *Defensor pacis* has repercussions for Marsiglio's distinction between the temporal and spiritual realms. In typical Christian Aristotelian fashion, Marsiglio acknowledges that human ends "fall into two kinds, of which one is temporal or earthly, while the other is usually called eternal or heavenly."[28] But the resemblance between Marsiglio and more mainstream medieval thinkers such as Thomas Aquinas is largely superficial. In Saint Thomas, there was a distinct hierarchy of ends: Temporal goals were to be encouraged inasmuch as they were conducive to the ultimate purpose of human salvation. The good ruler's highest duty was always the promotion of spiritual happiness and eternal salvation among his subjects.[29]

By contrast, Marsiglio is far more circumspect in his analysis of the part that can be played by the civil body in the realization of spiritual goodness. He advances a remarkable argument for a strict division of the spiritual concerns of religion from the mundane aims of politics. In the second discourse of the *Defensor pacis*, he defines temporal matters as stemming from "those human actions and passions which are voluntary and transient, resulting in benefit or harm to someone other than the agent."[30] It is such "transient" acts—"other-regarding" may be the modern equivalent[31]—that are the proper object of regulation by the laws and rulers of the political community, according to Marsiglio.[32] When transient behavior is performed "in due proportion," it results in benefit to others as well as to oneself; this is the basis of the reciprocity at the core of the functionally healthy community. But when transient action is "excessive," harmonious cooperation is injured, and the need for correction arises.

This definition of the temporal sphere is directly contrasted with the spiritual realm by Marsiglio. The term "spiritual" refers to every immanent action or passion of human cognitive or appetitive power,[33] where "immanent" acts are understood as "actions or passions" that "do not pass over into a subject other than the doer, nor are they exercised through any external organs or locomotive members; of this kind are human thoughts and desires or affections."[34] Because they are wholly internal—self-regarding—immanent acts are not susceptible to public inspection and control; they are spiritual in the sense that they do not transgress the boundaries of the soul, hence are invisible to human observation and are known only to God.

In light of his sharp distinction between transient and immanent acts, Marsiglio is able to limit quite dramatically the legitimate connection between temporal politics and spiritual goodness. At best, the community can ensure that the faithful enjoy the opportunity and resources to worship God, insofar as their attention is not deflected from divine purposes by material deprivation and bodily suffering. Given the centrality of function to Marsiglian politics, it is difficult to envision any more extensive public role for spiritual aims. It is not religion that holds the secular community together, but instead the civil body permits enhanced opportunities for worship. The strictly biological end of human association, in conjunction with the wholly inward concern of religion, requires for Marsiglio a pronounced separation between spiritual and temporal domains.

This view is supported by Marsiglio's account of the origins and nature of the priesthood. Priests arose in the wake of the Fall, Marsiglio contends, "to teach and educate men in those matters which, according to evangelical law, it is necessary to believe, do, and refrain from in order to attain eternal salvation and avoid misery."[35] The instructional focus of Marsiglio's concept of the priesthood is crucial. All priests are teachers: They inform the faithful what *must* be done (commands) and what *might* be done (counsels) to merit divine grace and ultimate salvation. It does not, however, pertain to the office of the priest to *enforce* a divine code on the faithful by physical or coercive means.

The priesthood is prohibited from compelling anyone to believe its lessons and from imposing temporal punishment for those who dispute its dogmas. Coercion pertains only to the citizen body or its authorized executive, the ruling segment of the community.[36]

Ironically, it seems to be as a consequence of his desire to uphold a strict separation of spiritual and temporal activities that Marsiglio counts the priesthood among the offices of the civil body, so that its conduct must thus be regulated for the sake of the common good. A perfected human community requires priests to minister to the souls of its members, just as it requires farmers to feed it and soldiers to defend it.[37] But this entails that the religious functions of the clergy must be treated as just another public office.

Community and Church

To afford official civil status to the priesthood might seem to imply support for establishmentarianism, a doctrine generally inimical to religious toleration. Certainly, Marsiglio holds that the Catholic faith is the one true faith.[38] But the point of his treatment of the priesthood as a public office is to control the temporal implications of religion, not to sanction the intrusion of religion into politics.[39] He wants to ensure that the priesthood remains confined to its proper instructional role and that it does not promote conduct dangerous to the common good. (To do the latter, of course, would be self-destructive in any event, because without peace and prosperity, the practice of religion is itself endangered for Marsiglio.) It is with public supervision thus in mind that Marsiglio retains for the community the right to license priests and to oversee their teachings.[40] More dramatically, he acknowledges the legitimacy of the priestly office in non-Christian regimes.[41] When judged from a civil perspective, the "truth" of Christianity is not immediately germane. What matters instead is that, whatever the religion practiced by a given civic body, its priests conform their activities to the welfare of the whole. The validity of the religion does not confer on the priesthood any greater authority over or autonomy from the community than is permitted to "false" religions.

Nevertheless, Marsiglio still appears to leave the door open to religious intolerance and persecution. Because he has set the activities of religious office in the public domain, might the priesthood not simply appeal to the community of citizens to punish in coercive fashion those who offend against divine law or ecclesiastical teachings? The *Defensor pacis* remains ambivalent about the use of coercion to penalize spiritual malefactors, as is evident from Marsiglio's discussion of the power of excommunication. He acknowledges that excommunication is both "punishment for the status of the future life" and "also a grave penalty . . . for the status of the present life, in that . . . one is deprived of civil communion and benefits."[42] In other words, it is coercive. Hence, if the priesthood were permitted to excommunicate individuals on its own authority, it could interfere with impunity in civil affairs and impose its wishes on the community through the threat or imposition of the ban. This violates the purely instructional role that Marsiglio ascribes to the priestly office.

One alternative logically available to Marsiglio would be to challenge the very principle that any person or group enjoys the authority of excommunicating citizens. This he avoids doing. Rather, he leaves the question of the propriety of excommunication up to the determination of the human legislator: "We do not wish to say that it is inappropriate that heretics or other infidels be coerced, but that the authority for this, if it be lawful, belongs only to the human legislator."[43] He thus shifts the power of declaring the ban from a spiritual to a temporal source. Note the studied ambiguity in Marsiglio's remark. On the one hand, he clearly does not regard excommunication as a necessity. Instead, the *Defensor pacis* entertains the possibility that a policy of full toleration might be extended to all forms of religious dissent: "If human law did not prohibit the heretic or other infidel from dwelling among the faithful in the same province, as heretics and Jews are now permitted to do by human laws even in these times of Christian peoples, rulers, and pontiffs, then I say that no one is allowed to judge or coerce a heretic or other infidel by any penalty in property or in person for the status of the present life."[44] Throughout his discussions, Marsiglio always employs conditional language and implies that he would be amenable (or at least not object) to the elimination of excommunication entirely.[45]

Yet at the same time, Marsiglio appears willing to defer to the decision of the civil community on the validity of excommunication. It falls without exception to "the whole body of faithful citizens . . . to make a judgment or to appoint a judge having coercive power to expel persons from the company of the community because of a disease of the soul, such as a notorious crime, although such a judgment ought to emerge from the counsel of priests, inasmuch as they are held to know the divine law by which is determined the crimes because of which the transgressor must be denied the society of crimeless believers."[46] Marsiglio seems perfectly content to countenance depriving individuals of their earthly goods and civic rights on account of spiritual transgressions, so long as this action has been lawfully authorized in advance and is undertaken by the community rather than the priesthood. Consequently, there may seem considerable merit in the inference drawn by some scholars that Marsiglio's theory is not especially friendly to toleration. As Brian Tierney concludes, "Marsilius's arguments could then have been applied in such a way as to justify the institutions of an authoritarian, persecuting state. . . . He did not develop any doctrine of an individual right to religious liberty."[47]

Yet this conclusion overlooks that fact that Marsiglio's willingness in the *Defensor pacis* to accept the temporal ramifications of excommunication is not strictly consistent with his communal functionalist stance. It is unclear why one's failure to accept the same religious doctrines as other members of the secular community must negatively affect one's own appropriate functions. Is a heretical farmer intrinsically any the less competent in performing his civil tasks and intercommunicating them with other citizens than an orthodox farmer? Is one necessarily better qualified as a soldier because one embraces Christian beliefs instead of some other confession? The concern evinced by the medieval Church about the "contamination" of the soul that might occur if apostates mingled freely with the faithful in secular affairs is not warranted by Marsiglio's strict separation of spiritual and temporal realms. For him the intercommunication of functions necessary for a physically sufficient life is entirely unrelated to acceptance of the instruction of priests about the worship of God. What matters in the secular sphere is simply whether one is performing one's tasks properly and in a manner consonant with the common good. One's faith is not germane to this judgment.

Excommunication and Exclusion

In the *Defensor pacis*, Marsiglio demonstrates no keen awareness of the incongruity in his theory. By the time he wrote the *Defensor minor* about fifteen years later, however, he had adopted a more internally consistent position, which led him to expound a communally grounded theory of religious toleration. That scholars have not taken note of this development reflects the extent to which attention has been focused exclusively on the *Defensor pacis*, perhaps on the unwarranted assumption that the *Defensor minor* reflects no intellectual change or maturation on Marsiglio's part.

In the *Defensor minor*, Marsiglio does confirm his previous claim that the priesthood lacks any rightful power whatsoever to declare any member of the church anathema: "Inasmuch as this authority must involve coercion over goods or persons or both, and thus must be applied (however moderately) in this world by the civil power, such authority never pertains to priests." Excommunication has a coercive dimension precisely because it imposes on the sinner "the punishment of exile" and it removes "the wealth and income" by which one sustains oneself and one's family.[48] The excommunicate stands outside the temporal community as well as the spiritual one. Hence, like all other applications of coercive authority, the decision to remove a person from civil association through excommunication can be the determination of only the whole body of citizens or its appointed executives.

Yet Marsiglio does not seem entirely satisfied with this solution. Rather, he poses the further question of "whether it is expedient to separate heretics from, or deprive them of, the fellowship of believers."[49] In other words, he wonders aloud about the validity of excommunication at all. Is it even appropriate that those who decline to accept the established tenets of religious dogma should be anathematized? The answer he offers is striking, for it rests on a denial of the temporal implications of spiritual dissent. To make this argument, Marsiglio must examine the purpose of excommunication. It cannot be the case that individuals are anathematized for the sake of compelling them to accept dogma. Marsiglio denies that nonbelievers can ever truly or effectively be coerced into accepting the faith: It is not a tenet of Christianity that "any individual ought to be compelled to profess the Christian faith." This is a view that he employs explicitly against the practice of crusading: "If a foreign journey is made or will be made in order to subdue or restrain infidels for the sake of the Christian faith, then such a foreign journey would in no way seem to be meritorious."[50] Thus, if the aim of excommunication is the coercion of heretics to return to the faith, this enterprise is likewise unjustified.[51] Compulsion is not to be employed as a means to return the heterodox to the faith.

Consequently, the only valid reason for excommunication must be the protection of the eternal souls of orthodox believers. Marsiglio admits that "heretics and other infidels . . . are to be shunned, especially in connection with domestic or social relations, or cohabitation or conversation, concerning those matters which pertain to the preservation of the rituals of the faith, . . . lest they taint the remaining believers."[52] He quotes several biblical passages in support of the practice of excommunication on these grounds, but he immediately emphasizes that the separation of believer from heretic should occur in connection with spiritual matters only: "This is to be understood in regard to belief and the observance of the rituals of the faith, rather than in regard to other domestic or civil intercourse."[53] The condemnation of heterodox belief is, Marsiglio contends, really "a sort of shame and disgrace" rather than a form of coercive punishment at all.[54] The Church (properly represented in its General Council) has the authority to fix its truths and to exclude from worship those who reject doctrinal principles. Thus, excommunication is a prohibition of spiritual association; orthodox members are never to talk with or heed the words of heretics about the faith.

Yet there is neither a scriptural nor a rational basis for extending this prohibition to the temporal domain of communal life. Marsiglio's defense of this claim assumes his functionalist conception of society. He points out that the final cause of human law and its coercive force "is the tranquillity and finite happiness of this world," with the result that such precepts shape "human beings insofar as they are disposed and affected towards tranquillity and power and many other [earthly] things."[55] If excommunication were to encompass temporal as well as spiritual affairs, then the legitimate concerns of public order and welfare would be disturbed. Indeed, the very purpose of excommunication, the well-being of the faithful, would be undermined. For by denying intercommunication of a purely secular nature between the orthodox and nonbelievers of all sorts, the faithful themselves are harmed: They will not be able to take advantage of those material benefits that constitute the very foundation of communal life. It is a violation of the social bond, the very law of nature that joins human beings together, to deprive anyone (let alone orthodox Christians) of

> civil comforts and associations, such as by purchasing bread, wine, meat, fish, pots, or clothes from them [persons guilty of heresy], if they abound in such items and others of the faithful lack them. This is likewise also true of the rest of the functions and comforts to which they might possibly be judged susceptible in connection with their positions or civil duties and services. For otherwise this punishment would redound in like fashion or for the most part to innocent believers.[56]

The extension of excommunication to civil association constitutes for Marsiglio an attack on the most basic principle of community rooted in the interchange of functions. Neither orthodox Christians nor religious dissenters would be permitted to perform those tasks that form the basis of their citizenship. Inevitably, the functional breakdown of the community, and the intranquillity that Marsiglio so feared, would ensue.

Toleration and Inclusion

The conclusion to be drawn from Marsiglio's thought is clear: It is no part of human law, or of divine law, to command that nonbelievers should be excluded from participation in civic life, whether in economic activity or in the civil rights that such activity confers.[57] A stable political order requires a principled policy of toleration for religious difference, where such diversity does no direct harm to the performance of those functions necessary for the common good. Orthodox believers may indeed be under a spiritual obligation to refrain from contact with infidels in matters of worship or conscience, but they cannot be prevented by their church (or by the civil body) from engaging in acts of exchange or association with nonbelievers. Indeed, marriage between Christians and heretics is even permissible, because Marsiglio regards marriage not as a sacrament but as a civil ceremony.[58] Nor can the Church rightfully demand that heretics by virtue of their religious views be denied their proper role in the community. This principle seems equally applicable to any sort of attitude toward supernatural matters: catholic or nonconforming Christian as well as non-Christian believer. Marsiglio's strict separation of spiritual from secular concerns means that no profession of faith provides an adequate justification for exclusion from the temporal community.

Detractors may immediately object that Marsiglio still clings to a certain measure of non-neutrality insofar as he continues to regard the priesthood as a necessary "part" of the civic body, rather than as an activity whose bearing is purely private. Excuse could, of course, be made on historical grounds that religion was so dominant a feature of Marsiglio's world (as it is not of our own) that he could not plausibly relegate it to the private sphere. Such special pleading is not really needed, however, because Marsiglio has completely repudiated the compulsory overtones normally associated with establishmentarianism of any sort (whether of a specific church or of a confession generally). Even if Marsiglio presumes the existence of a single "official" (in the sense of civilly sanctioned) church, citizens cannot as a condition of their citizenship be made to observe the teachings or obey the orders of its priests. Although profession of certain official beliefs could be demanded for one's continued status as a church member, no such profession could be a legal requirement of civic identity. Even when the instruction of the priesthood about divine law merely repeats or reaffirms the requirements of secular law (for example, in the prohibition of acts such as theft and murder), clerical lessons acquire no coercive force. The teachings of priests apply to the inward condition of the soul (immanent acts), whereas the coercive sanctions imposed by the community and its executive agents have the temporal goal of regulating transient acts so as to promote the peaceful interchange of functions.

It might nevertheless seem that toleration of religious difference remains for Marsiglio a wholly contingent matter. Surely his argument could just as readily justify suppression of religious difference on functionalist grounds, say, should the community of citizens freely decide that a particular practice stemming from one's mode of worship is incompatible with the common good. The response to this objection depends largely on the specific practice that one has in mind. A form of worship that substantially interferes with the ability of other citizens to perform their civilly oriented tasks or that limits one's capacity to contribute one's appropriate function to the community might well come in for curtailment or prohibition. In the *Defensor pacis*, Marsiglio mentions monastic and clerical orders that claim "immunities from public or civil burdens," such as taxation or obedience to certain secular laws. Marsiglio argues on functional grounds that "he who enjoys civil honors and advantages, like peace and the protection of the civil legislator, must not be exempt from civil burdens and jurisdiction."[59] This principle indicates that the community retains reasonable control over practices that intrude on the smooth operation of the community. Similarly, in the *Defensor minor*, Marsiglio denies that the Church has "the authority or power to order or command any of the faithful to perform any fast regardless of length or to forbid food to anyone, nor to command likewise a holiday from manual or civil labors on account of the festivals of saints, nor conversely to forbid such decrees."[60] Such matters touch directly on transient acts associated with the secular functions necessary for the maintenance of a common life and thus are appropriately subject to public, rather than religious, regulation.

We are not justified, however, in concluding that, because such communal toleration is not absolute, Marsiglio's idea of tolerance of religious difference is weak or contingent. Even in modern society, clear limits are set on actions that are protected by freedom of religion. In liberal regimes, most conduct that violates the law—conscientious objection to military service is a rare and notable exception (and even the conscientious objector must perform alternative service)—cannot be excused on the grounds that obedience to statutory law conflicts with observance of the "higher" or "divine" dictates of one's religion. Indeed, official neutrality is hardly so clear-cut as liberals would have us believe. A law that orders business closings on Sundays may seem to favor devout Christians (or at least Christians who accept certain dominant beliefs); but a law that permits businesses to operate all weekend can equally be seen to favor nonreligious proprietors over observant ones.[61] It is perhaps more honest to confront directly the dilemmas posed by the impossibility of adopting the utterly neutral stance demanded by perfect tolerance, rather than to gloss over such difficulties, as liberals would often have us do.

Conclusion

As a matter of historical interpretation, it seems reasonable to characterize Marsiglio of Padua as not merely a forceful opponent of persecution but as a budding advocate of religious toleration. Simply put, his position is completely unconcerned with the connections between politics and spiritual orientation, except where individual conduct impedes or threatens the tranquillity of the community. The attempt to establish the indifference of the civil body and its laws and rulers toward competing conceptions of human goodness and salvation by introducing an absolute separation between the various human ends permits the communal functionalist case for religious toleration to proceed. The politics of the common good are confined to the narrower goal of ensuring conditions that permit a sufficient life for all citizens.

As a result, the Marsiglian position presumes the indispensability of liberty and its consistency with reason and faith. In Marsiglio's view, individuals must be free both to judge and to worship independently as a prerequisite for discerning a conception of the good life. The assurance of inner freedom is the logical precondition for the attainment of any form of spiritual virtue and personal salvation. A functionally healthy community is conducive to this goal because it permits such exercise of individual freedom and does not impose an exclusive public conception of goodness. Marsiglio's communal functionalism recognizes that political life is a valuable and positive (if indirect and limited) force for promoting human goodness. The goal is to establish a balance between public and private realms, not to keep politics at a distance from the individual and to constrain it in its most narrow justifiable confines. Yet communal functionalism does not hold that civic inclusion and identification must entail acceptance of a single comprehensive conception of the good: Meaningful citizenship, because it concentrates on matters of material cooperation, is logically compatible with an array of religious viewpoints.

It must be stressed that, even in comparison with succeeding early modern theories of toleration, Marsiglio's communally based version is constructed at a high level of generality. First, there is no sense in which his account is "concordant" rather than truly tolerant. Marsiglio regards the status of one's membership in (or relation to) the Christian faith or Church to be entirely irrelevant to the maintenance of the community. Nothing in his theory prevents individuals from remaining contumacious heretics in perpetuity; it violates the foundations of citizenship for anyone to be compelled to recant. Consequently, Marsiglio has opened the door for religious pluralism, so long as it does not break out into the sort of armed conflict that early modern Europe was to witness. Indeed, the logic of his argument encompasses all manner of nonconformance to Christian orthodoxy: Infidels as well as heretics are included, and in principle there is nothing to stop even agnostics and atheists from being counted as members of the temporal political community (although Marsiglio never entertains the latter notion, of course). Such a view may profitably be contrasted with the seventeenth-century theories of John Locke and Pierre Bayle, for whom toleration was to be extended to a far more constrained range of confessions (or nonconfessions).[62] Finally, it may be argued that because Marsiglio's approach to religious tolerance was grounded in a broader set of distinctions between public and private realms and other-regarding and self-regarding acts, his theory readily extends into a defense of difference broadly construed—not simply in matters of faith, but in lifestyle, cultural identity, sexual orientation, and so forth. It is, of course, untenable to suggest that Marsiglio ever had such a wide-ranging conception of toleration in mind when he was composing the two *Defensors*. Yet it is often the case that powerful theories prove capable of taking on a life of their own and come to be applied in ways never imagined by their authors. The theoretical case propounded by Marsiglio in support of religious toleration seems to be a prime example of how such an unintended application may nonetheless be validly made.[63]

6

NATIONALITY AND THE "VARIETY OF RITES" IN NICHOLAS OF CUSA

Nationality and Difference

Nationalism in the modern world has come to be counted among the prime causes of hatred, violence, and repression—a source of intolerance toward people of differing geographic, ethnic, and religious backgrounds. Nationalistic fervor has so often given birth to militaristic expansionism, persecution of minorities, or both, that Western societies now tend to greet its expression (at least in more extreme forms) with suspicion. During the Middle Ages, however, nationalism had a quite different complexion. In light of the Christian penchant for a universal and uniform religion, culture, and society, the medieval idea of "nationality" posed a novel form of identity that challenged the self-image of the *Respublica Christiana*. National monarchies (and in southern Europe, city-states) sought to lay claim to a rudimentary territorial sovereignty, extending their legal, administrative, and ideological apparatus over subjects and demanding primitive expressions of loyalty. Vernacular languages and literatures grew in use and self-confidence, displacing the omnipresence of Latin in political as well as cultural affairs.[1] In short, self-awareness of socio-geographic diversity became a significant organizing principle in Europe, opening up new opportunities for the acceptance of human difference.

These developments raised troubling dilemmas for the claims of Christian universalism. As we have seen, Christianity posited a close alignment among religion, culture, and politics as "universal" forms of experience. If one admitted the validity of divergent forms of cultural and political life, then one also at least tacitly acknowledged the possibility of different confessions, associated with territorial or regional particularisms, existing in harmony with one another. The recognition that politics and culture need not be grounded on a unitary foundation betokened, at minimum, the idea of a "national" church unbeholden to a single, supreme ecclesiastical authority, in other words, religious conviction attached to other forms of social identity. One notes precisely such associations at work, for instance, in the cooperation between French monarchs (especially Philip the Fair) and the French clergy in their opposition to the papacy.[2] By the end of the fourteenth century, the image of a "Gallican" Church, possessed of its own distinctive rites and traditions, had captured a wide audience. The convergence of nationalism and religion was to climax 150 years later, of course, when King Henry VIII of England took the step of breaking entirely with Roman universalism and establishing an actual national church.[3]

Emergent nationalism also attracted the attention of medieval philosophers at a relatively early stage. From 1300 onward, one encounters an increasingly pronounced readiness among authors to endorse the natural necessity of regional variations in government according to the diverse propensities and dispositions of local populations.[4] Scholastics such as John of Paris challenged the logic of universalism in the temporal sphere by adapting Aristotelian naturalism to explain diversity in the political order. Although all human beings are inclined to civil life, John reasons, "they choose different types of rulers to oversee the well-being of their communities to correspond with the diversity of these communities . . . in respect to differences of climate and conditions."[5] The spiritual purposes imposed by a common religion, according to John, by no means "require that the faithful be united in any common state. There can be different ways of living and different kinds of state conforming to differences in climate, language, and the conditions of men, since what is suitable for one nation may not be so for another."[6] John in effect detaches the demands of Christian universalism in the spiritual sphere from any secular political implications, on the grounds that the arrangement of civil life is a natural matter that corresponds with physical and geographic differences between groups. This thesis gained a wide following over the course of the fourteenth century. Even authors such as Engelbert of Admont and Marsiglio of Padua, who had intellectual and polemical reasons to support the claims of the Holy Roman Empire, averred that distinct communities could legitimately authorize the political institutions most appropriate to their circumstances.[7] By the end of the century, it was a commonplace in scholastic tomes as well as civilian legal treatises to adopt the view that systems of government were flexible according to the natural diversity in the human race.[8]

Implicit in the assertion of natural human difference was a measure of social and cultural toleration. As Kate Forhan has argued in connection with another early theorist of nationality, Christine de Pizan, "The idea of nationalism can prepare an environment conducive to the growth of tolerance."[9] Yet a further move, from the temporal to the spiritual realm, was necessary for such forbearance to include issues of religion, constructing the foundations for "nationally" based differences of faith and rite. This shift seems to come only in the fifteenth century, and from a very unlikely source: the ecclesiastical reformer and eventual cardinal, Nicholas of Cusa. In a little treatise entitled *De pace fidei*, composed in 1453,[10] Nicholas constructs a bridge from the national differences that were by now an accepted part of medieval thought to a diversity of religious practices and forms of worship. The immediate stimulus for the composition of *De pace fidei* was initial word of the fall of Constantinople together with stories of Turkish atrocities that soon spread throughout Europe. Nicholas had earlier served on a diplomatic mission to Constantinople and was clearly shocked by reports (for the most part exaggerated) of the destruction of the ancient city and its Christian inhabitants. Consequently, *De pace fidei* laments and condemns persecutions stemming from religious diversity and calls for a peaceful harmonization of discordant faiths, motivated by a sincere desire to see all the world's peoples reconciled in amiable coexistence. Nicholas's passion for harmony does not blind him to (indeed, it encourages him to speculate on) the causes of conflict and discord. In doing so, he admits the intractability of political and cultural divisions; yet he proposes that this is a strength rather than a weakness of humanity, even suggesting that "national" diversity may in fact serve to strengthen reverence for God. Ultimately, Nicholas adopts the view that, given the permanent character of social differences, religious concord can be achieved only in a partial and muted fashion—"one religion in a variety of rites," to use his now famous phrase.[11] *De pace fidei* in effect reverses the principle of Christian universalism by constructing a kind of sociology of religious toleration: Because earthly nations can never be reduced to a single universal order, many aspects of divergent confessions must be respected for the sake of peace.

Nicholas in the History of Toleration

To a greater extent than most of the writings examined in the present study, Nicholas of Cusa's *De pace fidei* has already been assured a place in scholarship on the history of toleration. According to the conventional interpretation of the work, pioneered by Ernst Cassirer in *Individuum und Kosmos in der Philosophie der Renaissance*, Nicholas belongs in a wholly original movement of Christian humanism that broke with the medieval past and promoted "truly grand tolerance,"[12] presaging more modern proponents of toleration such as Jean Bodin.[13] In this vein, *De pace fidei* has been proclaimed "to be one of the finest and most practical treatises on the question of religious tolerance, . . . free from the typical Scholastic provincialism and lack of toleration."[14] One ought not to overlook the premise built into such readings of *De pace fidei*: It must be a work "before its time" because the beliefs typical of the Latin Middle Ages were entirely incompatible with tolerant attitudes and doctrines.

The "modernizing" interpretation of *De pace fidei* has been convincingly challenged on a number of counts: For instance, it diminishes the significance of numerous medieval precedents for inter-religious dialogue, such as Abelard and Llull (Nicholas seems to have known the works of the latter); it ignores the hostility that Nicholas expressed toward Islamic religion in his later *Cribratio Alkorani*; and it dismisses his dedication to traditional neo-Platonic philosophy.[15] In place of the view that Nicholas was an early advocate of a modern idea of religious toleration, many recent scholars have emphasized that the teachings of *De pace fidei* extend and elaborate his philosophy and theology as well as his ecclesiology.[16] In particular, attention has been directed to the substance of Nicholas's case for a "single easy harmony" between apparently disparate faiths.[17] On this account, *De pace fidei* applies the Cusan methods of "concordance" and *coincidentia oppositorum* to the issue of religious conviction, yielding a decidedly Christian unity of belief in matters of salvation. Nicholas is thereby shown to retain a concerted universalism in his attitude to religion: The primary tenets of Christianity are vindicated over the course of the dialogue, and proponents of divergent faiths (including polytheism, Judaism, Islam, and Hinduism) are induced to admit the superior wisdom of Christian theology. At best, then, what distinguishes *De pace fidei*'s idea of religious pluralism is its irenicism; violent persecution and coerced conversion must be replaced with rational debate and proof as the means for realizing the universal truth of Christian doctrine.[18] No wonder that scholars who adopt this interpretation remark on Nicholas's "optimistic impulse."[19]

Recognition of the debt owed by *De pace fidei* to central elements of Nicholas's philosophy, theology, and ecclesiology certainly provides a vital corrective to previous, excessively modernizing interpretations of the work. As a consequence, however, current scholars have become reluctant to speak of the relevance of *De pace fidei* to the history of toleration. Presumably, they accept the same premise as their predecessors, namely, that a defense of tolerance can be constructed only on certain distinctively modern grounds.[20] To the extent that this assumption is flawed, it becomes possible to view *De pace fidei* as a work issuing from characteristically medieval forms of discourse *and* simultaneously as a contribution to the development of tolerant principles in European thought. As with other medieval authors, Nicholas is primarily concerned with criticizing the premises that gave rise to intolerant actions and attitudes, such as were in evidence in the purported bloodshed and repression at Constantinople. He therefore sought to explain how differences in matters of religious belief need not result in violence and persecution, but could be accorded tolerance. Nicholas's distinctive contribution was to connect his critique of intolerance to differences of nationality. This fact becomes evident when we step away from the intricacies of Nicholas's proposals for concord among the many confessions and consider the framework of cultural and political difference in which the treatise proceeds.

Principles of Nationality

De pace fidei purports to recount a vision experienced by Nicholas himself—an answer to his prayer for the peaceful resolution to the bloodshed accompanying the Turkish sack of Constantinople—in which God determines to hold a conclave of wise men for the purpose of achieving universal agreement about matters of faith. The body of the work is an account of a dialogue between representatives (although Nicholas does not use that term) of the world religions and spokesmen for Heaven (including Peter, Paul, and the Word). Scholarship has seldom commented on one of the most intriguing features of the dramatic structure of *De pace fidei:* The wise men are usually identified not as members of particular confessions, but by their cultural, ethnic, or political heritage. God calls together delegates from "the individual provinces and sects of the world,"[21] and in the course of the discussion we are introduced to a Greek, an Italian, an Arab, an Indian, a Chaldean, a Jew, a Scythian, a Frenchman, a Persian, a Syrian, a Spaniard, a Turk, a German, a Tartar, an Armenian, a Bohemian, and an Englishman. The fact that these characters are designated primarily by national or sociocultural identities distinguishes *De pace fidei* from other medieval (and indeed early modern) inter-religious dialogues, where the participants are generally named according to or are directly associated with their specific doctrinal viewpoints.

What is the significance of Nicholas's unique designation of his dramatis personae? Throughout *De pace fidei*, this dramatic structure permits him to filter issues of religious difference through the lens of disparate "nations." Nationalism and the bases of national identities remained emergent and fluid concepts in the mid-fifteenth century.[22] At times, Nicholas employs the term *natio* to describe an entire religion or faith, as when the Tartar states that "the Jews say they have [God's] commandments through Moses, the Arabs through Mohammed, the Christians through Jesus, and the other nations perhaps venerate their own prophets by whose hands they claim to have received the divine commandments."[23] Yet on numerous occasions, *De pace fidei* distinguishes a religion as practiced by given nations and populations—among Christians as well as non-Christians—from the religion itself, acknowledging the impact of local conditions and institutions in the manner of the scholastic discussions of national difference with which he was surely familiar. Thus, for instance, the Greek comments, "A faith other than that which a nation has defended with its very blood will, it seems to us, be accepted with difficulty."[24] Likewise, when speaking of the Eucharist, the Bohemian remarks, "It is not easy to believe that other nations which do not have the custom of sacrificing in this way will accept this way of doing things."[25] Certainly, *natio* lacked some of the precision in Nicholas's language that it tends to enjoy in modern, state-oriented discourse.[26] Nonetheless, he ordinarily imputes to *natio* a sociopolitical dimension quite distinct from a unified religious conviction that binds people of diverse heritages, on the order of the *Respublica Christiana*.

Nicholas's appeal to nationality in a political and cultural sense derives, in turn, from his adaptation and amplification of the scholastic thesis that earthly human life is inherently and inescapably diverse. This principle is explicitly defended from the beginning of *De pace fidei* on two grounds, which I shall call "historicity" and "inequality." Nicholas prefaces his explanation of the origins of religious difference by asserting: "A great multitude cannot exist without considerable diversity, and almost everyone is forced to lead a life burdened with sorrows and full of miseries and to live under servile subjection to rulers who lord over them."[27] This statement, I think, contains the key to Nicholas's unique approach to toleration. The first part refers to the circumstances of human culture ("historicity"), the second to the nature of earthly political life ("inequality").

Nicholas acknowledges, in the first place, that human cultures necessarily diverge according to time and place. As he remarks elsewhere in *De pace fidei*,

"In the sensible world nothing remains stable and, because of time, opinions and conjectures as well as languages and interpretations vary as things transitory."[28] Although Nicholas consistently maintains that there is only a single ultimate truth in central religious doctrines, he is aware that understandings of that truth are bound to change and diverge because of the fragility of human intelligence and the particular patterns of cultural practice. Thus, for instance, "difference in the manner of speech" produces distinctive confessions and rites, even if the true meaning that each religion intends to convey is identical.[29] Religious rites, Nicholas says, "have been instituted and received as sensible signs of the truth of faith. But signs are subject to change; not however that which is signified."[30] This is perhaps best illustrated by an intriguing passage of *De pace fidei* in which Peter explains to the German that certain sections of the Qur'an that seem offensive to European Christians must not be taken literally: "It says in the Qur'an that beautiful black maidens with very large white eyes are found [in Paradise]; no German in this world, even if given to the vices of the flesh, would desire them. Hence, it is necessary that these things be understood allegorically (*similitudinaliter*)."[31] Differing cultural and linguistic contexts demand the expression of the same idea—in this case, the desirability of the afterlife—according to usages and expectations appropriate to their specific conditions. Nicholas appears to regard such historical particularity as unavoidable. He thereby implicitly rejects the possibility of a universal human language and culture through which religious truths might be unambiguously expressed. At best, *De pace fidei* advocates the translation of ultimate truth into terms comprehensible to diverse peoples and strives to demonstrate how this may occur.

Inequality, especially between the wise leaders and the ignorant masses (*rudes*), forms the other cornerstone of human diversity. As Nicholas observes, "Only a few have enough leisure that they can proceed to a knowledge of themselves using their own free choice. For [most people] are distracted by many bodily cares and duties; and so they are not able to seek you, who are a hidden God."[32] This principle of the inequality of human condition is a theme that runs throughout Nicholas's writings. In *De concordantia catholica*, written a decade before *De pace fidei*, he declared, "Almighty God has assigned a certain natural servility to the ignorant and the stupid, so that they readily trust the wise to help them preserve themselves. . . . The ignorant could not govern themselves and so become servile to the wise out of necessity."[33] Although Nicholas admits a certain basic equality of human intelligence and choice,[34] he insists that these faculties are insufficient to permit most people to rule their own lives without the guidance of individuals of superior wisdom. This constitutes for him the origin of both political jurisdiction and religious rite. Speaking directly to God, he says: "You appointed for your people different kings and seers, who are called prophets; in carrying out the responsibility of your mission many of them have instituted worship and laws in your name and taught the ignorant (*rudum*). . . . You sent to the different nations different prophets and teachers, some at one time and others at another."[35] Political and ecclesiastical institutions ought therefore to be viewed as divinely inspired remedies for the incapacities of human nature. Human beings for the most part require guidance to attain their earthly survival, let alone their salvation; the daily burdens of life demand acquiescence to the wise in matters of the public welfare, just for the sake of the ignorant themselves.[36] This entails that particular practices and rituals are imposed on the masses, a fact that accounts for the many systems of government and worship that have emerged throughout the world.

Indeed, the division between the wise and the ignorant shapes the whole course of *De pace fidei*. Recall that the heavenly conclave contains a cross-national selection of the "wise," who are in turn charged with taking the results of the assembly back to their various peoples and leading them to concord.[37] Various speakers express concern, however, that what can perhaps be understood by wise individuals is beyond the reach of the multitude. As the Chaldean comments, "Even if the wise people could somewhat grasp these things, nevertheless they would exceed the common people."[38] Likewise, Nicholas traces many of the metaphorical characteristics of the Qur'an to its reluctance "to state to the ignorant people (*rudi populum*) other more hidden matters but only those matters that seem happier according to the sense, lest the people, who do not relish spiritual things, would disparage its promises."[39] As in the instance of historicity, Nicholas appears to regard inequality as an essential feature of the human condition on earth. As feeble and encumbered human beings, we require wise rulers who establish and interpret law (human as well as divine) for our particular benefit to guide us toward our temporal and eternal goals. For this wise leadership to be effective, Nicholas takes for granted that it must be localized, thus contributing to the patchwork of national identities.

Diversity and Religious Conflict

The two pillars of *natio* are the prime supports of the religious conflicts and persecution that Nicholas abhors. Having explained the intractable character of historicity and inequality in his opening plea to God, he admits, "Yet the way it is with the earthly human condition, a long-standing custom that is taken as having become nature is defended as truth. Thus, not insignificant dissensions occur when each community (*communitas*) prefers its faith to another."[40] Religion in this sociocultural sense is regarded as a purely conventional phenomenon, flowing from the traditions and rituals that have accrued in a society as the result of contingent historical usage and the requirements of inequality. Inasmuch as these forms of worship become a kind of "second nature" among established political and cultural units, nations are unwilling to change or alter them and indeed will go to war and die to preserve them. Later in *De pace fidei*, the Tartar (who presents himself as an outsider to these disputes) remarks, "I do not grasp how there could be a unity in these matters which vary also according to place and time; and unless it occurs, persecution will not end. For diversity gives birth to division and to hostility, hatred, and warfare."[41] This, then, frames the salient dilemma of *De pace fidei:* how to achieve agreement about true doctrine without submerging cultural and political differences that arise ineluctably from the human condition. Nicholas's concord must be of a very special sort—not the unbridled universalism of the *Respublica Christiana*, but a unity attuned to distinctions of *natio* that ought not to be, and at any rate cannot be, eradicated.

In matters at the core of Christian faith, of course, Nicholas is unwavering in his observance of orthodoxy. *De pace fidei* thus insists on absolute acceptance of Latin Christian teachings on monotheism, idolatry, the Trinity, and so forth. Once the reasonableness of these doctrines is demonstrated to wise men of other faiths, Nicholas believes, they will naturally and uncontentiously embrace them.[42] There is still wide latitude in matters of "rite," that is, the socially conditioned practices that distinguish worship among different faiths. Nicholas counts circumcision, baptism, marriage, the Eucharist, and other Christian sacraments among such rites.[43] In his view, once faith as the chief source of salvation "is acknowledged, the variety of rites will not be a cause of turbulence."[44] Rather, he avers that "it is very often necessary to condescend to human weakness if it does not offend against eternal salvation. For to seek conformity in all things is rather to disturb the peace."[45] Consequently, Nicholas allows that the sacrament of the Eucharist is unnecessary for the salvation of the "rudes."[46]

This is not to suggest that he does not express a preference for Christian rites in cases where conformity can be achieved. As Paul responds to the Tartar's concerns about circumcision:

How peace could be preserved among the faithful if some are cir-
cumcised and others are not is a major question. Hence, because the
larger part of the world is uncircumcised and circumcision is not necessary [for salvation], I consider it fitting that in order to preserve peace
the smaller part should conform to the larger, with whom they are
united in faith. But if on account of peace the larger part should conform to the smaller and accept circumcision, it ought to be done vol-
untarily so that peace thus might be established by mutual
interchanges. For if in the cause of peace other nations accept faith
from Christians and the Christians circumcision from them, peace
would be better made and strengthened.[47]

Yet Nicholas is by no means sanguine that such "mutual interchanges" will
occur. Instead, he admits that, given the demands of *natio*, respect for a "variety of rites" is more likely to produce the elimination of cross-cultural conflict:
"Still I think that the practice of this [conformity regarding circumcision]
would be difficult. Therefore, it should suffice that peace be established in faith
and in the law of love and that such rites be thereafter tolerated (*tolerando*)."[48]
It would be mistaken to view this as mere pragmatism on Nicholas's part, in
light of the ineliminable foundations of *natio* that we have previously examined. Rather, toleration of diverse rites is elevated by him to the status of a
principle as a result of the processes associated with human historicity and
inequality: "Where no conformity in manner (*modo*) can be found, nations
should be permitted their own devotional practices and ceremonies."[49] To compel agreement in rites when no convergence is possible is to impose a false resolution on the earthly human predicament. Given the clear intractability that
Nicholas imputes to differences among nations, any approach short of tolerance is not only unrealistic and counterproductive, it violates the plan that
God Himself has prescribed for human existence.

   Of course, it may well be objected that toleration for cultural and political diversity as proposed by *De pace fidei* is still wholly negative in character,
advocated only to further the goal of maintaining peace among human nations.
But Nicholas in fact finds virtue in the necessity of religious diversity. A variation of rites according to the differences among nations is capable of promoting worship, he holds, by permitting a creative competition among the
peoples of the world. Nicholas tentatively suggests this possibility near the
beginning of *De pace fidei*: "Perhaps the difference of rites cannot be removed
or it is not expedient to do so in order that diversity may contribute to devotion, as when any region expends more attentive effort in performing its cer-

emonies as if they would become more pleasing to you, the King."[50] If human beings worship in a manner appropriate to their national traditions and customs, that is, they will take pride in their confession and will be more inclined to praise and serve God. Nicholas thus approaches the equation of local religious ritual with national self-awareness; a people acknowledges itself to be such through the practice of its own distinctive forms of worship. He returns to this point at the close of *De pace fidei*, when Paul proclaims: "A certain diversity will perhaps even increase devotion when each nation will strive to make its own rite more splendid through zeal and diligence in order thus to surpass another and so to obtain greater merit with God and praise in the world."[51] Note that the purpose of a variation of rites is not simply religious in character; it redounds to the earthly glory and reputation of nations. Nicholas conveys a vision of a tolerant internationalism in which national differences in worship are treated not as sources of hostility but as the basis for the mutual recognition of dignity and respect among nations. Of course, Nicholas stipulates that the possibility of achieving such a vision requires prior agreement on the essential matters of faith that he discusses in *De pace fidei*—unity precedes diversity. But this still leaves considerable leeway for human beings to organize their everyday religious activities as suits the conventions of various nations, without fear that their peace will be disturbed or their forms of worship persecuted. Inasmuch as Paul's comments about the positive aspects of diverse rites are the final words spoken among the participants in the heavenly assembly, they may be accorded particular force as a statement of Nicholas's belief in the potentially positive value implicit in a policy of systematic toleration between nations.

Conclusion

Certainly, it is evident that *De pace fidei* is not a work *de tolerantia* in the modern sense that an earlier generation of scholars proposed. Nicholas makes no room for individual rights or liberty of conscience, as later thinkers would. Rather, his account of toleration is constructed in a framework of what may be termed "group rights" typical of the Latin Middle Ages.[52] But this fact ought not to detract from the importance of *De pace fidei*'s contribution to the discourse of toleration that ran through medieval Europe. Indeed, Nicholas's attempt to challenge religious intolerance on the basis of *natio* represents a wholly realistic recognition of the emerging self-consciousness of medieval people about the pronounced differences in political and cultural "ways of life" that existed in Europe as well as on a more global scale. It is not so much "optimism" as accommodation to thoroughly ingrained forms of group identity that lies behind his call for "one religion in a variety of rites." The medieval ideal of the *Respublica Christiana* is at least tacitly shown to be unworkable in its traditional formulation.[53] In place of this ideal comes a recognition that the unity of faith is not undermined—in fact, may be enhanced—by the multiplicity of national practices and identities.

In some ways, then, the path to toleration pioneered by *De pace fidei* has surprising resonance at the end of the twentieth century. In recent years, the characteristic modern defense of tolerance, couched in terms of the personal liberty to think and act with reference to individual judgment alone, has proved increasingly untenable and irrelevant. Conflicts over group rights—religious, cultural, ethnic, national—have taken center stage in both the Western and non-Western worlds, while modern conceptions of autonomous human agency and the unencumbered self have been challenged by a wide range of philosophies, from neo-Aristotelianism to poststructuralism and feminism. Nicholas of Cusa's work sets the stage for many of these developments, inasmuch as *De pace fidei* addresses the preconditions and consequences of an important form of group identity.[54] Perhaps most significantly, Nicholas argues that *natio*—which may be understood broadly, rather than merely equated with the nation-state—is a constitutive part of human experience. Humanity ought not to be treated simply at the level of an amalgamation of individuals, for the identity of persons rests heavily on their "nationality." This view forms precisely the basis for his underlying critique of the universalistic *Respublica Christiana:* The human condition rests as much on essential differences as on a single identity, whether that identity is constituted by religious faith or by naturalistic distinctiveness. If the necessity of such communal diversity is not admitted and addressed—if, in other words, we cling to a belief in universal human similitude alone—the result will be conflict, persecution, and oppression, in sum, unending warfare, arising from the presumption that the identity of one group equates to the identity of all peoples. By contrast, Nicholas teaches that acceptance of the impossibility of eliminating group difference can lead to tolerant attitudes. The participants in the assembly imagined in *De pace fidei* come to recognize that their particular paths to their goal—the true God and the true faith—are in most cases equally worthy of respect and forbearance.

Of course, Nicholas is no relativist. He presumes, as we have seen, the existence of pre-existing universal verities. Yet even if we do not accept his Christian account of truth, the principle that rests behind his lesson—that knowledge of truth provides an insufficient justification for conflict and per-secution—remains compelling. Nicholas resisted the uncritical equation of religious truth with oppression of difference. There is more to his position than an abhorrence of violence and a preference for irenic solutions, however. *De pace fidei* seeks to expose the misguided premises that have appeared to warrant the commission of atrocities such as those that reportedly occurred at Constantinople (and are certainly perpetrated even today). Once we come to terms, as Nicholas does, with the realization that divergent expressions of *natio* form a salient feature of human life, we may begin to articulate and negoti-ate principles of toleration that conform to patterns of difference. In the absence of such recognition, Nicholas of Cusa knew, the practice of tolerance itself could never be achieved as anything more than a temporary cease-fire in the midst of a perpetual war. The historical record of recent times—from Europe to Africa, Asia, and the Americas—seems to validate his conclusion.

7

EQUALITY, CIVILIZATION, AND THE AMERICAN INDIANS IN THE WRITINGS OF LAS CASAS

Barbarism and Intolerance

It seems to be ordinarily presumed that the European encounter with the indigenous populations of the Americas occasioned a wholly new chapter in the history of Western religious toleration.[1] On the face of it, the people of the "Indies" seemed to sixteenth-century thinkers to stand at a considerable remove from the traditions and practices of Mediterranean religions, even pre-Christian paganism. Not only did the inhabitants of the Americas worship many gods and engage in palpable idolatry, but they lacked a literate (text-based) faith and performed rites (such as human sacrifice) deemed incompatible with a civilized way of life. In sum, to many Europeans, Native American ways of life were simply "barbarous," and the peoples of the "New World" were therefore "barbarians," a term that, with its Aristotelian connotations, implied their natural servitude: people incapable of governing themselves and hence susceptible to legitimate domination by a superior (European) race.[2]

Stressing the novelty of the dilemmas posed by the European confrontation with the inhabitants of the Americas, however, captures only one side of the West's response to the New World. As we have seen, from the twelfth to the fifteenth century, direct Christian contact with non-Christian religions and cultures stirred thoughtful attempts to come to terms with religious difference and to reject outright intolerance as a solution to a pluralism of creeds. Nor was the European experience of non-Christian faiths limited to the monotheistic, Abrahamic convictions of Judaism and Islam. During the High Middle Ages, the Roman Church was forced to consider its position with regard to many groups of infidels whose beliefs were completely alien to the Judeo-Christian tradition, including the Lithuanians and the Mongols.[3] William of Rubruck's report of his debate with the polytheistic *tuins* at the court of the Mongol chan Mangu is perhaps the most dramatic recounting of an actual dialogue between Christians and infidels during the Latin Middle Ages, but it was by no means sui generis. Nicholas of Cusa's *De pace fidei* casts its net to include all the world's religions and cultures known to its author, even those that were acknowledged to be pantheistic or polytheistic.

As a consequence, the cultural, political, and moral traditions and theories endemic to the Latin Middle Ages were capable of proving extremely useful to authors who stood in opposition to the wholesale conquest by the European powers (and especially Spain) of the indigenous peoples encountered in the Americas. Of course, given the size of the stakes, it may seem surprising that anyone in the late fifteenth or sixteenth century dared offer opposition to European expansionism in the New World. After all, authors prepared to sanction bloodshed and confiscation of Indian wealth might be well rewarded for their efforts.[4] Yet a debate over the status of the Indians, and their appropriate treatment by Westerners, reverberated through the corridors of secular as well as spiritual power in Europe.

In Spain, particularly, where the earliest imperial successes were registered, many voices resistant to military domination and exploitation of the American peoples were heard loudly and widely. Some, such as Francisco de Vitoria, were figures with impeccable scholastic credentials; his arguments rested on the dispassionate logic of someone lacking direct experience of the misery and depredation wrought on the Indians by the Spanish.[5] Others, most notably Bartholomé de Las Casas, had observed the process of conquest at first hand and could draw on empirical as well as philosophical evidence to refute justifications of Spanish imperialism. Las Casas provides an especially compelling case, because he began his career as a member of the conquering Spanish elite, but renounced his own holdings in "New Spain," joined the Dominican order, and achieved the office of bishop of Chiapas.[6] In more than half a century of concerted attack on Spanish dominion over the indigenous population of the Americas, he unleashed a broad range of arguments against the policies and conduct of his fellow Europeans and has thus earned a much deserved reputation as an important proponent of religious (and also cultural) toleration.[7] Over the course of his lengthy career, Las Casas produced a vast body of works in defense of the Indians, including polemical tracts, historical and anthropological treatises, and his famous refutation of Juan Ginés de Sepúlveda's scholastic apology for the Spanish conquest.

In surveying the writings of Las Casas, one is struck by their constant and heavy dependence on the multiple conventional "languages" of philosophy, politics, and law in currency during the Latin Middle Ages.[8] Scholars have already highlighted important elements of this debt to medieval tradition. Some commentators emphasize Las Casas's appropriation of the medieval philosophical frameworks of Aristotelianism and Thomism to serve the cause of protecting Indian culture.[9] Other readers stress his reliance on medieval canon law and indeed ascribe to him a "subjective natural rights" theory derived from canonist thought.[10] Less frequently noted, however, is Las Casas's employment of a third type of discourse in wide circulation during the Latin Middle Ages: Ciceronian.[11] Throughout his corpus, in his polemical tomes as well as his anthropological studies, Las Casas returns repeatedly to central themes of Ciceronian moral and political thought, a fact upon which scholars seldom remark.[12] In turn, failure to consider this debt to Cicero means that our understanding of Las Casas's teachings is distorted, inasmuch as his criticisms of Spanish conquest, and ultimately his arguments for toleration, are profoundly imbued with ideas of manifestly Ciceronian provenance.

Las Casas was by no means unique among European proponents of tolerance in finding support for his views among Cicero's writings. We have seen in Chapter 3 how John of Salisbury appropriated the moderate skepticism of the Ciceronian New Academy as a cornerstone for his defense of intellectual toleration, and Gary Remer has shown that the rhetorical theory of Cicero shaped Renaissance reflections on tolerant dialogue.[13] But Las Casas seems to have been distinctive in drawing on yet another strain of Ciceronian thought: the principle of fundamental human equality, founded on an account of the universality of reason, religion, and society among human beings. When modern scholars acknowledge the egalitarian dimension in Cicero's theory of natural human capacities,[14] they merely retrace the footsteps of Las Casas, for whom that doctrine formed a cornerstone in the brief against Spanish conquest and on behalf of respect and forbearance by Europeans toward the Indians. In summary, Las Casas follows Cicero in arguing that human beings are distinguished by an ability to reason, to perceive divinity, and to associate in an organized fashion; these functions define them as members of the human race and accord them basic individual and cultural rights. Although Las Casas insists that acceptance of Christianity (as the one true religion) is the ultimate token of mature human civilization, he contends that the use of force to "civilize" so-called barbarians (or alternatively, to destroy them) is not only self-defeating, but both inhumane and uncivilized. To employ coercion is inhumane because it fails to take into account that humanity is defined by possession of certain inborn, but imperfectly realized, potentialities; it is uncivilized because it mistakes Occidental cultural development for a singular process that no other people is capable of recapitulating, except perhaps at sword's point. The bulk of Las Casas's attack on intolerant policies toward the Indians and his defense of toleration rests on these Ciceronian premises. Indeed, one might make the case that Las Casas was more consistent and thoroughgoing in his promotion of a Ciceronian intellectual program than Cicero himself.[15]

Principles of Equality

Las Casas's familiarity with Cicero rivals that of any later medieval (or even Renaissance humanist) author. In the course of his works, he cites a full range of Cicero's philosophical treatises available during the mid-sixteenth century—including *De officiis*, *De legibus*, *De natura deorum*, *Disputationes Tusculanum*, and *De divinatione*—as well as his treatises on rhetoric (*De inventione*, *De oratore*) and various of his speeches and letters. In many instances, Las Casas mentions Cicero simply as a source of historical information about the beliefs and rituals of ancient religions in Greece, Rome, and the oriental world. The *Apologetic History*, in particular, relies heavily on Cicero's works for evidence about the names and natures of Greek and Roman deities; about the forms of superstition, idolatry, sacrifice, and divination employed by the ancients; and about the diverse rites and sacraments that Mediterranean and Asian peoples practiced.[16] Las Casas's purpose is to demonstrate the extraordinary number of parallels between classical religions and those faiths found among the American Indians, toward the end of deflecting the Eurocentric view that the inhabitants of the New World are incorrigibly primitive and thus unworthy of respect. To uphold the latter position, he implies, denies the humanity of the pagan forebears of Christian Europeans and the presence among them of a mature civilization, inasmuch as the Greco-Roman world subscribed to many of the same beliefs and rituals as indigenous Americans. Likewise, because the pagans of the West were susceptible to conversion by the gentle and patient teachings of Christianity and hence were capable of cultural development without recourse to coercion or decimation, then so must be the peoples of the Americas.

The empirical force of this case is bolstered throughout Las Casas's corpus by reference to a set of theoretical arguments, derived from Cicero, about the natural equality of the human race. Las Casas has been hailed by modern scholars for his repeated declaration that "all the nations of the world are human beings."[17] What is more rarely noticed is that he ordinarily asserts this claim in the context of a discussion of Ciceronian principles of human nature. Indeed, Las Casas's most extensive defense of the doctrine of equality, in the *Apologetic History,* ascribes the idea expressly to Cicero himself: "Tully posited in Book 1 of *De legibus* [that] . . . all the nations of the world are human beings, and all human beings and each one of them form no less the definition [of humanity] than any other, and this is that they are rational."[18] Las Casas then enumerates the psychological qualities on the basis of which human beings are deemed to possess reason—some suggested by Cicero (the senses, the capacity for knowledge and virtue), others supported by Christian teaching (free will). The passage underscores the Ciceronian provenance of human reason by advancing an extensive (if extraneous) series of quotations from *De legibus.*[19] The phrase "all the nations of the world are human beings" is entirely Las Casas's own invention. Yet it follows directly from his appropriation of Cicero: The powers of the human mind being identical in all cases, and the faculty of reason being therefore universal, "all the lineage of humanity is one, and all human beings as regards their creation and natural existence are alike."[20] The ascription of human equality Las Casas finds in Cicero's writings becomes the cornerstone of his defense of Indian peoples against European oppression.

This egalitarian precept effectively undercuts any attempt to withhold the status of humanity from certain peoples on the grounds that their conditions of life are barbarous. Although Las Casas not does overtly invoke Cicero's authority on this point in his reply to Sepúlveda—because he confines himself there largely to the languages of his opponent (namely, Aristotelianism and scholastic theology)—the principle of equal human reason is nonetheless evident in the *Apology,* helping to explain its apparently idiosyncratic understanding of Aristotle's concept of the barbarian.[21] Las Casas takes for granted what Aristotle manifestly did not: that a certain uniformity exists in the natural world such that the qualities of human nature are distributed more or less equally and without ethnic, racial, or cultural distinction. Hence, Las Casas denies that any people as a whole could be barbarian in the strict Aristotelian sense of "slaves by nature" incapable of self-governance. As he concludes in the *Apologetic History*, "It is an impossibility of all impossibilities that an entire nation may be incapable or so barbaric and of little judgment or lesser or diminished reason that it does not know how to govern itself."[22] Underlying this claim is the Ciceronian conviction that human nature is inherently and universally rational.

One might still object, as Philippe André-Vincent has done, that Las Casas is simply addressing the condition of entire populations rather than of discrete individuals.[23] That is, the wording of his treatises appears to suggest a concern with the equality of groups, not of each of their particular members. But on occasion Las Casas does explicitly specify that his claim about the equal powers of reason applies to persons as individuals:

> Human beings are more rational than other creatures and are conferred in their souls, upon their creation, with the seeds and beginnings and natural inclinations of the senses and the virtues, and they are by no means deficient in the exercise of these qualities . . . ; and the entire human race and *every individual member of it* [possesses] . . . all these characteristics, dispositions, and natural human inclinations [that] are natural and universally the same in all human beings, as was affirmed above by the declared judgment of Tully.[24]

The essentially invariant presence of a rational faculty among individual human beings is confirmed for Las Casas by the extreme rarity of persons who are impeded in their use of reason. He maintains in both the *Apology* and the *Apologetic History* that those few persons whose souls do not equip them to exercise reason are to be counted among the monstrosities of nature, comparable to people born with extra limbs or organs, whose existence is commonly explained by reference to divine (extranatural) causes.[25] That such deformities—whether of the body or the soul—occur so infrequently simply provides further proof that nature is consistent in granting the same properties—psychological as well as physiological—to each and every human being. Only God's direct intervention in nature can disrupt this pattern.

A related token of human equality for Las Casas is the universal acknowledgment of the existence of a divine being or supernatural power. Again, his argument does not rely merely on induction; it is a theoretical case framed in Ciceronian language. The most extensive articulation of this position is located in the *Apologetic History*, where Las Casas quotes lavishly from *De natura deorum* as well as from *Disputationes Tusculanum* and *De legibus*, in support of the claim that "all the nations in the world, no matter how barbarous and wild they may be, can and may be moved to know and understand that some Lord exists, a creator, mover, and consecrator of all things, who is more excellent than humanity, whom all human beings call God."[26] Such "knowledge of the gods," Las Casas insists (on Cicero's authority), "is naturally formed, impressed, and carved upon the souls of human beings."[27] Such awareness of divinity, in turn, depends on "the light of reason and the agency of understanding," that is, natural properties of "all human beings of the world, no matter how barbarous, uncivilized, and wild and isolated on lands or islands or far-flung places they may be."[28] To the extent that human reason is universal, so knowledge of the divine manifests itself without exception. Consequently, evidence of the worship of some deity or deities can be found throughout human history in all cultures, including that of the Indians, without regard for their locale. (The implied rational impossibility of atheism is hardly exceptional; it pervaded even the most tolerant thinkers of later centuries, such as Locke.) As Las Casas remarks in the *Apology* against Sepúlveda—again, with reference to *De legibus* and *Disputationes Tusculanum*—"No matter how wild or barbarous a nation may be, it cannot live without the worship of the true or of a false deity."[29] The connection between reason and the knowledge of divinity was postulated by Cicero on identical grounds: Because reason "exists both in humanity and in God," human beings uniquely of all creatures are able to apprehend their creator and recognize that they spring from a supernatural ancestry.[30] This view is consonant with the Christian teaching that people have intellect and understanding because "they are formed in the image and likeness of God."[31] The shared quality of reason extends to the whole human race and is reflected in the universal awareness of the divine presence regardless of the contingent differences of culture that divide humankind. Hence, the worship of deities that one encounters at all times and places constitutes for Las Casas one of the primary signs—indeed, perhaps the pre-eminent sign—of human equality.

Reason and Civilization

At the same time as Las Casas upholds the principle of human equality, he is by no means insensitive to or unrealistic about differences among the world's cultures and peoples. He admits that some of the inhabitants of America apparently lack the defining marks of the most rudimentary civilization: They "are found to live separately and remotely, and have no dwelling-place in the form of a city, . . . but live vagrantly without order like savages,"[32] ignorant of political affairs, law, commerce, friendship, and the other salient characteristics of civilized life.[33] Moreover, Las Casas realizes that even among more highly developed Indian communities religious rites and beliefs stand at very great distance from the Christian faith; their understanding of divinity remains "a confused and general knowledge, neither clear nor distinct, without having the light of faith."[34] Consequently, many of their forms of worship, such as the commission of human sacrifice, are rightly repugnant to Christians.[35] As is already evident, Las Casas does not shy from describing the indigenous nations of the "New World" as "primitive," "crude," "uncivilized"—indeed, "barbarous." But he concludes that their present condition is not a permanent or intractable state. Rather, he discerns a universal process of historical progress, a recognizable pattern of cultural development, followed by all peoples of the world, Europeans no less than Indians, stemming from the natural faculties possessed by each and every human being. Inasmuch as human knowledge is grounded on reason and the attendant knowledge of divinity, all members of the race possess an identical capacity to attain a fully civilized life, although these potentialities are realized in a historically contingent fashion. Thus, it may be said of even the most ostensibly primitive peoples "that they would not fail to be rational human beings, and reducible to order and reason, but that they still have not begun and are in such a pristine rude state that they are earlier than all the other nations that exist."[36] Although Las Casas doubts that many completely primordial groups will actually be discovered, he maintains that, should such a nation be encountered, it will still exhibit just as great a potential for achieving a civilized way of life as any European population.

In part, Las Casas founded his account of the historicity of the civilizing process on psychological observations about human ontogeny. Individuals in their earliest stages of life are governed by "sensuous and animalistic" inclinations, such as "eating and drinking and other acts that are common to ourselves and beasts, without any time or work or deliberation or application of reason"; by contrast, "rational [activities] require time, work, deliberation, and the application of reason." In other words, all human beings move from a prerational to a rational stage, maturing intellectually through passage of time and effort. "The acts of reason are more recent and less used, because we do not know nor can we use reason until we are older, nine, ten, or eleven years; and as a consequence, certain acts are performed more easily, and those of reason with difficulty, and thus, for acting in certain ways we do not need any guide, aid, tutor, and director, and for others for which a guide, attractor, aid, and persuader is required, we have a great need."[37] Prerational modes of action are, in effect, instinctual and unlearned, whereas the use of reason depends on tuition and practice. Las Casas's implication is clear: Phylogeny recapitulates ontogeny. Human civilizations progress toward completion as they replace their animalistic standards of behavior with a set of rational precepts—social, political, legal, and religious. Just as no person is born with the powers of reason entirely operative, so no people begins its communal life in a fully formed condition, but rather undergoes a process of collective education.

This psychological claim correlates directly to Cicero's famous account of the foundations of human society. In his early rhetorical treatise, *De inventione,* Cicero narrated how human beings in their most primitive state lived a quasi-bestial existence: They "wandered at large in the fields like animals and propagated their lives on wild fare," depending on physical strength instead of reason, ignorant of religious worship, social institutions, morality, and law. Only by means of the persuasion and instruction of a wise and eloquent man— Cicero's primeval archetype of the orator—did they come to discover and implement all the fruits of communal life: "When through reason and eloquence they listened with greater attention, he transformed them from brutes into kind and gentle creatures."[38] Cicero repeated versions of this story in other works (including a nearly verbatim transcription in *Pro Sestio*),[39] and it enjoyed great currency throughout the Middle Ages and Renaissance.[40] Indeed, it is arguable that Cicero's philosophical anthropology, and not Aristotle's analogous but more fragmentary and compressed account, represented the dominant view of Latin Christendom from c. 1100 onward about the origins of human community.

In the course of his writings, Las Casas returns time and again to Cicero's narrative of social development. For example, his first published work, *De unico modo,* presents a sketch of

> a wise philosopher who, employing considerable art, induced primitive human beings, who lived in a savage state and very similar to wild animals, to a more human life, to education, to instruction in good morals, to knowledge of God and worship of divine religion in the form it then existed, and they were convened in communal living through the institution of the community and the city; he persuaded them of the individual utility and fruits that result from a more human life, attracting them by his eloquence and graceful oration and thus by art.[41]

Thereafter, Las Casas quotes the relevant passage from the prologue of *De inventione* in its entirety and then highlights what he takes to be the salient lessons of Cicero's account. First, if human beings are found in a condition of savagery or wildness, this does not reflect their "true" nature, but rather is a consequence of "second nature," that is, custom. Primitive human existence is not a "state of nature," but an aberration thereof. Second, the ferocity of primordial people can be tamed, and the seeds of civilization can be cultivated in them, "through the force of natural reason" supplemented by the persuasion of "honeyed, sweet, and patient words." Finally, any transformation from a primitive to a civilized condition is only properly achieved by "compelling the human intellect rationally . . . not by armed attack or violence."[42] All these conclusions have considerable import for the key theme of *De unico modo:* That the sole valid and efficacious way of converting the inhabitants of America to Christianity is through "the persuasion of the understanding by means of reasons."[43] Las Casas's appeal to Cicero supports the position that no people is so primeval that it is unable to receive the words of Christian preachers and is thus susceptible to enforced conversion or extinction. Rather, the most "natural" method of spreading Christianity among the Indians is to recapitulate the educative process by which their social order was first formed.

The deployment of Cicero's account of social development in *De unico modo* remains focused, however, on Las Casas's polemical aims and as such never receives full statement as a theoretical principle. In his historical and anthropological treatises, by contrast, the Ciceronian reconstruction of the origins of communal life moves to a more central place in the argument. For instance, *The History of the Indies*, a work that primarily chronicles the early occidental voyages of discovery, prefaces its detailed recounting of European contact with the Indians by reminding its audience of the historical experience common to all peoples. Las Casas initially presents his view of the civilizing process as simply an inductive generalization that may be gleaned by anyone who takes "notice of the ancient histories, not only the divine and ecclesiastical ones, but also the profane ones."[44] He frames his reading of these historical accounts in overtly Ciceronian language. "No generation or nation of the past, neither before nor after the deluge," he observes, was so advanced "that at its beginnings it did not suffer from very many flaws of wildness and irrationality, such that it lived without politics (*policia*)." Yet, although all the peoples of the earth first "lived without houses and without cities and as brute animals," still "they came together by the use of reason and took hold of those things pertaining to human capacity." In this connection, Las Casas introduces a favored metaphor: that human beings in their primitive state are like "uncultivated land" that yields "thorns and thistles"; but when domesticated through persuasion and instruction, they are capable of producing the most useful and pleasing fruits.[45]

As authority for these broad assertions, Las Casas quotes but a single source—the preface to *De inventione*—and proceeds to expand on and extrapolate from it at length. On the basis of this analysis of Cicero's doctrine, he announces the principle that will guide his investigations throughout the considerable body of *The History of the Indies*:

> And thus it appears that although human beings at the beginning were totally uncultivated, and, as they did not work the land, ferocious and bestial, but by the natural discretion and talent that was innate in their souls, since God created them rational creatures, being ordered and persuaded by reason and love and good industry, which is the proper way for rational creatures to be attracted to the exercise of virtue, there is no nation whatsoever, nor could there be, regardless of how barbarous, wild, and depraved its customs may be, that cannot be attracted and ordered to all the political virtues and all the humanity of domesticated, political, and rational human beings, and notably to the Catholic faith and Christian religion.[46]

As illustration of this theoretical point, Las Casas reports that no less a civilized nation than Spain itself originated from a "barbaric" people whose ferocity rivaled that ascribed to the Indians. If the Spanish could arrive at a mature culture, he implies, then so surely can the indigenous inhabitants of America.[47] Although Las Casas may have intended to invoke such a comparison to provoke and even shock his fellow Spaniards, one may notice that it follows directly from his antecedent proposition that all societies emerge gradually from a barbaric into a civilized condition.

By far the most pronounced use Las Casas made of this Ciceronian framework may be found in the *Apologetic History*, his contribution to what Anthony Pagden terms "comparative ethnology."[48] There Cicero's teaching about the historicity of civilization is not only stated at greater length than in any of Las Casas's other writings, but is reiterated throughout. In addition to the sheer extent of the recitation of the Ciceronian account of human development in the *Apologetic History*—couched not primarily in quotations from *De inventione*, but in the words of Las Casas himself—several factors distinguish that presentation from the appropriations made elsewhere. First, Las Casas weaves the principle of human equality derived from *De legibus* and other works and the doctrine of cultural evolution borrowed from *De inventione* into a single coherent and seamless account. Having narrated the pattern according to which human beings are transformed from bestial to civilized creatures, he asserts that the "truth" of this view rests on the antecedent claim of Cicero that human beings are united—across all geographical and cultural divides—by reason.[49] Because people invariantly possess the capacity for rationality, they are susceptible to "sweet words and the vehement force of powerful reason," by means of which they "come together out of their dispersion in mountains and fields, one with the others, to a certain place in order to live in company and assemble themselves in society."[50] Equality of reason thus entails for Las Casas that every nation experiences an identical process leading to full human association, including political institutions and (eventually) worship of the true God. Once again, he employs the analogy of the barren field: A "wild" people is "like uncultivated land that produces simply weeds and useless spines, but has within itself such natural virtue that it may, by work and cultivation, yield healthy and advantageous domesticated fruits."[51] Yet, at the same time, Las Casas stresses the contingency of the occurrence of communal organization: It did not happen at the same time among all the peoples of the world nor was the transition necessarily a smooth one. Rather, "rudeness, coarseness, and quasi-bestiality lasted much later" among some nations than among others, depending on a wide range of entirely unpredictable local circumstances.[52] Las Casas emphasizes that the formation of human societies was by no means an inexorable, unconscious event; it depended, instead, on *art*, in particular the persuasive skills of the primitive wise orator in overcoming the habitual behavior of uncivilized people unaccustomed to social order and harmony. When and where such talented speakers might appear, and how arduous their labors might be, are matters that resist systematic human explanation. The most that can be said is that all human beings share the potential to achieve a completely acculturated way of life and that all nations follow essentially the same pattern in attaining this condition.

Civilization and Toleration

The line Las Casas draws from his Ciceronian interpretation of human capabilities and social development to a full-blooded theory of toleration is direct and unmistakable. If all people (and peoples) possess rudimentary reason and knowledge of God, as well as the potential to partake of civilized association, then every nation must be left to follow its own "natural" and appropriate route to maturity. The use of coercive force—either to destroy supposedly incorrigible barbarians or to speed the process of cultural evolution—is wrong and self-defeating: No population is so brutish that it cannot be improved, yet the sole way in which this may be achieved is through patient, rational persuasion. Of course, Las Casas's theory remains weakly teleological—and therefore susceptible to the accusation of being "merely concordant"—to the extent that he posits acceptance of the Christian faith as the final sign of a civilized nation. But this is of little importance to the fundamental principles of his theory, inasmuch as he insists that forbearance of non-Christian, native forms of worship must be extended indefinitely until the Indians *themselves* are convinced of the truth of Christianity and embrace it. There is no set timeline for this process, just as there is none for the course of human development generally. Hence, tolerance is not a practical expedient to remedy a temporary religious rift without recourse to violence; rather, it must be respected as long as people refrain from adopting the Christian faith, even if the physical capacity exists to impose Christianity on them. From his Ciceronian raw materials, therefore, Las Casas constructs a principled yet still Christian theory of toleration. Indeed, he is sufficiently able to grasp the logic of his own position that he is at times willing to countenance the legitimacy of non-Christian nations defending by arms their own religious convictions and rites against the coercive attacks of Christians.

So far from condemning or reviling the "barbarous" condition of indigenous Americans, Las Casas maintains, Europeans perhaps owe them greater respect and forbearance than is due to more advanced cultures. (The latter presumably includes non-Christians of the Mediterranean world, such as Muslims, as well as schismatics and heretics—perhaps Reformers—in Latin Christianity.) He reasons that

> whatever peoples, however many more, are in a primitive and rude state—as were we and were all the nations of the world—they are much less blameworthy than those who have departed this state and taken up order and political conversation, and imbibed and were instructed in religion; they have bestial, barbaric, and depraved customs that are no more or less detestable or worse than others that we and the other peoples had in the same state; we are not to suspect their order and rational attraction to a state of worship and politics, since we were formed and rejoiced in order and so did many other nations as barbaric as ourselves.[53]

Las Casas bids his fellow Europeans (especially Spaniards) to extend tolerance to the Indians, then, on the basis of the universality of humanity. Not only do circumstances in the Americas closely resemble those in the West during earlier times, but the potential for civilized development is identical among all the world's peoples. To foreclose this potential by violent conquest is, in effect, to deny that Latin Christianity possesses an intrinsic rationality and truth superior to other forms of belief. Las Casas's repeated insistence on rational persuasion as the "only way" of inducing the Indians to enter the Christian fold reflects his belief that Christianity is the most humane religion, the confession most consonant with human nature (conceived in Ciceronian terms); and coercion is antithetical to this human nature. To treat the Indians differently than, say, the Spaniards were treated by early Christian missionaries would be to affront and ultimately to invalidate the very basis of the superiority that Las Casas claims for Christianity.

As a consequence, the Spanish and other Christian nations entirely lack a right (*ius*) to make war on and dispossess the peoples of the New World, according to Las Casas. Scholars have generally dissected this assertion from the perspective of either scholastic theories of *dominium* or civilian and canonistic conceptions of property rights.[54] But Las Casas's deployment of technical philosophical and legal arguments should not blind us to an equally important feature of his theory of toleration, namely, that such warfare against the Indians violates the divinely endowed principles of human nature. Conquest, he says in *De unico modo*,

> is contrary to the natural way in which divine wisdom deals with all created beings and, more especially, contrary to that which is established for naturally moving and guiding rational beings towards goodness. It is contrary to the natural art of inducing human beings to goodness, which natural reason dictates that all doctors or other teachers ought to possess. It is contrary to the methods used by the wise philosophers, taught and illuminated by the natural light, for winning over the most barbarous people to the way of living humanely.[55]

The prosecution of an unjust war is, quite simply, against nature. Indeed, it is so unnatural, Las Casas insists on the authority of Cicero's *De officiis*, that even one's own death is to be preferred to the violent injury of the life, limb, and estate of innocent persons.[56] For to dispossess or otherwise harm our fellow human beings is, Las Casas states repeatedly, to "violate the *ius* of human society," the fundamental bond that links human beings together through a common precept of reason.[57] The realization and maintenance of this right of society rest, as we have seen, on the assent of human beings to the political, legal, moral, and religious conditions necessary for association, attained through rational persuasion. The dissemination of Christianity—the final stage in the civilizing process—must follow the established "natural" course of human development by recapitulating in the sphere of religion what earlier had been achieved in the other dimensions of social intercourse. "All human beings in common ought in this way to be invited to, led to, and gain the law of Christ and the Christian religion, namely, naturally and rationally, according to the endowment which all possess, that is, consonant with the persuasion of the rational intellect and the enticement, movement, and stimulation of the will."[58] Not only does Las Casas assert this as a moral principle to reach the ultimate goal of spreading the gospel to the indigenous peoples of America; he also insists that the Indians are owed recompense for the misery and deprivation that have already been inflicted on them by the violent conduct of unjust warfare. "The observance of justice," he declares, "necessarily requires compensation to be made, therefore they [Europeans] are obligated to make restitution."[59] The right of society will not be restored until the material consequences of intolerance have been reversed and that which has been unjustly appropriated is returned to its legitimate possessors. Adherence to the "natural" path of toleration demands that the impact of "unnatural" violent persecution be erased wherever possible.

As a corollary to the duty of Christians to cease unjust war on Native Americans, Las Casas occasionally proposes a rudimentary right of resistance to conquest on the part of Indians.[60] In some measure, this is justified by the long-standing legal dictum (derived from Roman law) that the illicit use of force may justly be repulsed by the exercise of similar force. But Las Casas seems to have more in mind, in particular, that given the universality of human reason, religion, and society, those who would oppress a populace with violence are in fact enemies of humanity who have renounced the right to be treated peacefully. Such oppressors are, literally, inhumane. The connection between a Ciceronian conception of human nature and the propriety of resisting those who act contrary to such nature is drawn explicitly, for instance, in *The History of the Indies*. Las Casas asks whether there exists "any reasonable people or nation in the world that, through the authority of natural law and reason, would not" respond to the violence of the Spanish conquest with force. He then immediately proclaims the universality of human nature with reference to *De legibus* and concludes that no nation—even a less than fully civilized one—is unjustified in responding to oppression, because all people by nature "hate evil and shun the painful and the harmful."[61] Las Casas talks in an analogous vein in other of his tracts, remarking with approval that "Tully understands that all human beings are obligated by natural *ius* to defend their God, or gods taken for the true God."[62] Likewise, he observes elsewhere, "When some people, kingdom, or city suffers oppression or molestation from some tyrant, it can justly contest him who tyrannizes over it, and be freed from its weighty yoke by killing him, according to Tully, *De officiis*, Book 3," from which he then quotes.[63] It may surely be debated whether such fleeting comments amount to a coherent theory of a right of resistance comparable to, say, Locke's. But Las Casas clearly intends to convey, at minimum, that the principles from which toleration proceeds also license human beings to defend themselves against the intolerant—a claim equally valid for all peoples alike, non-Christian as well as Christian. Although certain earlier Christian thinkers had been prepared to authorize the physical resistance of subjects to manifestly unjust uses of power,[64] none, to my knowledge, extended this principle to the legitimacy of non-Christian peoples repulsing oppression by Christians. On this count, Las Casas takes an important step forward—a step fully warranted in light of his Ciceronian premises.

Conclusion

On the whole, Las Casas's appropriation of Ciceronian discourse proves a fertile ground for challenging intolerant religious and cultural practices toward the peoples of the Americas. Cicero's teachings about reason, religion, and society—in sum, about human equality and diversity—afforded an effective counter to those of Las Casas's opponents who equated barbarism with natural servitude and an incapacity for self-rule. Yet his credentials remain solidly medieval: His source materials—Cicero included—typify the scholastic's intellectual arsenal, and his writings do not consistently uphold the doctrine of modern subjective natural rights theory. Although he never surrenders his own commitment to the ultimate validity of orthodox Roman Christianity, Las Casas requires tolerance *as a matter of principle* to achieve a dialogue between believers and nonbelievers, the conclusion of which may not be artificially imposed by extradiscursive compulsion. By positing that conversion to Christianity must follow a path consonant with human nature—that is, through rational persuasion and voluntary assent—he eliminates the possibility that the "magistrate" may ever coerce either conscience *or* the practice of nonconforming (even non-Christian) rites. Without appealing to the later language of religious liberty—which was in any case employed inconsistently and imperfectly even among seventeenth-century theorists of toleration[65]—Las Casas voices a conclusion that powerfully advocates tolerance: It is by the power of persuasion alone, the forceless force of the better argument, that human beings may be led to alter their convictions about the deity they worship. No application of political might can properly resolve religious discord or substitute coercive sanction for rational discourse.

CONCLUSION

Tolerating Different Worlds

The entrenched view that toleration is a phenomenon distinctive of modern Western thought cannot be sustained. The evidence from a wide range of medieval sources clearly reveals the folly of connecting ideas and practices of tolerance in exclusive fashion to notions of the freedom-bearing individual and the sovereign nation-state—in sum, to political liberalism. Liberal thought posits an intrinsic relation between toleration and political liberalism. Should one encounter an apparent doctrine of toleration generated on the basis of some nonliberal principle or source, therefore, it either is rejected as not "truly tolerant" or is seen to be the outgrowth of some "forward-thinking" mind who has anticipated elements of full-fledged political liberalism. However, the preceding investigations have shown neither claim to be the case among medieval proponents of tolerance: They *are* as "truly tolerant" as modern thinkers, yet they by no means "anticipate" the doctrines of political liberalism. In each of the writers discussed, we have discovered some strategy to criticize intolerance and to defend forbearance that is *principled* (that is, not simply pragmatic or *politique*) without subscribing to a *modern* principle.

Are any generalizations possible about the distinctiveness of a medieval, as distinguished from a modern, outlook on toleration? It is evident from the foregoing that the strategies employed by medieval authors to counter intolerance vary widely. Yet in glancing backward at the texts surveyed in this study, several common features stand out. First, the defense of toleration is couched as a necessary outgrowth of God's plan, inasmuch as the practical and moral illegitimacy of intolerance is traced to some element of human nature. All the authors addressed in this volume would agree that it is contrary to the natural makeup of the human creature (however construed) to impose fundamental beliefs by force or fear. As Christians, moreover, they would never have doubted that humanity was a part (indeed, a central part) of divine creation and that people owe their natures (both in their original perfection and in their postlapsarian willfulness) to the Creator Himself. The phrase "natura, id est Deus" expressed a formula that was universally accepted during the Latin Middle Ages.[1] The writings that we have examined effectively turned this principle on its head by arguing that the natural diversity of created human beings must have been part of the divine design, and therefore difference demands our respect as a matter of piety. That some medieval thinkers could have embraced such a doctrine may reflect, in turn, the remarkable anthropocentrism (some scholars have dared to say "humanism") characteristic of much medieval thought after 1100.[2] Interest in the mental and physical capacities of human beings, and in human nature generally, waxed during the Latin Middle Ages, in the wake of the so-called Renaissance of the Twelfth Century and the rise of scholasticism. Recognition of the differences that naturally separate human beings—whether arising from the frailty of their mental capacities or the divergences in their sociocultural development—surely helps to explain how medieval texts could confidently attack the persecutorial impulse and hold out toleration as a viable alternative. Tolerance was by no means impious, but instead reflected the honor owed to God.

Second, the various medieval theories of toleration under consideration tend to adopt a "contextualized" or "situational" approach to toleration similar to the idea of "judgemental toleration" that Michael Sandel has lately proposed. By this phrase, Sandel appears to mean that tolerance is afforded to minority groups or practices for the sake of some other, greater human good.[3] To embrace a contextual conception of forbearance is to acknowledge, for instance, that truth (including religious truth) cannot be grasped without respect for differing opinions and rites. It is also to recognize that the material well-being of citizens subscribing to all confessions (the supposedly "orthodox" as well as the heretics) is threatened when persecution occurs. The medieval conception of tolerance as embedded in particular contexts denies, to be sure, that tolerance is a value in and of itself. Yet this is not to imply that the authors whom we have investigated were simply forerunners of a wholly utilitarian idea of toleration. Rather, from the twelfth century through to the sixteenth, these writers sought to articulate an overarching "moral" principle capable of providing for "peaceful coexistence" and thus for "basic human rights," to borrow Michael Walzer's terminology.[4] Such moral principles were, as we have seen, derived from an account of human nature, but they tended not to posit an abstract and universalized human essence, such as "natural rights" or "personal autonomy." Medieval notions of human nature that promoted tolerance instead tended to give primacy to the features of the species that made its members and communities different rather than identical. Thus, the very contextualization of tolerant attitudes and practices had the effect of generating a powerful rationale for extending toleration to differing (even repugnant) teachings and forms of worship.

Third, where there is a pronounced tendency in post-Enlightenment thought to regard tolerance in matters of religion as necessary because faith itself is irrational, medieval authors seem generally convinced that religious belief can be subjected to rational evaluation.[5] It is this belief in the relevance of *logos* (in its classical sense) to religion that clearly stands behind the inter-religious dialogue literature of the Middle Ages, as well as the epistemological and culturalist defenses of tolerance: People can profitably talk about their religious differences, but such discussion requires mutual respect and intellectual liberty if there is the slightest hope of reaching understanding. Persecution, as the violent alternative to rational debate, accomplishes nothing precisely because the only possibility of discovering the truths of religion lies in the faculty of reason. Of course, the medieval authors presently under examination admitted that such rational discussion was not an easy process and was unlikely to generate rapid and universally accepted resolution to difficult problems. Still, they held that free and open discourse about religious matters remained the most potentially fruitful method of addressing diverse confessions, in comparison with coercion.

Finally, many medieval authors directly acknowledged the complexity of the interactions and ties between differences of religion and other modes of human differentiation (for instance, national and cultural manifestations). In the modern world, faith tends to be counted as a matter of purely individual choice or conscience, independent of the historical inheritance or circumstances of the believer. By contrast, medieval authors from Abelard and Llull to Cusa and Las Casas realized that what people believed about God was inextricably linked to their heritage and social identity. A Latin Christian could readily locate the source of human religious and cultural difference in the Fall—not in the sense that diversity is evil, but in the sense that it stems from humanity's active effort to maintain "a spark of the natural good" by means of discovering "many disciplines," in the words of the twelfth-century monk Peter of Celle.[6] Again, the implications for toleration are fairly straightforward. If different peoples evolve divergent manners of living, expressed in their religion as well as their social institutions, to recover some semblance of their true prelapsarian nature, then such diversity demands our forbearance. Such differences reflect the historical dilemma that all human beings have confronted since the expulsion from Paradise: how best to serve God as they understand Him, both in conscience and in rite.

Given the unique characteristics of medieval ideas of tolerance, we may well ask whether theorists today have anything to learn from these predecessors. Are the texts of the Latin Middle Ages worth studying for anything more than antiquarian purposes? Are they mere historical curiosities? I wish to defend the position, broadly speaking, that medieval thinkers do indeed offer worthwhile alternative pathways to tolerance in matters of religion as well as in other forms of human difference relevant to contemporary concerns.

This is most obviously the case for societies in which political liberalism is not a primary value, such as the many theocratic or highly communitarian nations that flourish outside the West. Here, the medieval approach is useful precisely because it begins from premises foreign to Western liberalism but congenial to social orders that subscribe to an orthodox religion or a constrained civil order. A reading of our medieval authors demonstrates that neither foundation for social organization necessarily entails rigid conformity in connection with faith or culture. Rather, just as convinced Christians living in an official Christian society could still find compelling reasons to defend human diversity, so other apparently unified societies may be able to generate moral principles conducive to toleration.

Likewise, the framework of tolerance developed by medieval authors seems fruitful in the contemporary pluralist context, where at least some minority groups do not subscribe to liberalism and its version of tolerance. This pertains to a large number of religious and social bodies of which many citizens of Western nations are currently members. Short of constraining the ability of such groups to practice their own ways of life in the name of freedom or equality or some other abstract principle—a response that itself strikes one as illiberal—the theoretical challenge rests on finding a balance among the competing demands posed by pluralism. In Rawlsian terms, this approach means the development of principles that extend the scope of the "overlapping consensus" necessary for stable and just social and political institutions.[7] Reflection on how other thinkers in past times, working outside the bounds of liberal premises, sought to ground their ideas of toleration may consequently have salutary results for theorists today. It would be a worthwhile project (but one outside the scope of the present volume) to apply the lessons of a medieval approach to toleration to, say, the complexities of the recent *chardor* controversy in France or to the political separatism of certain ethnic and cultural groups.

To claim that the products of medieval thought may retain resonance in current times must, however, be distinguished from sheer "presentism" or uncritical anachronism. It is folly to turn to the past (ancient, medieval, or modern) to solve all the problems of current political life, but confronting the intellectual power and range of medieval authors expands our own vistas, helping us to appreciate both the particular dilemmas and the more enduring challenges posed by politics, while also supplementing and enriching the discourses and frameworks available to us.[8] In speaking of the role that political theory ought to play in the inquiries of political scientists, Terence Ball has called for Lakatosian pluralism and tolerance toward a variety of theoretical research programs.[9] It seems that a similar plea must be made for the study of the ideas of the Latin Middle Ages among philosophers and political theorists.

Careful investigation of medieval writings, then, can only proliferate and diversify the tools that political thinkers today have at their disposal for discussion and debate about the fundamental issues of politics. It is hoped that the examination of one especially unlikely and surprising instance in which this holds true—toleration—encourages other scholars to consider the opportunities afforded by the Latin Middle Ages to expand their conceptual horizons on similar fronts. After all, medieval authors were deeply concerned with such issues as group and individual rights, diversity, community, and economic and social exclusion and deprivation that continue to be salient in recent times. To undertake such study is not, it should be re-emphasized, identical with a search for lost ancestors. In many instances, differences of perspective outstrip similarities, but the lessons one may learn from precisely such distancing are neither irrelevant nor negligible. What Janet Coleman has said of William of Ockham's philosophy holds no less true at the dawn of the twenty-first century: "By knowing one's past, one understands one's present and one makes one's future."[10] For just this reason, the Middle Ages forms a promising field of study for political theorists and philosophers regardless of their intellectual interests or orientations. There is simply no future for any theoretical attempt to understand political life, whether in the West or globally, that does not appreciate and take seriously the past.

NOTES

INTRODUCTION

1. In the decade of the 1990s and in the English language alone, readers may consult Michael Walzer, *On Toleration* (New Haven: Yale University Press, 1997); Richard Vernon, *The Career of Toleration: John Locke, Jonas Proast, and After* (Montreal and Kingston: McGill-Queen's University Press, 1997); Mehdi Amin Razavi and David Ambuel, eds., *Philosophy, Religion, and the Question of Intolerance* (Albany: SUNY Press, 1997); Andrew R. Murphy, "Tolerance, Toleration, and the Liberal Tradition," *Polity* 29 (Summer 1997): 593–623; David Heyd, ed., *Toleration: An Elusive Virtue* (Princeton: Princeton University Press, 1996); Michael Sandel, "Judgemental Toleration," in Robert P. George, ed., *Natural Law, Liberalism, and Morality* (Oxford: Clarendon Press, 1996), 107–12; Ole Peter Grell and Robert W. Scribner, eds., *Tolerance and Intolerance in the European Reformation* (Cambridge: Cambridge University Press, 1996); Ingrid Creppell, "Locke on Toleration: The Transformation of Constraint," *Political Theory* 24 (1996): 200–229; George P. Fletcher, "The Case for Tolerance," *Social Philosophy and Policy* 13 (1996): 229–39; Levent Köker, "Political Toleration or Politics of Recognition," *Political Theory* 24 (1996): 315–20; Glenn Tinder, *Toleration and Community* (Columbia: University of Missouri Press, 1995); George Khushf, "Tolerant Intolerance," *Journal of Medicine and Philosophy* 19 (1994): 161–81; Norma Claire Moruzzi, "A Problem with Headscarves: Contemporary Complexities of Political and Social Identity," *Political Theory* 22 (1994): 653–79; John Horton, ed., *Liberalism, Multiculturalism, and Toleration* (New York: St. Martin's Press, 1993); Stephen Kautz, "Liberalism and the Idea of Toleration," *American Journal of Political Science* 37 (1993): 610–32; Anna Elisabetta Galeotti, "Citizenship and Equality: The Place for Toleration," *Political Theory* 21 (1993): 585–605; Nick Fotion and Gerald Elfstrom, *Toleration* (Tuscaloosa: University of Alabama Press, 1992); John Horton and Peter Nicholson, eds., *Toleration: Philosophy and Practice* (Aldershot, England: Avebury, 1992); J. Budziszewski, *True Tolerance* (New Brunswick, N.J.: Transaction Press, 1992); Gary Remer, "Hobbes, the Rhetorical Tradition, and Toleration," *Review of Politics* 54 (1992): 5–33; Russell L. Hanson, "Deliberation, Tolerance, and Democracy," in George E. Marcus and Russell L. Hanson, eds., *Reconsidering the Democratic Public* (State College: The Pennsylvania State University Press, 1992); Ethel Groffier and Michel Pardis, eds., *The Notion of Tolerance and Human Rights* (Ottawa: Carleton University Press, 1991); Ole Peter Grell, Jonathan I. Israel, and Nicholas Tyacke, eds., *From Persecution to Toleration: The Glorious Revolution and Persecution in England* (Oxford: Clarendon Press, 1991); Andrew R. Cecil, *Equality, Tolerance, and Loyalty* (Dallas: University of Texas at Dallas Press, 1990); Maurizio Passerin d'Entreves, "Communitarianism and the Question of Tolerance," *Journal of Social Philosophy* 21 (1990): 77–91; Kirstie McClure, "Difference, Diversity, and the Limits of Toleration," *Political Theory* 18 (1990): 361–91.

2. A similar policy of linguistic interchangeability is adopted by Heyd, *Toleration*, 17, note 1. For a recent attempt to reassert the importance of the distinction between "tolerance" and "toleration," see Murphy, "Tolerance, Toleration, and the Liberal Tradition," 596–602.

3. McClure, "Difference, Diversity, and the Limits of Toleration," 381–87; Galeotti, "Citizenship and Equality," 597–602.

4. See the account given by John Rawls, *Political Liberalism* (New York: Columbia University Press, 1993), xxii–xxvi. A more extensive version of this position may be found in James Muldoon, "The Development of Group Rights," in Jay A. Sigler, *Minority Rights: A Comparative Analysis* (Westport, Conn.: Greenwood Press, 1983), 53–60.

5. Rawls, *Political Liberalism*, xxiv: "The historical origin of political liberalism (and of liberalism more generally) is the Reformation and its aftermath, with the long controversies over religious toleration." See McClure, "Difference, Diversity, and the Limits of Toleration," 361; Galeotti, "Citizenship and Equality," 588–91; and Murphy, "Tolerance, Toleration, and the Liberal Tradition," 615–23.

6. See Susan Mendus and John Horton, "Locke and Toleration," in Mendus and Horton, eds., *John Locke: A Letter Concerning Toleration in Focus* (London: Routledge, 1991), 3, 6–7. Gordon J. Schochet has argued ("John Locke and Religious Toleration," in Lois G. Schwoerer, ed., *The Revolution of 1688–1689: Changing Perspectives* [Cambridge: Cambridge University Press, 1992], 147–64) that Locke's real novelty lay in his advocacy of "religious liberty," rather than "toleration." But Schochet's point about Locke as the founding figure of liberal theory about religious pluralism and diversity—that he was "decidedly different" from his contemporaries (148)—seems ultimately identical to that made by other authors. For a dissenting view, see Walzer, *On Toleration*, 4: "Nor can we say that state neutrality and voluntary association, on the model of John Locke's 'Letter on Toleration,' is the only or the best way of dealing with religious or ethnic pluralism. It is a very good way, one that is adapted to the experience of Protestant congregations in certain sorts of societies, but its reach beyond that experience and those societies has to be argued."

7. Preston King, *Toleration* (London: Allen and Unwin, 1976), 73.

8. Henry Kamen, *The Rise of Toleration* (New York: McGraw-Hill, 1967), 18.

9. Grell, Israel, and Tyacke, eds., *From Persecution to Toleration: The Glorious Revolution and Religion in England*, 1.

10. Brian Tierney, "Freedom and the Medieval Church," in R. W. Davis, ed., *The Origins of Modern Freedom in the West* (Stanford: Stanford University Press, 1995), 98.

11. Mario Turchetti, "Religious Concord and Political Tolerance in Sixteenth- and Seventeenth-Century France," *Sixteenth Century Journal* 22 (1991): 15.

12. Klaus Schreiner, "Toleranz," in Otto Bruner, Werner Conze, and Reinhart Koselleck, eds., *Geschichtliche Grundbegriffe* (Stuttgart: Klett-Cotta, 1990), 6:448.

13. Bernard Hamilton, *The Medieval Inquisition* (London: Edward Arnold, 1981), 19.

14. As Rawls remarks in *Political Liberalism*, xxiii.

15. Tierney, "Freedom and the Medieval Church," 97.

16. Scott L. Waugh and Peter D. Diehl, eds., *Christendom and Its Discontents: Exclusion, Persecution, and Rebellion, 1000–1500* (Cambridge: Cambridge University Press, 1997), 5.

17. Ibid., 1.

18. Alasdair MacIntyre, *After Virtue*, 2d ed. (London: Duckworth, 1981), 165.

19. Constantin Fasolt, *Council and Hierarchy* (Cambridge: Cambridge University Press, 1991), 103.

20. Raoul Vaneigem, *The Movement of the Free Spirit* (New York: Zone Books, 1998), 58.

21. István Bejczy, "Tolerantia: A Medieval Concept," *Journal of the History of Ideas* 58 (1997): 374.

22. Alexander Murray, *Excommunication and Conscience in the Middle Ages* (London: University of London, 1991), 34–37; Brian Tierney, *The Idea of Natural Rights* (Atlanta: Scholars Press, 1997), 43–89; Colin Morris, *The Discovery of the Individual, 1050–1200* (London: SPCK, 1972); Alan Harding, "Political Liberty in the Middle Ages," *Speculum* 55 (1980): 423–43; and George Makdisi, Dominique Sourdel, and Janine Sourdel-Thomine, eds., *La Notion de liberté au Moyen Age Islam, Byzance, Occident* (Paris: Société Édition "Les Belles Lettres," 1985), 89–118, 191–213.

23. For example, Stephen Lahey, "Toleration in the Theology and Social Thought of John Wyclif," and Kate Langdon Forhan, "Respect, Interdependence, Virtue: A Medieval Theory of Toleration in the Works of Christine de Pizan," both in Cary J. Nederman and John Christian Laursen, eds., *Difference*

and Dissent: Theories of Toleration in Medieval and Early Modern Europe (Lanham, Md.: Rowman & Littlefield, 1996), 39–82; Gary Remer, "Ha-Me'iri's Theory of Religious Toleration," in John Christian Laursen and Cary J. Nederman, eds., *Beyond the Persecuting Society: Religious Toleration Before the Enlightenment* (Philadelphia: University of Pennsylvania Press, 1998), 71–91.

24. On the distinction between "concordance" and "true tolerance," see Mario Turchetti, *Concordia o tolleranza? François Bauduin (1520–1573) e i "Moyenneurs"* (Geneva: Droz, 1984).

25. Sandel, "Judgemental Toleration," 107–9. Sandel views Saint Thomas Aquinas's attitude toward the Jews as a prime example of such judgmental toleration.

26. R. I. Moore, *The Formation of a Persecuting Society: Power and Deviance in Western Europe, 950–1250* (Oxford: Blackwell, 1987).

27. Walzer, *On Toleration*, 3, 4. A similar approach to the juxtaposition of diverse "regimes of toleration" is advocated by Will Kymlicka, "Two Models of Pluralism and Tolerance," in Heyd, ed., *Toleration*, 81–105.

CHAPTER 1

1. Robert I. Moore, *The Formation of a Persecuting Society: Power and Deviance in Western Europe, 950–1250* (Oxford: Blackwell, 1987).

2. On these developments, see also the contributors to Scott L. Waugh and Peter D. Diehl, eds., *Christendom and Its Discontents: Exclusion, Persecution, and Rebellion, 1000–1500* (Cambridge: Cambridge University Press, 1997). Among those supporting the general outline of Moore's position, see Mark R. Cohen, *Under Crescent and Cross: The Jews in the Middle Ages* (Princeton: Princeton University Press, 1994); Jeffrey Richards, *Sex, Dissonance, and Damnation: Minority Groups in the Middle Ages* (London: Routledge, 1990); and David Nirenberg, *Communities of Violence: Persecution of Minorities in the Middle Ages* (Princeton: Princeton University Press, 1996). Moore's most recent restatement of his views may be found in "An Accident of Birth? Social Foundations of Persecution and Toleration in Western Europe," Working Papers Series, no. 15 (1997/1998), Advanced Study Center, International Institute, University of Michigan.

3. For what follows, I am heavily indebted to G. E. M. de Ste. Croix, "Why Were the Early Christians Persecuted?" along with the "Amendment" by A. N. Sherwin-White and the "Rejoinder" by de Ste Croix, all published in M. I. Finley, ed., *Studies in Ancient Society* (London: Routledge and Kegan Paul, 1974), 210–62; W. H. C. Frend, *Martyrdom and Persecution in the Early Church* (Oxford: Clarendon Press, 1965); and Peter Garnsey, "Religious Toleration in Classical Antiquity," in W. J. Sheils, ed., *Persecution and Toleration* (Oxford: Blackwell, 1984), 1–27.

4. Peter Schäfer, *Judeophobia: Attitudes Toward the Jews in the Ancient World* (Cambridge, Mass.: Harvard University Press, 1997).

5. Louis H. Feldman, *Jew and Gentile in the Ancient World* (Princeton: Princeton University Press, 1993), 124.

6. Garnsey, "Religious Toleration in Classical Antiquity," 10.

7. Saint Augustine, *Political Writings*, ed. Henry Paolucci (Chicago: Regnery, 1962), 219–20.

8. Ibid., 184–89.

9. The following paragraphs draw on Charles Norris Cochrane, *Christianity and Classical Culture* (Oxford: Oxford University Press, 1957).

10. Saint Augustine, *On Christian Doctrine*, trans. D. W. Robertson Jr. (Indianapolis: Bobbs-Merrill/Library of Liberal Arts, 1958), 2.40.

11. On this point, see Henry Kamen, *The Rise of Tolerance* (New York: McGraw-Hill, 1967), 12–17.

12. Raoul Vaneigem, *The Movement of the Free Spirit* (New York: Zone Books, 1998), 7–10, 55–57; he speaks of "a grotesque legend of a Middle Ages drenched in Christian faith like sardines in oil" (55).

13. A good deal of the extant evidence for the thirteenth century and beyond has been gathered

in ibid., 95–232. Vaniegem's census reveals much about the failure of orthodox Christianity to permeate the peasant population of Europe, even in the fourteenth century.

14. See the appraisal of Alexander Murray, "Piety and Impiety in Thirteenth-Century Italy," *Studies in Church History* 8 (1971): 83–106; and idem, "Religion Among the Poor in Thirteenth-Century France," *Traditio* 30 (1974): 285–324.

15. The continuity of the medieval reforming sentiment is surveyed by Steven Ozment, *The Age of Reform, 1250–1550: An Intellectual and Religious History of Late Medieval and Reformation Europe* (New Haven: Yale University Press, 1980). See also R. I. Moore, *The Origins of European Dissent* (London: Penguin, 1977), 46–82.

16. Gerhart B. Ladner, "Terms and Ideas of Renewal," in Robert L. Benson and Giles Constable, eds., *Renaissance and Renewal in the Twelfth Century* (Cambridge, Mass.: Harvard University Press, 1982), 19.

17. Giles Constable, "Renewal and Reform in Religious Life: Concepts and Realities," in Benson and Constable, eds., *Renaissance and Renewal in the Twelfth Century*, 62–66. See also Giles Constable, *The Reformation of the Twelfth Century* (Cambridge: Cambridge University Press, 1998).

18. See Malcolm Lambert, *Medieval Heresy: Popular Movements from Bogomil to Hus* (London: Edward Arnold, 1977), 39–47; and Heinrich Fichtenau, *Heretics and Scholars in the High Middle Ages, 1000–1200*, trans. Denise A. Kaiser (University Park: The Pennsylvania State University Press, 1998).

19. Carol Lansing, *Power and Purity: Cathar Heresy in Medieval Italy* (New York: Oxford University Press, 1998), 81–157.

20. Anathematization came during the Middle Ages to be construed as a form of ecclesiastical penalty distinct from simple excommunication; see Elisabeth Vodola, *Excommunication in the Middle Ages* (Berkeley and Los Angeles: University of California Press, 1986), 14; and Murray, *Excommunication and Conscience in the Middle Ages* (London: University of London, 1991), 23–24.

21. See Vodola, *Excommunication in the Middle Ages*, 28–43.

22. Murray, *Excommunication and Conscience in the Middle Ages*, 16–17.

23. Ibid., 26–33.

24. Bernard Hamilton, *The Medieval Inquisition* (London: Edward Arnold, 1981), 19–20.

25. Vodola, *Excommunication in the Middle Ages*, 140, 161.

26. See Constant J. Mews, "Philosophy and Theology, 1100–1150: The Search for Harmony," in Françoise Gasparri, ed., *Le XIIe Siècle: Mutations et renouveau en France dans le première moitié du XIIe siècle* (Paris: Le Léopard d'Or, 1995), 159–203.

27. One thinks, in particular, of Peter Abelard and William of Ockham, both of whose difficulties with ecclesiastical authorities probably stemmed in large measure from personal and/or "political" animosities. See Constant J. Mews, *Peter Abelard* (London: Variorum, 1995), 11–12; and C. K. Brampton, "Personalities in the Process Against Ockham at Avignon, 1324–26," *Franciscan Studies* 25 (1966): 4–25.

28. R. R. Bolgar, *The Classical Heritage and Its Beneficiaries* (Cambridge: Cambridge University Press, 1954), 202–7.

29. Michael Herren, *Medieval Thought*, 2d ed. (Toronto: University of Toronto Press, 1992), 194–211.

30. On the proceedings against Gilbert at the Council of Rheims, see John of Salisbury, *Historia Pontificalis*, ed. M. Chibnall (Oxford: Oxford University Press, 1986), 15–41.

31. Jacques Le Goff, *Time, Work, and Culture in the Middle Ages*, trans. Arthur Goldhammer (Chicago: University of Chicago Press, 1980), 135–49.

32. Gordon Leff, *Paris and Oxford Universities in the Thirteenth and Fourteenth Centuries* (New York: Wiley, 1968), 167–73.

33. Saint Thomas Aquinas, *Sententia super Librum De Caelo et Mundo*, ed. R. M. Spiazzi (Turin: Marietti, 1952), 1:22 n. 3.

34. See the discussion of this by John Finnis, *Aquinas* (Oxford: Oxford University Press, 1998), 10–13 and notes.

35. Saint Thomas Aquinas, *De Perfectione Spiritualis Vitae*, in R. M. Spiazzi and M. Calcaterra, eds., *Opuscula Theologica* (Turin: Marietti, 1954), chap. 26.

36. Joseph R. Strayer, *The Reign of Philip the Fair* (Princeton: Princeton University Press, 1980).

37. H. S. Offler, "Empire and Papacy: The Last Struggle," *Transactions of the Royal Historical Society* 6th ser., 10 (1956): 21–47.

38. R. W. Southern, *Western Views of Islam in the Middle Ages* (Cambridge, Mass.: Harvard University Press, 1962).

39. Vivan B. Mann, Thomas F. Glick, and Jerrilynn D. Dodds, eds., *Convivencia: Jews, Muslims, and Christians in Medieval Spain* (New York: George Braziller, 1992).

40. Joel L. Kraemer, *Humanism in the Renaissance of Islam* (Leiden: E. J. Brill, 1993), 28–30; Bat Ye'or, *The Dhimmi: Jews and Christians Under Islam*, trans. D. Maisel, P. Fenton, and D. Littman (Rutherford, N.J.: Fairleigh Dickinson University Press, 1985), 43–77.

41. On this process, see Jean Jolivet, "The Arabic Inheritance," in P. Dronke, ed., *A History of Twelfth-Century Western Philosophy* (Cambridge: Cambridge University Press, 1988), 113–48; and M. R. Dod, "Aristoteles Latinus," in Norman Kretzmann, Antony Kenny, and Jan Pinborg, eds., *The Cambridge History of Later Medieval Philosophy* (Cambridge: Cambridge University Press, 1982), 45–79.

42. The account contained in this and the following paragraph is especially indebted to Kenneth R. Stow, *Alienated Minority: The Jews of Medieval Latin Europe* (Cambridge, Mass.: Harvard University Press, 1992).

43. Even where the Jews had been expunged from a Western locale (as in England), they could not be eliminated from the popular imagination; see Donnalee Dox, "Medieval Drama as Documentation: 'Real Presence' in the Croxton *Conversion of Ser Jonathas the Jewe by the Myracle of the Blissed Sacrament*," *Theatre Survey* 38 (May 1997): 97–115.

44. Walter Pakter, *Medieval Canon Law and the Jews* (Ebelsbach: Gremler, 1988).

45. Stow, *Alienated Minority*.

46. See Cohen, *Under Crescent and Cross*, 20–21.

47. Vodola, *Excommunication in the Middle Ages*, 47 note 20.

48. James Muldoon, *Popes, Lawyers, and Infidels* (Philadelphia: University of Pennsylvania Press, 1979), 10–11.

49. See Gavin I. Langmuir, *Toward a Definition of Anti-Semitism* (Berkeley and Los Angeles: University of California Press, 1990).

CHAPTER 2

1. A Jewish author, Yehuda Halévi, a twelfth-century Spanish rabbi, wrote *The Kosari* (trans. Yehuda Even Shmuel [Tel-Aviv: Dvir, 1972]) around 1140. The various contributions to inter-religious discussion made by Islamic scholars of the tenth and eleventh centuries are documented by Joel L. Kraemer, *Humanism in the Renaissance of Islam* (Leiden: E. J. Brill, 1993), 102–206 passim. On the context for medieval inter-religious dialogue in the Latin world, see G. R. Evans, *Anselm and a New Generation* (Oxford: Oxford University Press, 1980), 34–68.

2. Gary Remer, "Dialogues of Toleration: Erasmus and Bodin," *Review of Politics* 56 (Spring 1994): 305, 306. See also the discussion in Remer's book, *Humanism and the Rhetoric of Toleration* (University Park: The Pennsylvania State University Press, 1996), 13–101.

3. Jay Newman, *Foundations of Religious Tolerance* (Toronto: University of Toronto Press, 1982), 104

4. Ibid., 103–4, 110.

5. Robert C. Stacey, "The Conversion of Jews to Christianity in Thirteenth-Century England," *Speculum* 67 (1992): 263–64.

6. See Odo of Tournai, *A Disputation with the Jew, Leo, Concerning the Advent of Christ, the Son of God*, in *Two Theological Treatises*, trans. Irven M. Resnick (Philadelphia: University of Pennsylvania Press, 1994).

7. As Gustav Mensching remarks (somewhat anachronistically) of these authors, "One gets the feeling that their motives spring . . . from a kind of rationalistic attitude, and that they anticipate ideas expressed later by the European Enlightenment" (*Tolerance and Truth in Religion*, trans. J.-J. Kleimkeit [University: University of Alabama Press, 1971], 75).

8. Mario Turchetti, *Concordia o tolleranza? François Baudin (1520–1573) e i "Moyenneurs"* (Geneva: Droz, 1984).

9. Newman, *Foundations of Religious Tolerance*, 107.

10. Evans, *Anselm and a New Generation*, 35, remarks that "Anselm was not moved to write a dialogue of his own," but Constant Mews has discovered and transcribed a *Disputatio inter Christianum et gentilem* that seems to have an Anselmian provenance; see "St. Anselm and Roscelin: Some New Texts and Their Implications, 1," *Archives d'histoire doctrinale et littéraire du moyen age* 58 (1991): 86–98.

11. Ibid., 86.

12. Ibid., 95.

13. Anna Sapir Abulafia and G. R. Evans, eds., *The Works of Gilbert Crispin, Abbot of Westminster* (London: Oxford University Press for the British Academy, 1986), 63.

14. Ibid., 64.

15. Ibid., 10.

16. Ibid., 9.

17. Constant Mews, "On Dating the Works of Peter Abelard," *Archives d'histoire doctrinale et littéraire du moyen age* 52 (1985): 104 note 1.

18. Peter Abelard, *Dialogue of a Philosopher with a Jew and a Christian*, trans. Pierre J. Payer (Toronto: Pontifical Institute of Medieval Studies, 1979). The standard Latin edition, by Rudolf Thomas (Stuttgart-Bad Canstatt: Friedrich Frommann Verlag, 1970), contains a number of errors; a new critical text is being prepared. At the suggestion of Dr. John Marenbon of Trinity College, Cambridge, who is the co-editor of the new edition of the *Dialogue*, I have followed Payer's translation because it draws on a superior manuscript ignored in the Thomas version. The dating of the *Dialogus* has usually been placed near the end of Abelard's life, sometime after 1136. See John Marenbon, "Abelard's Ethical Theory: Two Definitions from the *Collationes*," in Haijo Jan Westra, ed., *From Athens to Chartres* (Leiden: E. J. Brill, 1992), 302–3. A convincing argument for an earlier dating (in the late 1120s or early 1130s) has been made by Mews, "On Dating the Works of Peter Abelard," 194–26.

19. Abelard, *Dialogue of a Philosopher with a Jew and a Christian*, 19–20.

20. Ibid., 20, 21.

21. Ibid., 24–27.

22. Ibid., 26.

23. Ibid., 21–22.

24. Ibid., 23.

25. Ibid., 23.

26. Ibid., 32–33.

27. A suggestion made by Anthony Bonner in his introduction to *The Book of the Gentile and the Three Wise Men* in *The Selected Works of Ramon Llull (1232–1316)*, 2 vols. (Princeton: Princeton University Press, 1985), 1:98–100. On the general project of Llull's evangelical program, see also Mark D. Johnston, *The Evangelical Rhetoric of Ramon Llull: Lay Learning and Piety in the Christian West Around 1300* (Oxford: Oxford University Press, 1996).

28. Bonner, ed., *The Selected Works of Ramon Llull (1232–1316)*, 1:110.

29. Ibid., 111–13.

30. Ibid., 113.

31. Ibid., 110.

32. This is given detailed exposition by Mark D. Johnston, *The Spiritual Logic of Ramon Llull* (Oxford: Oxford University Press, 1987).

33. Bonner, ed., *The Selected Works of Ramon Llull (1232–1316)*, 1:113–16.

34. Ibid., 116.

35. Ibid., 117.

36. Ibid., 118.

37. Ibid., 148.

38. Ibid., 149.

39. Ibid., 149–50.

40. Ibid., 260.

41. Ibid., 171–75.

42. Ibid., 288–92.

43. Abulafia and Evans, eds., *The Works of Gilbert Crispin*, 81.

44. Abelard, *Dialogue of a Philosopher with a Jew and a Christian*, 19, 21.

45. Ibid., 99.

46. Bonner, ed., *The Selected Works of Ramon Llull (1232–1316)*, 1:110.

47. Ibid., 116.

48. Abelard, *Dialogue of a Philosopher with a Jew and a Christian*, 71.

49. See the discussion by Payer in ibid., 5, 6–7.

50. Constant Mews, "Peter Abelard and the Enigma of Dialogue," in John Christian Laursen and Cary J. Nederman, eds., *Beyond the Persecuting Society: Religious Toleration Before the Enlightenment* (Philadelphia: University of Pennsylvania Press, 1998), 42.

51. Peter Abelard, *Sic et Non*, ed. Blanche Boyer and Richard McKeon (Chicago: University of Chicago Press, 1976), 103.

52. Mews, "Peter Abelard and the Enigma of Dialogue," 42.

53. Bonner, ed., *The Selected Works of Ramon Llull (1232–1316)*, 1:294–99.

54. Ibid., 300–301.

55. Ibid., 301–2.

56. Ibid., 302.

57. Ibid., 303.

58. Ibid., 303.

59. Ibid., 304.

60. Jean Bodin, *Colloquium of the Seven About Secrets of the Sublime*, trans. Marion L. Kuntz (Princeton: Princeton University Press, 1975), 471.

61. See Quentin Skinner, *The Foundations of Modern Political Thought*, 2 vols. (Cambridge: Cambridge University Press, 1978), 2:249; Georg Roellenbleck, "Les Poèmes intercalés dans L'Heptaplomeres," in *Jean Bodin: Actes du Colloque Interdisciplinaire d'Angers*, 2 vols. (Angers: Presses de l'Université d'Angers, 1985), 2:448.

62. See Remer, "Dialogues of Toleration," 324–31; and Marion Leathers Kuntz, "The Concept of Toleration in the *Colloquium Heptaplomeres de rerum sublimium arcanes abditis* of Jean Bodin," in Laursen and Nederman, eds., *Beyond the Persecuting Society*, 125–44.

63. Newman, *Foundations of Religious Tolerance*, 109.

64. Ibid., 105–8.

CHAPTER 3

1. For example, see Quentin Skinner, *The Foundations of Modern Political Thought*, 2 vols. (Cambridge: Cambridge University Press, 1978), 2:245–49; and Karl Popper, "Toleration and Intellectual Responsibility," in Susan Mendus and David Edwards, eds., *On Toleration* (Oxford: Clarendon Press, 1987), 17–18.

2. Preston King, *Toleration* (London: Allen and Unwin, 1976), 120; for the full argument, see 122–31.

3. The two most prominent examples are Richard Tuck, "Scepticism and Toleration in the Seventeenth Century," in Susan Mendus, ed., *Justifying Toleration: Conceptual and Historical Perspectives* (Cambridge: Cambridge University Press, 1988), 21–35; and Alan Charles Kors, *Atheism in France, 1650–1729, Volume I: The Orthodox Sources of Disbelief* (Princeton: Princeton University Press, 1990).

4. A brief history of the diffusion of skepticism in the pagan and early Christian worlds is provided by Charles Schmitt, *Cicero Scepticus: A Study of the Influence of the "Academica" in the Renaissance* (The Hague: Martinus Nijhoff, 1972), 5–42. Also see John Christian Laursen, *The Politics of Skepticism in the Ancients,*

Montaigne, Hume, and Kant (Leiden: E. J. Brill, 1992), 14–32; and R. J. Hankinson, *The Sceptics* (London: Routledge, 1995).

5. Tuck, "Scepticism and Toleration in the Seventeenth Century," 21.

6. The nature of John's "humanism" is admirably summarized by Hans Liebeschütz, *Mediaeval Humanism in the Life and Writings of John of Salisbury* (London: Warburg Institute, 1950).

7. See Schmitt, *Cicero Scepticus*, 36–38; Birger Munk-Olsen, "L'Humanisme de Jean de Salisbury, un Ciceronien au 12e siècle," in Maurice de Gandillac and Edouard Jeauneau, eds., *Entretiens sur la Renaissance du 12e siècle* (Paris: Mouton, 1968), 53–83; and Edouard Jeauneau, "Jean de Salisbury et la lecture des philosophes," in Michael J. Wilks, ed., *The World of John of Salisbury* (London: Basil Blackwell, 1984), 77–108.

8. On the Ciceronian foundations of the Erasmian approach to toleration, see Gary Remer, *Humanism and the Rhetoric of Toleration* (University Park: The Pennsylvania State University Press, 1996), 13–101.

9. Cary J. Nederman, "The Aristotelian Doctrine of the Mean and John of Salisbury's Concept of Liberty," *Vivarium* 24 (1986): 128–42.

10. John of Salisbury, *Policraticus*, ed. C. C. J. Webb, 2 vols. (1909; reprinted New York: Arno Press, 1979), 7.25 (176–77). The Webb edition will soon be replaced with one by K. S. B. Keats-Rohan, the first volume of which has now appeared (Turnhout: Brepols, 1993). Unfortunately, because virtually all the citations from the *Policraticus* in the present chapter are from its later books, I have been compelled to use Webb's edition. Translations throughout are my own, sometimes derived from my published partial translation of the *Policraticus* (Cambridge: Cambridge University Press, 1990), in which case I have given a page reference parenthetically.

11. John of Salisbury, *Policraticus*, 7.25 (176).

12. Ibid., 7.25 (179).

13. Ibid., 7.25 (176).

14. John of Salisbury, *Policraticus*, 4.9 (53–54). Coincidentally, he makes the same charge in his letters against Thomas Beckett; see Cary J. Nederman, "Aristotelian Ethics and John of Salisbury's Letters," *Viator* 18 (1987): 171–72.

15. Indeed, John explicitly rejects this position at *Policraticus* 8.9 when he attacks the Roman tribune who once proclaimed in a speech that there is no value to "liberty if it is not permitted to those who desire to ruin themselves by luxury." Such "liberty" would have been regarded by John to be instead "license"; see Nederman, "The Aristotelian Doctrine of the Mean and John of Salisbury's Concept of Liberty," 139.

16. John of Salisbury, *Policraticus*, 7.25 (180).

17. Ibid., 7.25 (175, 180).

18. Ibid., 6.24 (132–35).

19. For a summary of these criticisms, see Cary J. Nederman and Catherine Campbell, "Priests, Kings, and Tyrants: Spiritual and Temporal Power in John of Salisbury's *Policraticus*," *Speculum* 66 (1991): 579–80, 584–86.

20. John of Salisbury, *Policraticus* 7.25 (180).

21. Ibid., 1.5.

22. Ibid., 6.26 (140).

23. Ibid., 7.25 (176–77, 179).

24. For a full appraisal of John's version of the organic metaphor, see Tilman Struve, "The Importance of the Organism in the Political Theory of John of Salisbury," in Wilks, ed., *The World of John of Salisbury,* 303–17; and Cary J. Nederman, "The Physiological Significance of the Organic Metaphor in John of Salisbury's *Policraticus*," *History of Political Thought* 8 (Summer 1987): 21–23.

25. John of Salisbury, *Policraticus*, 5.2 (66). John compares the priesthood to the soul, which strictly speaking he does not count among the "parts" of the body.

26. See Paul Edward Dutton, "*Illustre civitatis et populi exemplum:* Plato's *Timaeus* and the Transmission from Calcidius to the End of the Twelfth Century of a Tripartite Scheme of Society," *Mediaeval Studies* 45 (1983): 79–119.

27. John of Salisbury, *Policraticus*, 6.26 (140).

28. Ibid., 6.26 (140).

29. Ibid., 8.17 (191).

30. Ibid., 7.25 (176).

31. Ibid., 4.2 (30–31).

32. Ibid., 7.25 (176).

33. Ibid., 6.25 (137).

34. Ibid., 6.25 (138–39).

35. Ibid., 6.26 (139–40).

36. Ibid., 6.24 (132).

37. Ibid., 6.24 (135).

38. On this point, see Gordon J. Schochet, "John Locke and Religious Toleration," in L. G. Schwoerer, ed., *The Revolution of 1688–1689: Changing Perspectives* (Cambridge: Cambridge University Press, 1992), 150–51; and Hans R. Guggisberg, "The Defense of Religious Toleration and Religious Liberty in Early Modern Europe: Arguments, Pressures, and Some Consequences," *History of European Ideas* 4 (1983): 36.

39. Ibid., 37.

40. On the details of Cicero's teachings in these works, see Paul MacKendrick, *The Philosophical Books of Cicero* (London: Duckworth, 1989), 114–30, 169–84. Medieval knowledge of the works containing Cicero's skepticism is examined by Schmitt, *Cicero Scepticus*, 33–42; and Mary A. Rouse and Richard H. Rouse, "The Medieval Circulation of Cicero's 'Posterior Academics' and the *De finibus bonorum et malorum*," in *Authentic Witnesses: Approaches to Medieval Texts and Manuscripts* (Notre Dame: University of Notre Dame Press, 1991), 61–98.

41. In addition to MacKendrick's work cited in note 40 above, see Olof Gignon, "Cicero und die griechische Philosophie," in H. Temporini, ed., *Aufstieg und Niedergang der Römischen Welt*, vol. 1 (*Von den Anfängen Roms bis zum Ausgang der Republik* vol. 4), (Berlin: Walter de Gruyter, 1973), 226–61; Neal Wood, *Cicero's Social and Political Thought* (Berkeley and Los Angeles: University of California Press, 1988), 58–61; Woldemar Görler, "Silencing the Troublemaker: *De legibus* I.39 and the Continuity of Cicero's Scepticism," in J. G. F. Powell, ed., *Cicero the Philosopher* (Oxford: Clarendon Press, 1995), 85–114; and John Glucker, "*Probabile, Veri Simile*, and Related Terms," in Powell, ed., *Cicero the Philosopher*, 115–44.

42. Cicero, *De natura deorum*, ed. H. Rackham (London: Heinemann, 1933), I.1.

43. Cicero, *Academica*, ed. H. Rackham (London: Heinemann, 1933), II.76–98.

44. Rodney M. Thomson, "What Is the *Entheticus?*" in Wilks, ed., *The World of John of Salisbury*, 300; Jan van Laarhoven, ed., *John of Salisbury's Entheticus Maior and Minor*, 3 vols. (Leiden: E. J. Brill, 1987), 1:50–51; Cary J. Nederman and Arlene Feldwick, "To the Court and Back Again: The Origins and Dating of the *Entheticus de Dogmate Philosophorum* of John of Salisbury," *Journal of Medieval and Renaissance Studies* 21 (Spring 1991): 129–45.

45. John of Salisbury, *Entheticus*, line 1138.

46. Ibid., lines 1144, 1147–54.

47. Schmitt, *Cicero Scepticus*, 37–38. This conclusion is seconded by Pasquale Porro, "Il *Sextus Latinus* e l'immagine dello scetticismo antico nel medioevo," *Elenchos* 15 (1994): 245–47.

48. In addition to articles cited in notes 9 and 14 above, see Cary J. Nederman, "Knowledge, Virtue, and the Path to Wisdom: The Unexamined Aristotelianism of John of Salisbury's *Metalogicon*," *Mediaeval Studies* 51 (1989): 268–86.

49. John of Salisbury, *Entheticus*, lines 1155–58.

50. Ibid., lines 1161–62.

51. John of Salisbury, *Metalogicon*, ed. J. B. Hall and K. S. B. Keats-Rohan (Turnhout: Brepols, 1991), Prologus; see also 2.20, 4.7.

52. Ibid., 4.31.

53. Ibid., 2.13.

54. Ibid., 4.34.

55. John of Salisbury, *Policraticus*, Prologus (7); see also 2.22, 7. Prologus (148), and 7.2 (152).

56. Ibid., 7.1 (148–49).

57. Ibid., 7.2 (150).

58. Ibid., 7.2. (151–52).

59. Ibid., 7.7 (153–56).

60. Ibid., 7.7 (154).

61. Ibid., 7.2 (152).

62. Ibid., 7.2 (152–53); for a shorter list in the same vein, see Prologus (7). The resemblance to Erasmus is especially striking: The Dutch humanist proposed a distinction between "fundamentals of faith" and "nonessentials" and maintained that discussion of all "nonessential" matters should be tolerated. See Remer, *Humanism and the Rhetoric of Toleration*, 50–54.

63. Ibid., 7.2 (153).

64. Saint Augustine, *Contra Academicos* (Indianapolis: Hackett, 1995), 3:4.30.

65. John of Salisbury, *Policraticus*, 7.2 (152).

66. John of Salisbury, *Entheticus*, 1.1142.

67. John of Salisbury, *Policraticus*, 7. Prologus (147–48).

68. For a sample of the debate, see Richard Tuck, *Natural Rights Theories—Their Origin and Development* (Cambridge: Cambridge University Press, 1979); and Brian Tierney, *The Idea of Natural Rights* (Atlanta: Scholars Press, 1997).

69. John of Salisbury, *Policraticus*, 2.22. Interestingly, immediately following this statement, John refers to "Paripateticus Palatinus," that is, Peter Abelard, for an example of how logical probability poses important issues of individual judgment. John, who studied with Peter at Paris, may well have taken Abelard's thought as a model for his own belief in intellectual freedom and forbearance.

70. John of Salisbury, *Policraticus*, 7.6.

71. Ibid., 7.8 (160).

72. John Stuart Mill, *On Liberty*, ed. Elizabeth Rapaport (Indianapolis: Hackett, 1978), 18.

73. John of Salisbury would thus succumb to Mill's scathing dismissal: "Strange it is that men should admit the validity of the arguments for free discussion, but object to their being 'pushed to the extreme.'. . . Strange that they should imagine that they are not assuming infallibility when they acknowledge that there should be free discussion of all subjects which can possibly be *doubtful*, but think that some particular principle or doctrine should be forbidden to be questioned because it is so *certain*, that is, because *they are certain* that it is certain" (ibid., 20).

74. On the relation between humanist dialogue and scholastic *disputatio*, see Remer, *Humanism and the Rhetoric of Toleration*, 97–100.

Chapter 4

1. See Vivian B. Mann, Thomas F. Glick, and Jerrilynn D. Dodds, eds., *Convivencia: Jews, Muslims, and Christians in Medieval Spain* (New York: George Braziller, 1992); Norman Daniel, *Islam and the West: The Making of an Image* (Edinburgh: Edinburgh University Press, 1960).

2. Igor de Rachewiltz, *Papal Envoys to the Great Chans* (Stanford: Stanford University Press, 1971).

3. The best recent analysis of Mongolian expansionism is Thomas T. Allsen, *Mongol Imperialism: The Policies of the Grand Qan Mongke in China, Russia, and the Islamic Lands, 1251–1259* (Berkeley and Los Angeles: University of California Press, 1987).

4. On these missions generally, see James Muldoon, *Popes, Lawyers, and Infidels* (Philadelphia: University of Pennsylvania Press, 1979), 41–45, 59–68.

5. John of Plano Carpini, *History of the Mongols*, in Christopher Dawson, ed., *Mission to Asia* (New York: Harper and Row, 1966), 46.

6. The development of the image of the Mongols among Latin Christendom has been studied by C. W. Connell, "Western Views of the Origin of the 'Tartars': An Example of the Influence of Myth

in the Second Half of the Thirteenth Century," *Journal of Medieval and Renaissance Studies* 3 (1972): 115–37.

7. This was true already in William's lifetime. Roger Bacon incorporated large extracts from William's letter into his *Opus Maior* as evidence for the behavior and beliefs of the Mongols; Bacon apparently encountered William in Paris after the return of the latter from the East.

8. *The Journey of William of Rubruck,* in Peter Jackson and David Morgan, ed., *The Mission of Friar William of Rubruck* (London: Hakluyt Society, 1990), 10.6, 9.1, 10.4, 27.8, 34.6. The translation is based on the Latin text edited by Anastasius van den Wyngaert, *Sinica Franciscana,* vol. 1: *Itinera et Relationes Fratrum Minorum Saeculum XIII et XIV* (Quaracchi: Franciscan Press, 1929).

9. *The Journey of William of Rubruck,* 1.14; the phrase is repeated at 9.1.

10. Ibid., 2.1–8.5.

11. The cosmopolitan population of the Mongol Empire, and its implications for the character of imperial rule, has been examined by Thomas T. Allsen, "Ever Closer Encounters: The Appropriation of Culture and the Apportionment of Peoples in the Mongol Empire," *Journal of Early Modern History* 1 (1997): 2–23.

12. *The Journey of William of Rubruck,* 11.1. 26.1, 30.10.

13. For example, William mentions discovering a "completely" Nestorian village, but this is clearly an unusual phenomenon (ibid., 27.1).

14. See ibid., 15.5–6, 24.1, 26.1, 26.11.

15. Ibid., 32.1.

16. Ibid., 25.9.

17. Ibid., 34.2; also 36.6.

18. Ibid., 34.2.

19. Ibid., 29.15.

20. On these "soothsayers," see 35.1–13.

21. See Will Kymlicka, "Two Models of Pluralism and Tolerance," in David Heyd, ed., *Toleration: An Elusive Virtue* (Princeton: Princeton University Press, 1996), 81–105; and Michael Walzer, *On Toleration* (New Haven: Yale University Press, 1997), 14–19.

22. For example, *The Journal of William of Rubruck,* 10.5, 15.5–6, 19.7, 25.7, 29.19–23.

23. Ibid., 34.7.

24. Ibid., 36.12.

25. Ibid., 10.5.

26. Ibid., 16.3, 19.7, 28.15, 28.18, 36.17.

27. Ibid., 22.2.

28. Ibid., 28.4.

29. Ibid., Epilogue.5.

30. Ibid., 25.8.

31. Ibid., 13.6.

32. Ibid., 10.5.

33. Ibid., 9.4.

34. Ibid., 12.2.

35. Ibid., 11.2.

36. Ibid., 26.14.

37. Ibid., 27.11.

38. Ibid., 29.54.

39. Ibid., 29.56.

40. Ibid., 32.11.

41. Ibid., 29.43.

42. Ibid., 28.12.

43. Ibid., 30.8.

44. Ibid., 30.10.

45. Ibid., 30.10, 30.12.

46. Ibid., 30.12.
47. Ibid., 30.14.
48. Ibid., 33.7.
49. Ibid., 33.12.
50. Ibid., 33.11.
51. Ibid., 33.14, 33.13.
52. Ibid., 33.16.
53. Ibid., 33.17–18.
54. Ibid., 33.21.
55. Ibid., 33.22.
56. Ibid., 34.2.
57. Ibid., 34.6.
58. Ibid., 38.10.
59. Ibid., 34.6.
60. Muldoon, Popes, Lawyers, and Infidels, 8–12.
61. Ibid., 16–17.

CHAPTER 5

1. For a useful discussion of the status of heresy in the medieval mind-set, see Gordon Leff, *Heresy in the Later Middle Ages*, 2 vols. (Manchester: Manchester University Press, 1967), 1–3.

2. The use of temporal penalties to supplement spiritual disengagement from the faithful is discussed by Elisabeth Vodola, *Excommunication in the Middle Ages* (Berkeley and Los Angeles: University of California Press, 1986), 165–67.

3. This is the general hypothesis proposed by R. I. Moore, *The Formation of a Persecuting Society: Power and Deviance in Western Europe, 950–1250* (Oxford: Blackwell, 1987).

4. See Antony Black, *Political Thought in Europe, 1250–1450* (Cambridge: Cambridge University Press, 1992), 48–58.

5. The best account of Marsiglio's life and career remains Carlo Pincin, *Marsilio* (Turin: Edizioni Giappichelli, 1967).

6. On the relation between the two works, see Cary J. Nederman, "From *Defensor pacis* to *Defensor minor*: The Problem of Empire in Marsiglio of Padua," *History of Political Thought* 16 (1995): 313–29.

7. The key elements of this "communal functionalist" framework are discussed by Cary J. Nederman, "Freedom, Community, and Function: Communitarian Lessons of Medieval Political Theory," *American Political Science Review* 86 (1992): 977–86; and idem, "Constitutionalism—Medieval and Modern: Against Neo-Figgisite Orthodoxy (Again)," *History of Political Thought* 17 (1996): 186–93.

8. Cary J. Nederman, *Community and Consent: The Secular Political Theory of Marsiglio of Padua's "Defensor Pacis"* (Lanham, Md.: Rowman & Littlefield, 1995), 29–34, 44–46.

9. Marsiglio of Padua, *Defensor pacis*, ed. C. W. Previté-Orton (Cambridge: Cambridge University Press, 1928), Discourse I, chapter 4, section 1. I have relied (with occasional modifications) on the standard English translation of the *Defensor pacis* by Alan Gewirth, *Marsilius of Padua—The Defender of Peace*, 2 vols. (New York: Columbia University Press, 1951–56).

10. Marsiglio, *Defensor pacis*, 1.4.2.

11. Aristotle, *Politics*, ed. H. Rackham (Cambridge, Mass.: Harvard University Press, 1932), 1252b29–31, 1280a26–28, and 1281a1–4.

12. Marsiglio, *Defensor pacis*, 1.2.3.

13. Ibid., 1.3.4.

14. Ibid., 1.4.3.

15. Ibid., 1.3.5.

16. Ibid., 1.4.5.

17. Ibid., I.6.9.

18. Ibid., I.5.2–11.

19. Ibid., I.2.3, I.19.2.

20. Ibid., I.6.9.

21. Ibid., I.4.5.

22. Ibid., I.5.1.

23. Ibid., I.4.4.

24. Ibid., I.13.4.

25. Aristotle, *Politics*, 1328a23–1329a2.

26. Marsiglio, *Defensor pacis*, I.12.3.

27. Ibid., I.12.6, I.13.5.

28. Ibid., I.4.3.

29. Saint Thomas Aquinas, *On Kingship*, trans. G. B. Phelan (Toronto: Pontifical Institute of Medieval Studies, 1949), 63–67.

30. Marsiglio, *Defensor pacis*, II.2.4.

31. As suggested by Brian Tierney, "Political and Religious Freedom in Marsilius of Padua," in Noel B. Reynolds and W. Cole Durham Jr., eds., *Religious Liberty in Western Thought* (Atlanta: Scholars Press, 1996), 64.

32. Marsiglio, *Defensor pacis*, I.5.7.

33. Ibid., II.2.5.

34. Ibid., I.5.4.

35. Ibid., I.6.8.

36. Ibid., I.12.2–3.

37. Ibid., I.5.10–11.

38. Ibid., I.5.14.

39. One ought never to forget the polemical background to the *Defensor pacis*. Marsiglio's stated intention is to challenge and rebut the pretensions of the Church, and particularly the papacy, to exercise modes of temporal power over property and persons (ibid., I.19.3–13). To permit the priesthood autonomy is in effect to encourage its belief in its own authority; hence, Marsiglio calls for regulation.

40. Ibid., II.21.15.

41. Ibid., I.5.10–13.

42. Ibid., II.6.12.

43. Ibid., II.5.7.

44. Ibid., II.10.3; see also II.28.17.

45. As has been pointed out by Gewirth, *Marsilius of Padua—The Defender of Peace*, 1:166–67; he also cites a large body of scholarly literature that identifies Marsiglio as an advocate of religious toleration (4 note 8). More recently, Diana Webb has declared: "That [Marsiglio] may have contemplated the possibility of toleration does not seem to lie beyond the bounds of the conceivable" ("The Possibility of Toleration: Marsiglio and the City States of Italy," in W. J. Sheils, eds., *Persecution and Toleration* [Oxford: Blackwell, 1984], 113).

46. Marsiglio, *Defensor pacis*, II.6.12; see II.10.3.

47. Tierney, "Political and Religious Freedom in Marsilius of Padua," 73, 74. Similar sentiments are expressed by Alexander Passerin d'Entrèves, *The Medieval Contribution to Political Thought* (Oxford: Oxford University Press, 1939), 77–84; and Georges de Lagarde, *La Naissance de l'esprit laïque au déclin du moyen âge*, new ed., 5 vols., *Le Defensor Pacis* (Louvain and Paris: Nauwelaerts, 1970), 3:255–60.

48. Marsiglio of Padua, *Defensor minor*, trans. Cary J. Nederman (Cambridge: Cambridge University Press, 1993), chapter 10, section 3.

49. Ibid., 10.5.

50. Ibid., 7.3.

51. Ibid., 15.7.

52. Ibid., 10.5.

53. Ibid., 10.5.

54. Ibid., 10.6.

55. Ibid., 15.5.

56. Ibid., 15.6.

57. Ibid., 15.7.

58. Ibid., 15.9–10.

59. Marsiglio, *Defensor pacis,* II.8.9.

60. Marsiglio, *Defensor minor,* 7.2.

61. A point made by Robert Audi, "The Separation of Church and State and the Obligations of Citizenship," *Philosophy and Public Affairs* 18 (1989): 263–64.

62. See John Christian Laursen, "Baylean Liberalism: Tolerance Requires Nontolerance," in Laursen and Cary J. Nederman, eds., *Beyond the Persecuting Society: Religious Toleration Before the Enlightenment* (Philadelphia: University of Pennsylvania Press, 1998), 197–215.

63. It seems to me that this is little different from extending Locke's (or even Mill's) principles to cover contemporary situations, as is often done by liberal political philosophers today; for example, see Susan Mendus, *Toleration and the Limits of Liberalism* (London: Macmillan, 1989).

CHAPTER 6

1. See Bernard Guenée, *States and Rulers in Later Medieval Europe,* trans. Juliet Vale (Oxford: Blackwell, 1985), 49–65; and Susan Reynolds, *Kingdoms and Communities in Western Europe, 900–1300* (Oxford: Oxford University Press, 1984), 262–331. Classic discussions of medieval nationalism are gathered together in Charles L. Tipton, ed., *Nationalism in the Middle Ages* (New York: Holt, Rinehart and Winston, 1972).

2. See Joseph R. Strayer, *The Reign of Philip the Fair* (Princeton: Princeton University Press, 1980).

3. On these developments generally throughout Europe, see Steven Ozment, *The Age of Reform, 1250–1550* (New Haven: Yale University Press, 1980), 187–89. The classic study of the early history of Gallicanism is by Victor Martin, *Les Origines du gallicanisme,* 2 vols. (Paris: Bloud & Gay, 1939).

4. Antony Black, *Political Thought in Europe, 1250–1450* (Cambridge: Cambridge University Press, 1992), 108–16.

5. John of Paris, *On Royal and Papal Power,* trans. Arthur Monahan (New York: Columbia University Press, 1974), chapter 3 (p. 14).

6. Ibid., chapter 3 (p. 15). I have amended the translation slightly in accordance with the Latin text of *De potestate regia et papali,* ed. Fritz Bleienstein (Stuttgart: Klett Verlag, 1969).

7. See Engelbert of Admont, *De ortu et fine Romani imperii,* chapters 14–15 (an English translation of this text by Thomas M. Izbicki and Cary J. Nederman is to be published by Thoemmes Press in 2000); Marsiglio of Padua, *Defensor pacis,* ed. C. W. Previté-Orton (Cambridge: Cambridge University Press, 1928), 1.17.10.

8. Black, *Political Thought in Europe,* 112–13.

9. Kate Langdon Forhan, "Respect, Interdependence, Virtue: A Medieval Theory of Toleration in the Works of Christine de Pizan," in Cary J. Nederman and John Christian Laursen, eds., *Difference and Dissent: Theories of Toleration in Medieval and Early Modern Europe* (Lanham, Md.: Rowman & Littlefield, 1996), 69.

10. This tract has been the object of a remarkable body of scholarship in the past several decades. The Latin text is available in two reliable recent editions: Raymond Klibansky and Hildebrand Bascour, eds., *Nicholai de Cusa: De pace fidei* (London: Warburg Institute, 1956); and Paul Wilpert, ed., *Nikolaus von Kues: Werke,* vol. 1 (Berlin: de Gruyter, 1967), 338–66. Moreover, there are four translations of the work into English alone: by John Patrick Dolan in his *Unity and Reform: Selected Writings of Nicholas of Cusa* (Notre Dame: University of Notre Press, 1962),. 195–237; Jasper Hopkins in his *Nicholas of Cusa's De pace fidei and Cribratio Alkorani* (Minneapolis: Banning, 1990); H. Lawrence Bond in James E. Biechler and H. Lawrence Bond, eds., *Nicholas of Cusa on Interreligious Harmony* (Lewiston, N.Y.: Edwin Mellen Press, 1990),

2–63; and William F. Wertz Jr. in his *Toward a New Council of Florence: 'On the Peace of Faith' and Other Works by Nicolas of Cusa* (Washington, D.C.: Schiller Institute, 1993), 231–72. Although I have consulted all editions and translations, my citations are to Bond's version, in part because it conveniently reproduces the translation with a facing Latin text. Nevertheless, I have often departed from Bond's rendering of the English.

11. The phrase "religio una in rituum varietate" or some variant thereof is repeated throughout *De pace fidei;* see, for instance, 7, 13, 62.

12. Ernst Cassirer, *Individuum und Kosmos in der Philosophie der Renaissance* (Berlin and Leipzig: Teubner, 1927), 31.

13. See Paul Oskar Kristeller, *Renaissance Thought, II: Papers on Humanism and the Arts* (New York: Harper, 1965), 64–65.

14. Dolan, *Unity and Reform*, 185, 187.

15. Among the studies that take issue with one or another feature of the "modernizing" interpretation of *De pace fidei* may be counted Michael Seidlmayer, "'Una religio in rituum varietate': Zur religionsauffassung des Nikolaus von Kues," *Archiv für Kulturgeschichte* 36 (1954): 145–207; Bruno Decker, "Nikolaus von Kues und der Friede unter der Religionen," in Josef Koch, ed., *Mystik und Kunst in der Welt des Mittelalters* (Leiden: Brill, 1959), 94–121; Eusebio Colomer, *Nikolaus von Kues und Raimond Llull* (Berlin: de Gruyter, 1961); Morimichi Watanabe, "Nicholas of Cusa and the Idea of Tolerance," in *Nicolò Cusano agli inizi del mondo moderno* (Florence: Sansoni, 1970), 409–18; Maurice de Gandillac, "Das Zeil der una religio in varietate rituum," in Rudolf Haubst, ed., *Der Friede unter den Religionen nach Nikolaus von Kues* (Mainz: Matthias-Grünwald, 1984), 192–204; Hopkins, "Introduction" to *Nicholas of Cusa's De pace fidei and Cribratio Alkorani*, 14–29;

16. See Paul E. Sigmund, *Nicholas of Cusa and Medieval Political Thought* (Cambridge, Mass.: Harvard University Press, 1963), 123–25, 292–95; Josef Stallmach, "Einheit der Religionen—Friede unter den Religionen," in Haubst, ed., *Der Friede unter den Religionen nach Nikolaus von Kues*, 61–75; Raymond Klibansky, "Die Wirkungsgeschichte des Dialogs 'De pace fidei,'" in Haubst, ed., *Der Friede unter den Religionen nach Nikolaus von Kues*, 113–25; Thomas P. McTighe, "Nicholas of Cusa's Unity-Metaphysics and the Formula *Religio una in rituum varietate*," in Gerald Christianson and Thomas M. Izbicki, eds., *Nicholas of Cusa in Search of God and Wisdom* (Leiden: Brill, 1991), 161–72; Wertz, *Toward a New Council of Florence*, 1–55; Jeannine Quillet, "La Paix de la foi: Identité et différence selon Nicolas de Cues," in Gregorio Piaia, ed., *Concordia Discors* (Padua: Antenore, 1993).

17. *De pace fidei*, 4.

18. The conclusion of Morimichi Watanabe, *The Political Ideas of Nicholas of Cusa with Special Reference to His De Concordantia Catholica* (Geneva: Droz, 1963), 185–86.

19. Biechler and Bond, *Nicholas of Cusa on Interreligious Harmony*, xii; also Hopkins, *Nicholas of Cusa's De pace fidei and Cribratio Alkorani*, 12.

20. See Bruno Decker, "Die Toleranzidee bei Nikolaus von Kues und in der Neuzeit," *Nicolò da Cusa* (Florence: Sansoni, 1962), 197–216; Watanabe, "Nicholas of Cusa and the Idea of Tolerance," 418.

21. *De pace fidei*, 4.

22. Denys Hay, *Europe: The Emergence of an Idea* (New York: Harper & Row, 1966), 76–83; Cary J. Nederman, "Aristotle as Authority: Alternative Aristotelian Sources of Late Medieval Political Theory," *History of European Ideas* 8 (1987): 39–41.

23. *De pace fidei*, 55.

24. Ibid., 11.

25. Ibid., 58.

26. See Guenée, *States and Rulers in Later Medieval Europe*, 216–20.

27. *De pace fidei*, 5.

28. Ibid., 9.

29. Ibid., 13.

30. Ibid., 52.

31. Ibid., 48.

32. Ibid., 5.

33. Nicholas of Cusa, *De concordantia catholica*, Book III, ed. Gerhard Kallen (Hamburg: Felix Meiner, 1959), secs. 271, 274.

34. In *De pace fidei*, Nicholas remarks, "Truth is one and it is not possible that it should not be understood by every free intellect" (10); cf. *De concordantia catholica*, sec. 127.

35. *De pace fidei*, 5–6.

36. See *De concordantia catholica*, sec. 275.

37. *De pace fidei*, 4, 62–63.

38. Ibid., 21.

39. Ibid., 49.

40. Ibid., 6.

41. Ibid., 51. The character of the "Tartar" is intriguing. Might Nicholas have encountered the narrative of William of Rubruck or one of the other thirteenth-century travelers to the Mongols? No specific evidence points to this, but the criticisms raised by the "Tartar" are suggestive.

42. See ibid., 12–13 (the Greek admits monotheism), 19–20 (the Indian accepts the prohibition against idolatry), 39 (the Persian affirms the divinity of Christ).

43. Ibid., 50–51.

44. Ibid., 51–52.

45. Ibid., 61.

46. Ibid., 60–61.

47. Ibid., 56.

48. Ibid., 56.

49. Ibid., 62.

50. Ibid., 7.

51. Ibid., 62.

52. See James Muldoon, "The Development of Group Rights," in Jay A. Sigler, *Minority Rights: A Comparative Analysis* (Westport, Conn.: Greenwood Press, 1983), 31–66.

53. Contrast this with Sigmund, *Nicholas of Cusa and Medieval Political Thought*, 292: "The yearning for a universal empire and universal church, and the hopes for a universal agreement among men . . . , remained with Nicholas until his death"; or Watanabe, *The Political Ideas of Nicholas of Cusa*, 144: "The 'fiasco of Nicholas' was also due to his failure to recognize the emergence of the idea of the nation state, which had been gradually gaining ground in Europe."

54. The argument of *De pace fidei* in some ways resembles one of the "regimes of toleration," namely, international society, identified by Michael Walzer, *On Toleration* (New Haven: Yale University Press, 1997), 19–22.

Chapter 7

1. On this, most generally, see Tzvetan Todorov, *The Conquest of America*, trans. Richard Howard (New York: Harper, 1985).

2. General treatments of European attitudes toward the newly encountered peoples of America are afforded by: Lewis Hanke, *The Spanish Struggle for Justice in the Conquest of America* (Philadelphia: University of Pennsylvania Press, 1949); idem, *Aristotle and the American Indians* (Chicago: Henry Regnery, 1959); and Anthony Pagden, *The Fall of Natural Man: The American Indian and the Origins of Comparative Ethnology* (Cambridge: Cambridge University Press, 1982).

3. See James Muldoon, *Popes, Lawyers, and Infidels* (Philadelphia: University of Pennsylvania Press, 1979), 320–48.

4. See Hanke, *Aristotle and the American Indians*, 76–78, who documents the rewards heaped on Sepúlveda for defending the case for Spanish conquest.

5. On Vitoria, see Pagden, *The Fall of Natural Man*, 60–80. Some of Vitoria's relevant writings have been collected and translated by Pagden and Jeremy Lawrance under the title *Political Writings* (Cambridge: Cambridge University Press, 1991).

6. There are a number of thorough biographical treatments of Las Casas in Spanish. In English, see Henry R. Wagner, *The Life and Writings of Bartolomé de las Casas* (Albuquerque: University of New Mexico Press, 1967). Also useful are the studies in Juan Friede and Benjamin Keen, eds., *Bartolomé de las Casas in History: Toward an Understanding of the Man and His Work* (DeKalb: Northern Illinois University Press, 1971).

7. Among recent advocates of Las Casas as an important figure in the history of toleration are Tzvetan Todorov, "Toleration and the Intolerable," in *The Morals of History*, trans. Alyson Waters (Minneapolis: University of Minnesota Press, 1995), 141–57; and Paul J. Cornish, "Spanish Thomism and the American Indians: Vitoria and Las Casas on the Toleration of Cultural Difference," in Cary J. Nederman and John Christian Laursen, eds., *Difference and Dissent: Theories of Toleration in Medieval and Early Modern Europe* (Lanham, Md.: Rowman & Littlefield, 1996), 99–117, esp. 112–13.

8. This discourse-oriented understanding of medieval thought has been elaborated by Anthony Black, *Political Thought in Europe, 1250–1450* (Cambridge: Cambridge University Press, 1992), 7.

9. Pagden, *The Fall of Natural Man*, 122. Similar views have been espoused by Hanke, *Aristotle and the American Indians*; Philippe André-Vincent, "La Concrétisation de la notion classique de droit naturel à travers l'oeuvre de Las Casas," in *Las Casas et la politique des droits de l'homme* (Aix-en-Provence: CNRS, 1974), 203–13; and Cornish, "Spanish Thomism and the American Indians."

10. Brian Tierney, "Aristotle and the American Indians—Again: Two Critical Discussions," *Cristianesimo nella storia* 12 (1991): 299. See also Kenneth Pennington, "Bartolomé de las Casas and the Tradition of Medieval Law," *Church History* 39 (1970): 149–61; and Muldoon, *Popes, Lawyers, and Infidels*, 132–52.

11. Black, *Political Thought in Europe*, 9.

12. Hanke makes no reference at all to Cicero in either of his classic books; Pagden, *The Fall of Natural Man*, 140, and Tierney, "Aristotle and the American Indians—Again," 319, make only fleeting mention of Las Casas's use of Cicero. Likewise, see the studies in *Las Casas et la politique des droits de l'homme* and *I dritti dell'uomo e la pace nel pensiero di Francisco de Vitoria e Bartolomé de las Casas* (Milan: Massimo, 1988).

13. Gary Remer, *Humanism and the Rhetoric of Toleration* (University Park: The Pennsylvania State University Press, 1996).

14. This claim was pioneered by R. W. Carlyle and A. J. Carlyle, *A History of Mediaeval Political Theory in the West*, vol. 1 (by A. J. Carlyle) (rpt. Edinburgh: William Blackwood & Sons, 1962), 1–18. More recently, see Marcia Colish, *The Stoic Tradition from Antiquity to the Early Middle Ages*, 2 vols. (Leiden: Brill, 1985), 1:99–102; Neal Wood, *Cicero's Social and Political Thought* (Berkeley and Los Angeles: University of California Press, 1988), 10; and David Luscombe, "City and Politics Before the Coming of the *Politics*: Some Illustrations," in David Abulafia, Michael Franklin, and Miri Rubin, eds., *Church and City, 1100–1500* (Cambridge: Cambridge University Press, 1992), 41–43.

15. Cicero's inconsistencies are remarked on, for instance, by Colish, *The Stoic Tradition from Antiquity to the Middle Ages*, 1:102.

16. Bartholomé de las Casas, *Apologética Historia Sumaria*, ed. Edmundo O'Gorman, 2 vols. (México City: Universidad Nacional Autónomia de México, 1967), 1:256, 391, 392, 397, 400, 409, 410, 414, 547, 549, 550, 567, 599, 600, 610, 615, 618, 630, 698; 2:38–39, 45–46, 55, 59, 67, 85–86, 101–2, 149, 249, 319, 320, 340, 411, 460.

17. Bartolomé de las Casas, *Historia de las Indias*, ed. Agustín Millares Carlo, 3 vols. (México City: Fondo de Cultura Economica, 1951), 2:96; see also *Apologética Historia Sumaria*, 1:257, 258. All translations from Spanish and Latin (except for the *Apologia*) are mine. Las Casas's egalitarianism is stressed, for instance, by Todorov, "Toleration and the Intolerable," 141–42.

18. Las Casas, *Apologética Historia Sumaria*, 1:257.

19. Ibid., 257–58.

20. Ibid., 258.

21. See Bartolomé de las Casas, *In Defense of the Indians* [the *Apology*], trans. Stafford Poole (DeKalb: Northern Illinois University Press, 1974), 28–53.

22. Las Casas, *Apologética Historia Sumaria*, 1:260; see *In Defense of the Indians*, 28.

23. André-Vincent, "La Concrétisation de la notion classique de droit naturel à travers l'oeuvre de las Casas," 205.

24. Las Casas, *Apologética Historia Sumaria*, 2:362.

25. Ibid., 1:259; Las Casas, *In Defense of the Indians*, 34–35.

26. Las Casas, *Apologética Historia Sumaria*, 1:374.

27. Ibid., 372.

28. Ibid., 375.

29. Las Casas, *In Defense of the Indians*, 75; also 227.

30. Cicero, *De legibus*, ed. C. W. Keyes (Cambridge, Mass.: Harvard University Press, 1928), I.23–24.

31. Las Casas, *Apologética Historia Sumaria*, 1:257.

32. Ibid., 260.

33. He enumerates these tokens of civilization in *In Defense of the Indians*, 42–43.

34. Las Casas, *Apologética Historia Sumaria*, 1:375.

35. Las Casas, *In Defense of the Indians*, 233–39.

36. Las Casas, *Apologética Historia Sumaria*, 1:260.

37. Ibid., 258–59.

38. Cicero, *De inventione*, ed. H. M. Hubbell (Cambridge, Mass.: Harvard University Press, 1949), I.2–3.

39. Cicero, *Pro Sestio*, ed. Robert Gardner (Cambridge, Mass.: Harvard University Press, 1958), 38.

40. See Cary J. Nederman, "Nature, Sin, and the Origins of Society: The Ciceronian Tradition in Medieval Political Thought," *Journal of the History of Ideas* 49 (January–March 1988): 3–26; idem, "The Union of Wisdom and Eloquence Before the Renaissance: The Ciceronian Orator in Medieval Thought," *Journal of Medieval History* 18 (March 1992): 75–95; idem, "Humanism and Empire: Aeneas Sylvius Piccolomini, Cicero, and the Imperial Ideal," *The Historical Journal* 36 (1993): 499–515.

41. Bartolomé de las Casas, *De unico vocationis modo omnium gentium*, ed. Agustín Millares Carlo (México City: Fondo de Cultura Economica, 1942), 98.

42. Ibid., 100.

43. Ibid., 6.

44. Las Casas, *Historia de las Indias*, 1:14.

45. Ibid., 14–15.

46. Ibid., 16.

47. Ibid., 16–19.

48. Pagden, *The Fall of Natural Man*, 122.

49. Las Casas, *Apologética Historia Summaria*, 1:257.

50. Ibid., 249.

51. Ibid., 258.

52. Ibid., 250.

53. Ibid., 2:362–63.

54. See Tierney, "Aristotle and the American Indians—Again," 299–304; Cornish, "Spanish Thomism and the American Indians," 109–12.

55. Las Casas, *De unico modo*, 502.

56. Ibid., 504; see Cicero, *De officiis*, ed. Walter Miller (Cambridge, Mass.: Harvard University Press, 1913), III.21.

57. Las Casas, *De unico modo*, 504, 542, 544.

58. Ibid., 390.

59. Ibid., 544.

60. See Las Casas, *In Defense of the Indians*, 244.

61. Las Casas, *Historia de las Indias*, 2:396–97.

62. Bartolomé de las Casas, *Una disputa o controversia*, in Las Casas, *Tratados*, 2 vols (México: Fondo de Cultura Economica, 1965), 1:408.

63. Bartolomé de las Casas, *Tratado comprobatorio del imperio soberano*, in Las Casas, *Tratados*, 2:1008–10.

64. See Cary J. Nederman, "A Duty to Kill: John of Salisbury's Theory of Tyrannicide," *Review of Politics* 50 (1988): 365–89.

65. As has been pointed out by Gordon J. Schochet, "John Locke and Religious Toleration," in Lois G. Schwoerer, ed., *The Revolution of 1688: Changing Perspectives* (Cambridge: Cambridge University Press, 1992), 150.

CONCLUSION

1. For example, James of Viterbo, *On Christian Government*, ed. R. W. Dyson (Woodbridge, Suffolk: Boydell Press, 1998), 103: "The institution of temporal power takes its origin from the natural inclination of men and, for this reason, from God, inasmuch as the work of nature is the work of God." On the background to this view, see Tina Stiefel, *The Intellectual Revolution in Twelfth Century Europe* (New York: St. Martin's Press, 1985), 44–46; and Gaines Post, *Studies in Medieval Legal Thought* (Princeton: Princeton University Press, 1964), 504–52.

2. On some elements of this "anthropocentrism," see Cary J. Nederman, "Nature, Ethics, and the Doctrine of 'Habitus': Aristotelian Moral Psychology in the Twelfth Century," *Traditio* 45 (1989–90): 87–89. Also see Sir R. W. Southern's classic essay "Medieval Humanism," in *Medieval Humanism and Other Studies* (Oxford: Blackwell, 1970), 29–60.

3. Michael Sandel, "Judgemental Toleration," in Robert P. George, ed., *Natural Law, Liberalism, and Morality* (Oxford: Clarendon Press, 1996), 107–12

4. Michael Walzer, *On Toleration* (New Haven: Yale University Press, 1997), 5.

5. I wish to thank Jim Muldoon for drawing my attention to this vital difference.

6. Peter of Celle, *Selected Works*, trans. Hugh Feiss (Kalamazoo: Cistercian Publications, 1987), 85.

7. John Rawls, *Political Liberalism* (New York: Columbia University Press, 1993). See Will Klymlicka, "Two Models of Pluralism and Tolerance," in David Heyd, ed., *Toleration: An Elusive Virtue* (Princeton: Princeton University Press, 1996), 81–105.

8. As Margaret Leslie has remarked, "The contemporary thinker, whether he calls himself political philosopher or political scientist, must suffer if he has not available to him for use in grasping the political experience of his own time the rich vocabulary of the past" ("In Defence of Anachronism," *Political Studies* 18 [1970]: 443).

9. Terence Ball, "Is There Progress in Political Science?" in Ball, ed., *Idioms of Inquiry: Critique and Renewal in Political Science* (Albany: SUNY Press, 1987), 13–44.

10. Janet Coleman, *Ancient and Medieval Memories: Studies in the Reconstruction of the Past* (Cambridge: Cambridge University Press, 1992), 537.

BIBLIOGRAPHY

PRIMARY SOURCES

Abelard, Peter. *Dialogus inter philosophum, Judaeum, et Christianum*. Ed. Rudolf Thomas. Stuttgart–Bad Canstatt: Friedrich Frommann Verlag, 1970.
———. *Sic et non*. Ed. Blanche Boyer and Richard McKeon. Chicago: University of Chicago Press, 1976.
———. *Dialogue of a Philosopher with a Jew and a Christian*. Trans. Pierre J. Payer. Toronto: Pontifical Institute of Medieval Studies, 1979.
Aquinas, Saint Thomas. *On Kingship*. Trans. G. B. Phelan. Toronto: Pontifical Institute of Medieval Studies, 1949.
———. *Sententia super Librum De Caelo et Mundo*. Ed. R. M. Spiazzi. Turin: Marietti, 1952.
———. *De perfectione spiritualis vitae*. In R. M. Spiazzi and M. Calcaterra, eds., *Opuscula Theologica*, vol. 2. Turin: Marietti, 1954.
Aristotle. *Politics*. Ed. Horace Rackham. Cambridge, Mass.: Harvard University Press, 1932.
Augustine of Hippo, Saint. *On Christian Doctrine*. Trans. D. W. Robertson Jr. Indianapolis: Bobbs-Merrill, 1958.
———. *Political Writings*. Ed. Henry Paolucci. Chicago: Regnery, 1962.
———. *Contra Academicos*. Indianapolis: Hackett, 1995.
Bodin, Jean. *Colloquium of the Seven About Secrets of the Sublime*. Trans. Marion L. Kuntz. Princeton: Princeton University Press, 1975.
Cicero, Marcus Tullius. *De officiis*. Ed. Walter Miller. Cambridge, Mass.: Harvard University Press, 1913.
———. *De legibus*. Ed. C. W. Keyes. Cambridge, Mass.: Harvard University Press, 1928.
———. *Academica*. Ed. Horace Rackham. London: Heinemann, 1933.
———. *De natura deorum*. Ed. Horace Rackham. London: Heinemann, 1933.
———. *De inventione*. Ed. H. M. Hubbell. Cambridge, Mass.: Harvard University Press, 1949.
———. *Pro Sestio*. Ed. Robert Gardner. Cambridge, Mass.: Harvard University Press, 1958.
Crispin, Gilbert. *The Works of Gilbert Crispin, Abbot of Westminster*. Ed. Anna Sapir Abulafia and G. R. Evans. London: Oxford University Press for the British Academy, 1986.
Engelbert of Admont. *De ortu et fine Romani imperii*. Trans. Thomas M. Izbicki and Cary J. Nederman. Bristol: Thoemmes Press, 2000.

Helévi, Yehuda. *The Kosari*. Trans. Yehuda Even Shmuel. Tel Aviv: Dvir, 1972.

James of Viterbo. *On Christian Government*. Trans. R. W. Dyson. Woodbridge, Suffolk, England: Boydell Press, 1995.

John of Paris. *De potestate regia et papali*. Ed. Fritz Bleienstein. Stuttgart: Klett Verlag, 1969.

———. *On Royal and Papal Power*. Trans. Arthur Monahan. New York: Columbia University Press, 1974.

John of Plano Carpini. *History of the Mongols*. In Christopher Dawson, ed., *Mission to Asia*. New York: Harper & Row, 1966.

John of Salisbury. *Policraticus*, 2 vols. Ed. C. C. J. Webb. Rpt. New York: Arno Press, 1979.

———. *Historia Pontificalis*. Ed. Marjorie Chibnall. Oxford: Oxford University Press, 1986.

———. *Policraticus: Of the Frivolities of Courtiers and the Footprints of Philosophers*. Trans. Cary J. Nederman. Cambridge: Cambridge University Press, 1990.

———. *Policraticus, I–IV*. Ed. K. S. B. Keats-Rohan. Turnhout: Brepols, 1993.

Las Casas, Bartolomé de. *De unico vocationis modo omnium gentium*. Ed. Agustín Millares Carlo. México City: Fondo de Cultura Economica, 1942.

———. *Historia de las Indias*, 3 vols. Ed. Agustín Millares Carlo. México City: Fondo de Cultura Economica, 1951.

———. *Tratados*, 2 vols. Ed. Lewis Hanke and Edmundo O'Gorman. México City: Fondo de Cultura Economica, 1965.

———. *Apologética Historia Sumaria*, 2 vols. Ed. Edmundo O'Gorman. México City: Universidad Nacional Autónomia de México, 1967.

———. *In Defense of the Indians*. Trans. Stafford Pool. DeKalb: Northern Illinois University Press, 1974.

Llull, Ramon. *The Selected Works of Ramon Llull (1232–1316)*, 2 vols. Ed. Anthony Bonner. Princeton: Princeton University Press, 1985.

Marsiglio of Padua. *Defensor pacis*. Ed. C. W. Previté-Orton. Cambridge: Cambridge University Press, 1928.

———. *The Defender of Peace*. Trans. Alan Gewirth. New York: Columbia University Press, 1956.

———. *Defensor minor*. Trans. Cary J. Nederman. Cambridge: Cambridge University Press, 1993.

Mill, John Stuart. *On Liberty*. Ed. Elizabeth Rappaport. Indianapolis: Hackett, 1978.

Nicholas of Cusa. *De pace fidei*. Ed. Raymond Klibansky and Hildebrand Bascour. London: Warburg Institute, 1956.

———. *De Concordantia Catholica, Liber III*. Ed. Gerhard Kallen. Hamburg: Felix Meiner, 1959.

———. *Werke*, vol. 1. Ed. Paul Wilpert. Berlin: Walter de Gruyter, 1967.

———. *On the Peace of the Faith*. Trans. H. Lawrence Bond. In James E. Beichler and H. Lawrence Bond, eds., *Nicholas of Cusa on Interreligious Harmony*. Lewiston, N.Y.: Edwin Mellen Press, 1990.

Odo of Tournai. *Two Theological Treatises*. Trans. Irven M. Resnick. Philadelphia: University of Pennsylvania Press, 1994.

Peter of Celle. *Selected Works*. Ed. Hugh Feiss. Kalamazoo: Cistercian Publications, 1987.

Van den Wyngart, A., ed. *Sinica Franciscana*, vol. 1: *Itinera et Relationes Fratrum Minorum Saeculum XIII et XIV*. Quaracchi, Italy: Franciscan Press, 1929.

Vitoria, Francisco de. *Political Writings*. Ed. Anthony Pagden and Jeremy Lawrance. Cambridge: Cambridge University Press, 1991.

William of Rubruck. *The Mission of Friar William of Rubruck*. Ed. Peter Jackson with David Morgan. London: Hakluyt Society, 1990.

SECONDARY SOURCES

Allsen, Thomas D. *Mongol Imperialism: The Policies of the Grand Qun Mongke in China, Russia, and the Islamic Lands, 1251–1259.* Berkeley and Los Angeles: University of California Press, 1987.

———. "Ever Closer Encounters: The Appropriation of Culture and the Apportionment of Peoples in the Mongol Empire." *Journal of Early Modern History* 1 (1997): 2–23.

André-Vincent, Philippe. "La Concrétisation de la notion classique de droit naturel à travers l'oeuvre de Las Casas." In *Las Casas et la politique des droits de l'homme.* Aix-en-Provence: CNRS, 1974.

Audi, Robert. "The Separation of Church and State and the Obligations of Citizenship." *Philosophy and Public Affairs* 18 (1989): 259–96.

Ball, Terence, ed. *Idioms of Inquiry: Critique and Renewal in Political Science.* Albany: SUNY Press, 1987.

Bejczy, István. "*Tolerantia:* A Medieval Concept." *Journal of the History of Ideas* 58 (July 1997): 365–84.

Benson, Robert L., and Giles Constable, eds. *Renaissance and Renewal in the Twelfth Century.* Cambridge, Mass.: Harvard University Press, 1982.

Black, Antony. *Political Thought in Europe, 1250–1450.* Cambridge: Cambridge University Press, 1992.

Bolgar, R. R. *The Classical Heritage and Its Beneficiaries.* Cambridge: Cambridge University Press, 1954.

Brampton, C. K. "Personalities in the Process Against Ockham at Avignon, 1324–26." *Franciscan Studies* 25 (1966): 4–25.

Brooke, Rosalind, and Christopher Brooke. *Popular Religion in the Middle Ages: Western Europe, 1100–1300.* London: Thames & Hudson, 1984.

Budziszewski, J. *True Tolerance.* New Brunswick, N.J.: Transaction Press, 1992.

Carlyle, R. W., and A .J. Carlyle. *A History of Mediaeval Political Theory in the West,* 6 vols. Rpt. Edinburgh: William Blackwood & Sons, 1962.

Cassirer, Ernst. *Individuum und Kosmos in der Philosophie der Renaissance.* Berlin and Leipzig: Teubner, 1927.

Cecil, Andrew R. *Equality, Tolerance, and Loyalty.* Dallas: University of Texas at Dallas Press, 1990.

Cochrane, Charles Norris. *Christianity and Classical Culture.* Oxford: Oxford University Press, 1957.

Cohen, Mark R. *Under Crescent and Cross: The Jews in the Middle Ages.* Princeton: Princeton University Press, 1994.

Coleman, Janet. *Ancient and Medieval Memories: Studies in the Reconstruction of the Past.* Cambridge: Cambridge University Press, 1992.

Colish, Marcia L. *The Stoic Tradition from Antiquity to the Early Middle Ages,* 2 vols. Leiden: Brill, 1985.

Colomer, Eusebio. *Nikolaus von Kues und Raimond Llull.* Berlin: Walter de Gruyter, 1961.

Condorelli, Mario. *I fondamenti giuridici della tolleranza religiosa nell'elaborazione canonistica dei secoli XIII–XIV.* Milan: Giuffre, 1960.

Connell, C. W. "Western Views of the Origin of the 'Tartars': An Example of the Influence of Myth in the Second Half of the Thirteenth Century." *Journal of Medieval and Renaissance Studies* 3 (1972): 115–37.

Constable, Giles. *The Reformation of the Twelfth Century.* Cambridge: Cambridge University Press, 1998.

Creppell, Ingrid. "Locke on Toleration: The Transformation of Constraint." *Political Theory* 24 (1996): 200–229.

Daniel, Norman. *Islam and the West: The Making of an Image.* Edinburgh: Edinburgh University Press, 1960.

Decker, Bruno. "Nikolaus von Kues und der Friede unter der Religionen." In Josef Koch, ed., *Mystik und Kunst in der Welt des Mittelalters.* Leiden: Brill, 1959.

———. "Die Toleranzidee bei Nikolaus von Kues und in der Neuzeit." In *Nicol da Cusa.* Florence: Sansoni, 1962.

D'Entrèves, Alexander Passerin. *The Medieval Contribution to Political Thought.* Oxford: Oxford University Press, 1939.

D'Entrèves, Maurizio Passerin. "Communitarianism and the Question of Tolerance." *Journal of Social Philosophy* 21 (1990): 77–91.

Dolan, John Patrick. *Unity and Reform.* Notre Dame: University of Notre Dame Press, 1962.

Dox, Donnalee. "Medieval Drama as Documentation: 'Real Presence' in the Croxton *Conversion of Ser Jonathas the Jewe by the Myracle of the Blissed Sacrament.*" *Theatre Survey* 38 (May 1997): 97–115.

Dronoke, Peter, ed. *A History of Twelfth-Century Western Philosophy.* Cambridge: Cambridge University Press, 1988.

Dutton, Edward Paul. "*Illustre civitatis et populi exemplum:* Plato's *Timaeus* and the Transmission from Calcidius to the End of the Twelfth Century of a Tripartite Scheme of Society." *Mediaeval Studies* 45 (1983): 79–119.

Evans, G. R. *Anselm and a New Generation.* Oxford: Oxford University Press, 1980.

Fasolt, Constantin. *Council and Hierarchy.* Cambridge: Cambridge University Press, 1991.

Feldman, Louis H. *Jew and Gentile in the Ancient World.* Princeton: Princeton University Press, 1993.

Fichtenau, Heinrich. *Heretics and Scholars in the High Middle Ages, 1000–1200.* Trans. Denise A. Kaiser. University Park: The Pennsylvania State University Press, 1998.

Finley, M. I., ed. *Studies in Ancient Society.* London: Routledge and Kegan Paul, 1974.

Finnis, John. *Aquinas.* Oxford: Oxford University Press, 1998.

Fletcher, George P. "The Case for Tolerance." *Social Philosophy and Policy* 13 (1996): 229–39.

Fotion, Nick, and Gerald Elfstrom. *Toleration.* University: University of Alabama Press, 1992.

Frend, W. H. C. *Martyrdom and Persecution in the Early Church.* Oxford: Clarendon Press, 1965.

Friede, Juan, and Benjamin Keen, eds. *Bartolomé de las Casas in History: Toward an Understanding of the Man and His Work.* DeKalb: Northern Illinois University Press, 1971.

Galeotti, Anna Elisabetta. "Citizenship and Equality: The Place for Toleration." *Political Theory* 21 (1993): 585–605.

Garnsey, Peter. "Religious Toleration in Classical Antiquity." In W. J. Sheils, ed., *Persecution and Toleration.* Oxford: Blackwell, 1984.

Gewirth, Alan. *Marsilius of Padua—The Defender of Peace,* 2 vols. New York: Columbia University Press, 1951–56.

Grell, Ole Peter, Jonathan I. Israel, and Nicholas Tyacke, eds. *From Persecution to Toleration: The Glorious Revolution and Persecution in England.* Oxford: Clarendon Press, 1991.

Grell, Ole Peter, and Robert W. Scribner, eds. *Tolerance and Intolerance in the European Reformation.* Cambridge: Cambridge University Press, 1996.

Groffier, Ethel, and Michel Pardis, eds. *The Notion of Tolerance and Human Rights.* Ottawa: Carleton University Press, 1991.

Guenée, Bernard. *States and Rulers in Later Medieval Europe.* Trans. Juliet Vale. Oxford: Blackwell, 1985.

Guggisberg, Hans. "The Defense of Religious Toleration and Religious Liberty in Early Modern Europe: Arguments, Pressures, and Some Consequences." *History of European Ideas* 4 (1983): 35–48.

Hamilton, Bernard. *The Medieval Inquisition.* London: Edward Arnold, 1981.

Hanke, Lewis. *The Spanish Struggle for Justice in the Conquest of America.* Philadelphia: University of Pennsylvania Press, 1949.

————. *Aristotle and the American Indians*. Chicago: Regnery, 1959.

Hankinson, R. J. *The Skeptics*. London: Routledge, 1995.

Hanson, Russell L. "Deliberation, Tolerance, and Democracy." In George E. Marcus and Russell L. Hanson, eds., *Reconsidering the Democratic Public*. University Park: The Pennsylvania State University Press, 1992.

Harding, Alan. "Political Liberty in the Middle Ages." *Speculum* 55 (1980): 423–43.

Harren, Michael. *Medieval Thought*, 2d ed. Toronto: University of Toronto Press, 1992.

Haubst, Rudolf, ed. *Der Friede unter den Religionen nach Nikolaus von Kues*. Mainz: Matthias-Grünwald, 1984.

Hay, Denys. *Europe: The Emergence of an Idea*. New York: Harper & Row, 1966.

Heyd, David, ed. *Toleration: An Elusive Virtue*. Princeton: Princeton University Press, 1996.

Hopkins, Jasper. *Nicholas of Cusa's De pace fidei and Cribratio Alkorani*. Minneapolis: Banning, 1990.

Horton, John, ed. *Liberalism, Multiculturalism, and Toleration*. New York: St. Martin's Press, 1993.

Horton, John, and Peter Nicholson, eds. *Toleration: Philosophy and Practice*. Aldershot, England: Avebury, 1992.

Johnston, Mark D. *The Spiritual Logic of Ramon Llull* Oxford: Oxford University Press, 1987.

————. *The Evangelical Rhetoric of Ramon Llull: Lay Learning and Piety in the Christian West Around 1300*. Oxford: Oxford University Press, 1996.

Kamen, Henry. *The Rise of Toleration*. New York: McGraw-Hill, 1967.

Kautz, Stephen. "Liberalism and the Idea of Toleration." *American Journal of Political Science* 37 (1993): 610–32.

Khushf, George. "Tolerant Intolerance." *Journal of Medicine and Philosophy* 19 (1994): 161–81.

King, Preston. *Toleration*. London: Allen and Unwin, 1976.

Köker, Levant. "Political Toleration or Politics of Recognition." *Political Theory* 24 (1996): 315–20.

Kors, Alan Charles. *Atheism in France, 1650–1729, Volume I: The Orthodox Sources of Disbelief*. Princeton: Princeton University Press, 1990.

Kraemer, Joel L. *Humanism in the Renaissance of Islam*. Leiden: E. J. Brill, 1993.

Kretzmann, Norman, Antony Kenny, and Jan Pinborg, eds. *The Cambridge History of Later Medieval Philosophy*. Cambridge: Cambridge University Press, 1982.

Kristeller, Paul Oskar. *Renaissance Thought II: Papers on Humanism and the Arts*. New York: Harper & Row, 1965.

Kymlicka, Will. "Two Models of Pluralism and Tolerance." In David Heyd, ed., *Toleration: An Elusive Virtue*. Princeton: Princeton University Press, 1996.

Lagarde, Georges de. *La Naissance de l'esprit laïque au déclin du moyen âge*, 5 vols., new ed. *Le Defensor Pacis*, vol. 3. Louvain and Paris: Nauwelaerts, 1970.

Lambert, Malcolm. *Medieval Heresy: Popular Movements from Bogomil to Hus*. London: Edward Arnold, 1977.

Langmuir, Gavin I. *Toward a Definition of Anti-Semitism*. Berkeley and Los Angeles: University of California Press, 1990.

Lansing, Carol. *Purity and Power: Cathar Heresy in Medieval Italy*. New York: Oxford University Press, 1998.

Laursen, John Christian. *The Politics of Skepticism in the Ancients, Montaigne, Hume, and Kant*. Leiden: E. J. Brill, 1992.

Laursen, John Christian, and Cary J. Nederman, eds. *Beyond the Persecuting Society: Religious Toleration Before the Enlightenment*. Philadelphia: University of Pennsylvania Press, 1998.

Leff, Gordon. *Heresy in the Later Middle Ages*, 2 vols. Manchester: Manchester University Press, 1967.

————. *Paris and Oxford Universities in the Thirteenth and Fourteenth Centuries: An Institutional and Intellectual History*. New York: John Wiley, 1968.

Le Goff, Jacques. *Time, Work, and Culture in the Middle Ages*. Trans. Arthur Goldhammer. Chicago: University of Chicago Press, 1980.

Liebeschütz, Hans. *Mediaeval Humanism in the Life and Writings of John of Salisbury*. London: Warburg Institute, 1950.

Leroy Ladurie, Emmanuel. *Montaillou: Promised Land of Error*. New York: Random House, 1974.

Leslie, Margaret. "In Defence of Anachronism." *Political Studies* 18 (1970): 433–47.

Luscombe, David. "City and Politics Before the Coming of the *Politics*: Some Illustrations." In David Abulafia, Michael Franklin, and Miri Rubin, eds., *Church and City, 1100–1500*. Cambridge: Cambridge University Press, 1992.

MacIntyre, Alasdair. *After Virtue*, 2d ed. London: Duckworth, 1981.

MacKendrick, Paul. *The Philosophical Books of Cicero*. London: Duckworth, 1989.

Makdisi, George, Dominique Sourdel, and Janine Sourdel-Thomine, eds. *La Notion de liberté au Moyen Age Islam, Byzance, Occident*. Paris: Société d'Édition "Les Belles Lettres," 1985.

Mann, Vivian B., Thomas F. Glick, and Jerrilyn D. Dodds, eds. *Convivencia: Jews, Muslims, and Christians in Medieval Spain*. New York: George Braziller, 1992.

Marenbon, John. "Abelard's Ethical Theory: Two Definitions from the *Collationes*." In Haijo Jan Westra, ed., *From Athens to Chartres*. Leiden: E. J. Brill, 1992.

Martin, Victor. *Les Origines du gallicanisme*, 2 vols. Paris: Bloud & Gay, 1939.

McClure, Kirstie. "Difference, Diversity, and the Limits of Toleration," *Political Theory* 18 (1990): 361–91.

McTighe, Thomas P. "Nicholas of Cusa's Unity-Metaphysics and the Formula *Religio una in rituum varietate*." In Gerald Christianson and Thomas M. Izbicki, eds., *Nicholas of Cusa in Search of God and Wisdom*. Leiden: E. J. Brill, 1991.

Mendus, Susan. *Toleration and the Limits of Liberalism*. London: Macmillan, 1989.

Mendus, Susan, and John Horton, eds. *John Locke: A Letter Concerning Toleration in Focus*. London: Routledge, 1991.

Mensching, Gustav. *Tolerance and Truth in Religion*. Trans. J.-J. Kleimkeit. University: University of Alabama Press, 1971.

Mews, Constant J. "On Dating the Works of Peter Abelard." *Archives d'histoire doctrinale et littéraire du moyen age* 52 (1985): 73–134.

———. "St. Anselm and Roscelin: Some New Texts and Their Implications, 1." *Archives d'histoire doctrinale et littéraire du moyen age* 58 (1991): 55–97.

———. "Philosophy and Theology, 1100–1150: The Search for Harmony." In Françoise Gaspari, ed., *Le XII Siècle: Mutations et renouveau en France dans le premiere moitié du XIIe siècle*. Paris: Le Léopard d'Or, 1995.

———. *Peter Abelard*. London: Variorum, 1995.

Moore, Robert I. *The Origins of European Dissent*. London: Penguin, 1977.

———. *The Formation of a Persecuting Society: Power and Deviance in Western Europe, 950–1350*. Oxford: Blackwell, 1987.

Morris, Colin. *The Discovery of the Individual, 1050–1200*. London: SPCK, 1972.

Moruzzi, Norma Claire. "A Problem with Headscarves: Contemporary Complexities of Political and Social Identity." *Political Theory* 22 (1994): 653–79.

Muldoon, James. *Popes, Lawyers, and Infidels*. Philadelphia: University of Pennsylvania Press, 1979.

———. "Group Rights." In Jay A. Sigler, *Minority Rights: A Comparative Analysis*. Westport, Conn.: Greenwood Press, 1983.

Munk-Olsen, Birger. "L'Humanisme de Jean de Salisbury, un Ciceronien au 12e siècle." In Maurice de Gandillac and Edouard Jeauneau, eds., *Entretiens sur la Renaissance du 12e siècle*. Paris: Mouton, 1968.

Murphy, Andrew R. "Tolerance, Toleration, and the Liberal Tradition." *Polity* 29 (Summer 1997): 593–623.

Murray, Alexander. "Piety and Impiety in Thirteenth-Century Italy." *Studies in Church History* 8 (1971): 83–106.

———. "Religion Among the Poor in Thirteenth-Century France." *Traditio* 30 (1974): 285–324.

———. *Excommunication and Conscience in the Middle Ages.* London: University of London, 1991.

Nederman, Cary J. "The Aristotelian Doctrine of the Mean and John of Salisbury's Concept of Liberty." *Vivarium* 24 (1986): 128–42.

———. "Aristotelian Ethics and John of Salisbury's Letters." *Viator* 18 (1987): 128–42.

———. "The Physiological Significance of the Organic Metaphor in John of Salisbury's *Policraticus*." *History of Political Thought* 8 (1987): 211–23.

———. "Aristotle as Authority: Alternative Aristotelian Sources of Late Medieval Political Theory." *History of European Ideas* 8 (1987): 31–44.

———. "Nature, Sin, and the Origins of Society: The Ciceronian Tradition in Medieval Political Thought." *Journal of the History of Ideas* 49 (1988): 3–26.

———. "A Duty to Kill: John of Salisbury's Theory of Tyrannicide." *Review of Politics* 50 (1988): 365–89.

———. "Knowledge, Virtue, and the Path to Wisdom: The Unexamined Aristotelianism of John of Salisbury's *Metalogicon*." *Mediaeval Studies* 51 (1989): 268–86.

———. "Ethics, Nature, and the Doctrine of 'Habitus': Aristotelian Moral Psychology in the Twelfth Century." *Traditio* 45 (1989/1990): 87–110.

———. "Freedom, Community, and Function: Communitarian Lessons of Medieval Political Theory." *American Political Science Review* 86 (1992): 977–86.

———. "The Union of Wisdom and Eloquence Before the Renaissance: The Ciceronian Orator in Medieval Thought." *Journal of Medieval History* 19 (1992): 75–95.

———. "Humanism and Empire: Aeneas Sylvius Piccolomini, Cicero, and the Imperial Ideal." *The Historical Journal* 36 (1993): 499–515.

———. "From *Defensor pacis* to *Defensor minor*: The Problem of Empire in Marsiglio of Padua." *History of Political Thought* 16 (1995): 313–29.

———. *Community and Consent: The Secular Political Theory of Marsiglio of Padua's "Defensor Pacis."* Lanham, Md.: Rowman & Littlefield, 1995.

———. "Constitutionalism—Medieval and Modern: Against Neo-Figgisite Orthodoxy (Again)." *History of Political Thought* 17 (1996): 179–94.

Nederman, Cary J., and Catherine Campbell. "Priests, Kings, and Tyrants: Spiritual and Temporal Power in John of Salisbury's *Policraticus*." *Speculum* 66 (1991): 572–90.

Nederman, Cary J., and Arlene Feldwick. "To the Court and Back Again: The Origins and Dating of the *Entheticus de Dogmate Philosophorum* of John of Salisbury." *Journal of Medieval and Renaissance Studies* 21 (1991): 129–45.

Nederman, Cary J., and John Christian Laursen, eds. *Difference and Dissent: Theories of Toleration in Medieval and Early Modern Europe.* Lanham, Md.: Rowman & Littlefield, 1996.

Newman, Jay. *Foundations of Religious Tolerance.* Toronto: University of Toronto Press, 1982.

Nirenberg, David. *Communities of Violence: Persecution of Minorities in the Middle Ages.* Princeton: Princeton University Press, 1996.

Offler, H. S. "Empire and Papacy: The Last Struggle." *Transactions of the Royal Historical Society* 6th ser., 10 (1956): 21–47.

Ozment, Steven. *The Age of Reform, 1250–1550: An Intellectual and Religious History of Late Medieval and Reformation Europe.* New Haven: Yale University Press, 1980.

Pagden, Anthony. *The Fall of Natural Man: The American Indian and the Origins of Comparative Ethnology.* Cambridge: Cambridge University Press, 1982.

Pakter, Walter. *Medieval Canon Law and the Jews.* Ebelsbach: Gremler, 1988.

Penna, Mario. *La parabola dei tre anelli e la tolleranza nel medio evo.* Turin: Rosenberg and Sellier, 1953.

Pennington, Kenneth. "Bartolomé de las Casas and the Tradition of Medieval Law." *Church History* 39 (1970): 149–61.

Pincin, Carlo. *Marsilio*. Turin: Edizioni Giappichelli, 1967.

Popper, Karl. "Toleration and Intellectual Responsibility." In Susan Mendus and David Edwards, eds., *On Toleration*. Oxford: Clarendon Press, 1987.

Porro, Pasquale. "Il *Sextus Latinus* e l'immagine dello scetticismo antico nel medioevo." *Elenchos* 15 (1994): 229–53.

Post, Gaines. *Studies in Medieval Legal Thought*. Princeton: Princeton University Press, 1964.

Powell, J. G. F., ed. *Cicero the Philosopher*. Oxford: Clarendon Press, 1995.

Quillet, Jeannine. "La Paix de la foi: Identité et différence selon Nicolas de Cues." In Gregorio Piaia, ed., *Concordia Discors*. Padua: Antenore, 1993.

Rachewiltz, Igor de. *Papal Envoys to the Great Khans*. Stanford: Stanford University Press, 1971.

Rawls, John. *Political Liberalism*. New York: Columbia University Press, 1993.

Razavi, Mehdi Amin, and David Ambuel, eds. *Philosophy, Religion, and the Question of Intolerance*. Albany: SUNY Press, 1997.

Remer, Gary. "Hobbes, the Rhetorical Tradition, and Toleration." *Review of Politics* 54 (1992): 5–33.

———. "Dialogues of Toleration: Erasmus and Bodin." *Review of Politics* 56 (1994): 305–36.

———. *Humanism and the Rhetoric of Toleration*. University Park: The Pennsylvania State University Press, 1996.

Reynolds, Susan. *Kingdoms and Communities in Western Europe, 900–1300*. Oxford: Oxford University Press, 1984.

Richards, Jeffrey. *Sex, Dissonance, and Damnation: Minority Groups in the Middle Ages*. London: Routledge, 1990.

Rollenbleck, Georg. "Les Poèmes intercalés dans L'Heptaplomeres." In *Jean Bodin: Actes du Colloque Interdisciplinaire d'Angers*, 2 vols. Angers: Presses de l'Université d'Angers, 1985.

Rouse, Mary A., and Richard H. Rouse. *Authentic Witnesses: Approaches to Medieval Texts and Manuscripts*. Notre Dame: University of Notre Dame Press, 1991.

Sandel, Michael. "Judgemental Tolerance." In Robert P. George, ed., *Natural Law, Liberalism, and Morality*. Oxford: Clarendon Press, 1996.

Schäfer, Peter. *Judeophobia: Attitudes Toward the Jews in the Ancient World*. Cambridge, Mass.: Harvard University Press, 1997.

Schmitt, Charles. *Cicero Scepticus: A Study of the Influence of the "Academica" in the Renaissance*. The Hague: Martinus Nijhoff, 1972.

Schochet, Gordon J. "John Locke and Religious Toleration." In Lois G. Schwoerer, ed., *The Revolution of 1688–1689: Changing Perspectives*. Cambridge: Cambridge University Press, 1992.

Schreiner, Klaus. "Toleranz." In Otto Brunner, Werner Conze, and Reinhart Koselleck, eds., *Geschichtliche Grundbegriffe*, vol. 6. Stuttgart: Klett-Cotta, 1990.

Seidlmayer, Michael. "'Una religio in rituum varietate': Zur religionsauffassung des Nikolaus von Kues." *Archiv für Kulturgeschichte* 36 (1954): 145–207.

Sigmund, Paul E. *Nicholas of Cusa and Medieval Political Thought*. Cambridge, Mass.: Harvard University Press, 1963.

Skinner, Quentin. *The Foundations of Modern Political Thought*, 2 vols. Cambridge: Cambridge University Press, 1978.

Southern, R. W. *Medieval Humanism and Other Studies* Oxford: Blackwell, 1970.

Stacey, Robert C. "The Conversion of Jews to Christianity in Thirteenth-Century England." *Speculum* 67 (1992): 263–83.

Stiefel, Tina. *The Intellectual Revolution in Twelfth-Century Europe*. New York: St. Martin's Press, 1985.

Stow, Kenneth R. *Alienated Minority: The Jews of Medieval Latin Europe*. Cambridge, Mass.: Harvard University Press, 1992.

Strayer, Joseph R. *The Reign of Philip the Fair*. Princeton: Princeton University Press, 1980.

Temporini, H., ed. *Aufstieg und Niedergang der Römischen Welt, I*, vol. 4. Berlin: Walter de Gruyter, 1973.

Tierney, Brian. "Aristotle and the American Indians—Again: Two Critical Discussions." *Cristianesimo nel storia* 12 (1991): 295–322.

———. "Freedom and the Medieval Church." In R. W. Davis, ed., *The Origins of Modern Freedom in the West*. Stanford: Stanford University Press, 1995.

———. "Political and Religious Freedom in Marsilius of Padua." In Noel B. Reynolds and W. Cole Durham Jr., eds., *Religious Liberty in Western Thought*. Atlanta: Scholars Press, 1996.

———. *The Idea of Natural Rights*. Atlanta: Scholars Press, 1997.

Tinder, Glenn. *Toleration and Community*. Columbia: University of Missouri Press, 1995.

Tipton, Charles L., ed. *Nationalism in the Middle Ages*. New York: Holt, Rinehart and Winston, 1972.

Todorov, Tzvetan. *The Conquest of America*. Trans. Richard Howard. New York: Harper, 1985.

———. *The Morals of History*. Trans. Alyson Waters. Minneapolis: University of Minnesota Press, 1995.

Tuck, Richard. *Natural Rights Theories—Their Origin and Development*. Cambridge: Cambridge University Press, 1989.

———. "Scepticism and Toleration in the Seventeenth Century." In Susan Mendus, ed., *Justifying Toleration: Conceptual and Historical Perspectives*. Cambridge: Cambridge University Press, 1988.

Turchetti, Mario. *Concordia o tolleranza? François Bauduin (1520–1573) e i "Moyenneurs."* Geneva: Droz, 1984.

———. "Religious Concord and Political Tolerance in Sixteenth- and Seventeenth-Century France." *Sixteenth Century Journal* 22 (1991): 15–25.

Vaneigem, Raoul. *The Movement of the Free Spirit*. New York: Zone Books, 1998.

Vernon, Richard. *The Career of Toleration: John Locke, Jonas Proast, and After*. Montreal and Kingston: McGill-Queen's University Press, 1997.

Vodola, Elizabeth. *Excommunication in the Middle Ages*. Berkeley and Los Angeles: University of California Press, 1986.

Wagner, Henry R. *The Life and Writings of Bartolomé de las Casas*. Albuquerque: University of New Mexico Press, 1967.

Walzer, Michael. *On Toleration*. New Haven: Yale University Press, 1997.

Watanabe, Morimichi. *The Political Ideas of Nicholas of Cusa with Special Reference to De Concordantia Catholica*. Geneva: Droz, 1963.

———. "Nicholas of Cusa and the Idea of Tolerance." In *Nicolò Cusano agli inizi del mondo moderno*. Florence: Sansoni, 1970.

Waugh, Scott L., and Peter D. Diehl, eds. *Christendom and Its Discontents: Exclusion, Persecution, and Rebellion, 1000–1500*. Cambridge: Cambridge University Press, 1997.

Webb, Diana. "The Possibility of Toleration: Marsiglio and the City States of Italy." In W. J. Sheils, ed., *Persecution and Toleration*. Oxford: Blackwell, 1984.

Wertz, William F., Jr. *Toward a New Council of Florence*. Washington, D.C.: Schiller Institute, 1993.

Wilks, Michael J., ed. *The World of John of Salisbury*. Oxford: Blackwell, 1984.

Wood, Neal. *Cicero's Social and Political Thought*. Berkeley and Los Angeles: University of California Press, 1988.

Ye'or, Bat. *The Dhimmi: Jews and Christians Under Islam*. Trans. D. Maisel, P. Fenton, and D. Littman. Rutherford, N.J.: Fairleigh Dickinson University Press, 1985.

Index

Abelard, Peter, 5, 6, 7, 10, 19, 26, 28–30, 33–34, 37, 53, 54, 88, 119, 132 n. 69
Academic School, 40, 41, 45–46, 47, 48, 49, 50, 51, 52, 101
Academica (Cicero), 46
Adrian IV, Pope, 42, 45
agnosticism, 84
Alans, 56, 59, 60
André-Vincent, Philippe, 102
Anselm of Canterbury, Saint, 6, 10, 27–28
Apologetic History (Las Casas), 102, 103, 104, 109
Aquinas, Saint Thomas, 19, 37, 74, 101
Arabic, 21
Arabs, 89, 90
Aristotle, 15, 18, 21, 71, 72, 74, 86, 99, 101, 103
Aremenians, 59, 60, 61, 62, 65, 89
"Art," the (Llull), 30–31, 34
atheism, 84, 105
Augustine of Hippo, Saint, 13–14, 18, 29, 40, 47, 49–50
Averroes, 21
Avicenna, 21

Bacon, Roger, 133 n. 7
Ball, Terrence, 121
baptism, 59, 93
barbarians, 99, 103, 105, 106, 109, 111

Batu, Chan, 54, 55
Bayle, Pierre, 84
Bejczy, István, 4
Bodin, Jean, 36, 40, 88
body politic, 43, 45, 50, 71, 130 n. 25
Bohemians, 89, 90
Bonaventure, Saint, 18
Boniface VIII, Pope, 20

canon law, 4, 17, 67, 101, 112
Caracorum, 56, 61, 62
Cassirer, Ernst, 88
Castellio, Sebastian, 40
Cathars, 15, 16–17, 22
Chaldeans, 89, 92
Chiapas, 90
Christine de Pizan, 87
Christianity, 1, 2, 3, 8, 12, 13, 14–16, 22, 25, 35, 37, 52, 55, 57, 59, 60, 61, 63, 65, 69, 76, 79, 82, 88, 90, 92, 102, 103, 105, 106, 108, 109, 111, 113, 118, 120
Cicero, Marcus Tullius, 7, 8, 18, 40, 41, 45–46, 48, 49, 72, 101–2, 103, 104, 105, 107, 108, 109, 110, 113, 114
circumcision, 93, 94
citizenship, 74, 77, 78, 80, 81, 82, 83, 118
civitas, 71, 73
Cluniacs, 16

coercion, 35, 42, 76–77, 79, 80, 81–82, 97, 102, 110–11, 114, 115
Coleman, Janet, 121
Colloquium of the Seven about Secrets of the Sublime (Bodin), 36–37
communal functionalism, 71, 72–74, 80, 82, 83
communitarianism, 1, 120
comos, 59, 60
conciliarism, 16
concordance, 5, 27, 32, 35, 36, 111
Constable, Giles, 16
Constant, Benjamin, 2
Constantinople, 8, 87, 89, 97
Contra Academicos (Augustine), 47
convivencia, 21, 30, 54
Cribratio Alkorani (Nicholas of Cusa), 88
Crispin, Gilbert, 26, 28, 30, 32, 33
Crusades, 15, 20

De concordantia catholica (Nicholas of Cusa), 91
decorum, 42
De divinatione (Cicero), 102
De doctrina christiana (Augustine), 14
De inventione (Cicero), 102, 107, 108, 109
De legibus (Cicero), 102, 103, 104, 109, 113
De natura deorum (Cicero), 46, 102, 104
De officiis (Cicero), 46, 102, 112, 114
De oratore (Cicero), 102
De pace fidei (Nicholas of Cusa), 87–97, 100
De unico vocationis modo omnium gentium (Las Casas), 107, 108, 112
Defensor minor (Marsiglio), 70, 71, 78–80, 82
Defensor pacis (Marsiglio), 70, 71–78, 82
dialogue, 26, 27, 29, 32, 35–36, 37, 51, 53–54, 55, 58, 63, 64, 91, 114, 119
Dialogus inter philosophum, Judaeum, et Christianum (Abelard), 26, 28–30, 31, 32, 33–34
Diehl, Peter, 4
Disputatio cum gentili (Crispin), 26, 28, 32

Disputatio inter Christianum et gentilem, 28, 32
Disputatio Judei et Christiani (Crispin), 26, 28
Disputationes Tusculanum (Cicero), 102, 104
divine law, 77, 81, 92
Dominicans, 65, 100
dominium, 112
Donatism, 13–14

Easter, 61–62
ecclesiology, 88
Engelbert of Admont, 86
England, 56, 89
Entheticus de dogmate philosophorum (John of Salisbury), 46–47, 48, 49, 50
Epistola de Tolerantia (Locke), 2
equality, 90, 91–92, 103–5, 109, 110, 114, 120
Erasmus, Desiderius, 41, 132 n. 62
establishmentarianism, 76, 81
Eucharist, 90, 93
excommunication, 8, 17, 69–70, 77, 78, 79–80

Fasolt, Constantin, 4
Feldman, Louis, 13
feminism, 1, 96
Forhan, Kate, 87
Formation of a Persecuting Society (Moore), 11
Fourth Lateran Council (1215), 11
France, 56, 86, 120
Franciscans, 16, 54

Gallican Church, 86
Garnsey, Peter, 13
Georgians, 56
Germany, 56, 70, 89, 91
Greece, 21, 89, 102
Greek Orthodox Church, 59
Gregory VII, Pope, 16
Grell, Ole Peter, 3
Guggisberg, Hans, 45

Hamilton, Bernard, 3
Henry VIII, King, 86

heresy, 6, 7–8, 11, 13–14, 16–17, 40,
    61, 69–70, 77, 78, 79–80, 81, 84, 111
Hindus, 88
History of the Indies (Las Casas), 108, 109,
    113
History of the Mongols (John of Plano
    Carpini), 54
Hostiensis, 66
humanism, 41, 52, 102, 118
Humboldt, Wilhelm von, 2
Hungary, 56

immanent acts, 75
In Defense of the Indians (*Apology*) (Las
    Casas), 103, 104
Indians, 8, 89, 99–114
*Individuum und Kosmos in der Philosophie der
    Renaissance* (Cassirer), 88
Innocent IV, Pope, 22, 54, 66
irenicism, 65, 88, 97
Islam. *See* Muslim
Italy, 89

Jerome, Saint, 14
Jesus, 90
Jews, 12, 13, 22, 26, 28, 29, 30, 31, 32,
    33, 34, 53, 77, 88, 89, 90, 100
John of Paris, 86
John of Plano Carpini, 54, 65
John of Salisbury, 5, 7, 10, 41–52
Journal of William of Rubruck, 54–67
Judaism. *See* Jews
justice, 113
Justin Martyr, 26

Kamen, Henry, 3
King, Preston, 3, 39–40

Lakatos, Imre, 121
Lansing, Carol, 16
Las Casas, Bartolomé de, 5, 8, 10,
    100–115, 119
Latin, 21
law, 72, 73, 77, 81, 82, 83, 92, 107
Le Goff, Jacques, 19

Liber de gentili et tribus sapientibus (Llull), 26,
    30–32, 34–36
liberalism, 1, 2, 9, 82–83, 117, 120, 124
liberty, 4, 6, 9, 29, 35, 40, 41–45, 49,
    50, 51, 52, 78, 83, 95, 96, 114, 117,
    119, 120, 124 n. 6, 130 n. 5, 132 n. 75
license, 130
Lithuanians, 100
Llull, Ramon, 6, 10, 26, 30–32, 33,
    34–36, 37, 53, 54, 88, 119
Locke, John, 2, 9, 84, 114, 124 n. 6
Louis IX, King, 54, 55, 57
Ludwig of Bavaria, King, 20, 70
Luther, Martin, 16

MacIntyre, Alasdair, 4
Mangu, Great Chan, 54, 55, 56–57, 59,
    60, 61, 62, 63, 64, 65, 66, 67, 100
Manicheanism, 61
marriage, 93
Marsiglio of Padua, 5, 7–8, 10, 70–84,
    86, 135 n. 39
Menucius Felix, 26
Metalogicon (John of Salisbury), 47, 48, 49
Mews, Constant, 33–34
Mill, John Stuart, 2, 9, 29, 52, 132
moderation, 47
Mohammed, 90
Mongols, 7, 54, 55–67, 100
Moore, Robert I., 5, 6, 11
Moses, 22, 57, 90
Murray, Alexander, 17
Muslims, 12, 20–21, 26, 30, 31, 32, 34,
    53, 54, 56, 57, 59, 60, 61, 63, 64, 65,
    88, 100, 111

nationalism, 85, 86, 87, 89–90, 95, 96,
    119
nature (human), 5, 8–9, 91–92, 101–2,
    103, 104, 106, 108, 112, 113, 114,
    117–18, 119
neo-Aristotelianism, 96
neo-Platonism, 88
Nestorians, 56, 57, 60, 61, 62, 63, 64,
    65

Newman, Jay, 26, 27, 37
Nicholas of Cusa, 5, 8, 10, 87–97, 90,
    119, 138 n. 53

Odo of Tournai, 26
On Liberty (Mill), 52
orator, 107, 110
Orvieto, 16
Ovid, 18

paganism, 14, 18, 22, 56, 99
pantheism, 100
papacy, 15, 70, 86, 135 n. 39
Paul, Saint, 89, 93, 95
Peter, Saint, 89
Peter of Celle, 119
Philip IV (the Fair), King, 20, 86
Plato, 18, 43
pluralism, 56, 84
Policraticus (John of Salisbury), 41–45,
    47, 48–51
polis, 72
polytheism, 64, 88, 100
Porrée, Gilbert de la, 19
postmodernism, 1
poststructuralism, 96
priesthood, 75–76, 77, 78–79, 81–82,
    135 n. 39
Pro Sestio (Cicero), 107

Qur'an, 91, 92

Rawls, John, 120
reason, 26–27, 28, 29, 31, 33, 36, 37,
    48–49, 51, 101, 103, 104, 105, 106–7,
    108, 109, 110, 112, 113, 115, 119
Reformation, 1–2, 111
Remer, Gary, 26, 101
Renaissance of the Twelfth-Century, 118
Respublica Christiana, 3–4, 11, 15, 23, 25,
    85, 86, 90, 93, 96
rights (human/natural), 4, 9, 45, 51, 95,
    101, 112, 114, 119, 121
Roman Church, 3, 7, 11, 17, 18, 22, 23,
    25, 43, 53, 62, 66, 67, 68, 79, 82, 98,
    135 n. 39
Roman Empire, 12, 13, 15, 41
Roman law, 113
Roman Republic, 102
Russians, 56, 59

Sandel, Michael, 5, 118
Saracens. See Muslims
Sartak, Chan, 54, 55, 65
Schmitt, Charles, 47
Schreiner, Klaus, 3
scholasticism, 4, 16, 19, 52, 86, 88, 90,
    101, 103, 112, 114, 118
Scythians, 89
Sececa, 18
Secreta secretorum (pseudo-Aristotle), 21
Sepúlveda, Juan Ginés de, 101, 103
Sic et Non (Abelard), 33–34
skepticism, 7, 39–41, 46–52, 101
Spain, 21, 30, 54, 89, 100, 101, 109, 111

Tartars, 54, 89, 90, 93, 138 n. 41
Terrence, 43
Tertullian, 14, 26
theology, 18, 19, 88, 103
Tierney, Brian, 3, 78
Timaeus (Plato), 43
transient acts, 74–75
truth, 19, 29, 39, 49, 50, 51, 76, 91,
    96–97, 110, 118
Tuck, Richard, 40
Turks, 87, 89
tuins, 60, 63, 64, 100
Turchetti, Mario, 3, 27, 32
tyranny, 44, 45

Uigurs, 56, 58
university, 19
University of Paris, 20, 47, 70

Vaneigem, Raoul, 4, 15
vice, 42, 43–44, 49
Virgil, 19

virtue, 42 , 49, 50, 71, 103, 109
Vitoria, Francisco de, 100
Vodola, Elizabeth, 17
Voltaire, 40

Walzer, Michael, 9, 118
Waugh, Scott, 4
Webb, Clement, C.J., 49
William of Ockham, 121
William of Rubruck, 5, 7, 54–67, 100